HORSE CRAZY

HORSE CRAZY

Girls and the Lives of Horses

JEAN O'MALLEY HALLEY

The University of Georgia Press ❧ Athens

Published by the University of Georgia Press
Athens, Georgia 30602
www.ugapress.org
© 2019 by Jean O'Malley Halley
All rights reserved
Designed by Erin Kirk New
Set in 10.5 on 14 Minion Pro
Printed and bound by Thomson-Shore
The paper in this book meets the guidelines for
permanence and durability of the Committee on
Production Guidelines for Book Longevity of the
Council on Library Resources.

Most University of Georgia Press titles are
available from popular e-book vendors.

Printed in the United States of America
19 20 21 22 23 P 5 4 3 2 1

Library of Congress Cataloging-in-Publication Data

Names: Halley, Jean O'Malley, 1967– author.
Title: Horse crazy : girls and the lives of horses / Jean O'Malley Halley.
Description: Athens : The University of Georgia Press, [2019] |
Includes bibliographical references and index.
Identifiers: LCCN 2018049582| ISBN 9780820355368 (hardcover : alk. paper)
| ISBN 9780820355276 (paperback : alk. paper) | ISBN 9780820355269 (ebook)
Subjects: LCSH: Horses—Social aspects—United States—History—20th century.
| Human-animal relationships. | Women—Identity.
Classification: LCC SF285 .H36 2019 | DDC 636.1—dc23 LC record
available at https://lccn.loc.gov/2018049582

For Snipaway and Jacob, my love, my family,
and to horses and their girls, everywhere.

ⅆⅆ

Contents

Acknowledgments

I am very thankful to more people than I can possibly name here. For the work of all my research assistants, who gathered and took detailed notes on sources and provided critical evaluation of my writing and ideas, I am especially grateful. In particular, I am indebted to Emily Scotti, an insightful young scholar who labored to make this a better book. Isaiah Halley-Segal helped me find important and relevant research material. Kara Johnson diligently found every possible source on horse lives and equine-assisted therapy. She is a research assistant extraordinaire. Danielle Lucchese, my talented research assistant and dear friend, helped from start to finish, throughout my five years working on this book.

I have learned so much from the scholarly work of and conversations with my many students and former-students-now-friends, especially Ramsha Begum, Bryan Joon Bickford, Erika A. Byrnison, Brooke Guinan, Laura Henrikson, Rej Joo, David Jordon, Anastasiya Panas, Amina Shikupilwa, Kristen Valletta, Naveena Waran, Heather Jean Wright, and Shayne Zaslow.

For their very helpful suggestions, I am also thankful to several anonymous reviewers of my proposal and, especially, two reviewers of my completed manuscript. Clearly, these reviewers took extensive time reading and thinking through and responding to my project. The City University of New York Office of Research Book Completion Award gave crucial support at just the right moment. My editor, Beth Snead, enthusiastically supported and guided me through the publication process. Superb librarians Mark Aaron Polger and Anne Hays helped me track down sources. Matthew Sharpe skillfully edited the full manuscript and greatly improved it. Carol Adams gave time for an enlightening interview and continues to inspire me with her work. Nan Sussman and Sarah Schulman, colleagues at the City University of New York, supported my work; Sarah kindly read an early draft of the manuscript and gave me clarifying and detailed feedback. Roz Bologh, Patricia Ticineto Clough, Hester Eisenstein, and Stuart Ewen substantially supported my work and, really, made my career possible. Jeffrey Bussolini, Grace Cho, Kate Crehan, Melissa Hope Ditmore, Amy Eshleman, Ozlem Goner, Richard Holland, Rose M. Kim, Ananya Mukherjea, Ron Nerio, Kathleen O'Malley, Brian Palmer, Rakesh Rajani, Chhaya Rajani-Bangser, and Beatrice Segal helped in innumerable ways, including connecting me to sources, sharing their ideas, and commenting on my writing. My writing group and dear friends, Jaime Amparo Alves, Francesca Degiuli, Rafael de la Dehesa, and Hosu Kim, gave me rich, honest, and smart criticism. Brilliant feminist journalist and author Leora Tanenbaum gave me insightful feedback. Lore Segal, both one of my favorite writers and a beloved family member, kindly read and reread several chapters and significantly improved the writing.

Remarkably generous, Lisa Maguire connected me with a dozen or more women who were horse crazy as girls, and she drove me, and Beatrice Segal who kindly came too, around upstate New York visiting stables and horse rescue organizations. Kathleen Halley-Segal drew and painted horses, shared loving horses, watched many episodes of *My Little Pony* with me, and accompanied me when I went back to horseback riding, so many years after my horse Snipaway's death. Getner Barn shared their insights, stories, skill, and horses with me. Many women and several men who love horses gave generously of their time, in interviews with me, to explain their experiences and their passion for horses. I am so grateful to them all.

Finally and foremost, Jacob Segal carefully read and gave me thoughtful feedback on numerous drafts of the complete manuscript. I would not have completed this book without his help. To the extent that it is well written and theoretically sound, it is largely because of him.

HORSE CRAZY

Prologue

Unexpected Kindness

❧ I don't know why my father, not very often but periodically, surprised me with unexpected kindness. Almost all the occasions, at least those that I remember, involved horses. Actually the first involved a pony, my small dusty brown and feisty Shetland pony, Dolly. Dolly was the name she came with, when my father purchased her from a Wyoming rancher, an hour's drive from Laramie where we lived. She was adorable to look at. And she was very smart. "They may be small but they ain't dumb," her former owner, the rancher, noted. I was eight and Dolly was a complete surprise. I am not sure if he had even told my mother who had left him two years earlier. As far as I remember, he did not give Dolly to me on a requiring-gifts occasion like my birthday or Christmas. My father just, out of the blue, bought her for me and drove me out to meet her. I was thrilled, overwhelmed with excitement really. I felt as much as a frozen little girl of eight, in the midst of a friendless third-grade year, can feel.

Exceptions, contradictions in my father's behavior still stick out in my memory, hard to place, and inexplicable. Yet my father, like every other human being, was capable of both cruelty and kindness. The reality of the one did not take away from the reality of the other.

My father was full of contradictions, much like a boy in my third-grade class who also stands out in my mind, also stands vividly, with a sense of contradiction. My memory of that boy is bound up in kindness, in contrast to cruelty—kindness and contradiction. Yet like my father, the memory of him refuses easy categorization. His name was something like Cory, a nice name, one that I might use for a child or animal companion. His desk was in the row next to mine although slightly further back. His clothes were grubby and in poor repair. And his kindness radiated out from him to me. We never spoke or played. We were not friends, and yet I felt a kinship with him.

I have a clear memory that Cory struggled with his schoolwork, although not for lack of good intentions on his part, or that of our teacher, a young Mrs. Something who clearly meant well. Cory struggled to understand our studies. While I saw numbers on a page of our mathematics book, the information blurred as it and he tried to meet together in his mind. The space around him held a sense of hopelessness. Neither he nor the teacher thought him capable of learning. One day this gentle, grubby boy lost his patience. He held his pencil like a knife to stop the heart of the math book. He stabbed the book, dug in, and swirled his pencil around and around on the page. The black made a lovely arch like a planet orbiting the sun. The teacher stood stunned. When Cory finished, we could all read the same thing on that gutted page, even Cory.

So my father giving me Dolly stands out in my mind, not quite fitting with all the other events of my life. The strangeness of it did not stop me from loving her, loving riding, loving the smell and feel and sight and sound of horses. My father also bought me a tiny, Shetland-pony-size saddle, and a small bridle, to use when I rode Dolly. For a year or two, we kept Dolly out at the ranch belonging to the rancher who had sold her to us. It was a long trip to get there over dusty roads that were barely visible—it sometimes seemed one drove over open prairie grass—and through a number of barbed-wire fences. Each time we came upon a gate, I would hop out of the car and begin wiggling the loop of wire holding the barbed-wire gate snug to the wooden fence post, drag the gate open so that the car could go through, drag it shut, and work the wire loop back in place. The worry over leaving a gate open, and risking losing the rancher's cows, held me tight.

When we arrived, my mother or father would let me out, turn the car around, and head back toward our little town of Laramie. The plan was that I would be back, and ready to go, when my parent arrived to pick me up. I do not remember the details. Did I wear a watch? In third grade, was I reasonably good at telling time? How did my parents manage that long drive back and forth to the ranch to drop me off, and later the same day, back and forth to pick me up? I do remember that I knew not to be late, not to be even a tiny bit late, if my father was the one picking me up.

Did my father love me? Was he capable of love? And anyhow, what does it mean to love someone? Does loving entail a series of actions, doing certain necessary things required by love? Is loving an emotion, anxiety or joy, anger or desire, or a physical sensation, tightness in the chest, a rush of energy, a warmth? Or is love a matter of seeing, truly seeing the fullness of another, recognizing the existence of a being outside one's self.

The intangibility of love has always bothered me. In a life full of pretending, one loses the capacity to be sure. Even the open and bloody body of the cat my father killed fell outside of sureness. Both questions, what happened, and did it happen, lurked around the corner of all my experience. So, surely, I could not be sure about love.

I remember bicycling out to my beautiful chestnut-red horse, another of my father's oddly out-of-place acts of kindness, and stopping on the side of the road, stunned by, dizzy with, uncertainty. Did I really love my horse, I wondered. Could I be sure? Yet without that love to hold onto, what did I have?

Cruelty, too, like love, leaves one unsure. Many of my father's cruel acts were unintentional. Does this unintentionality mean that the acts were not, really, cruel? If not intended, is the harm caused by accident or inability or mistake? Perhaps the harm that springs from a failure to see, a failure to recognize another at the other side of one's actions, is not cruelty at all, except in its results.

In our childhood, my little sister perhaps most often experienced this kind of cruelty, cruelty by default. Once it involved riding ponies.

Soon after my father bought me Dolly, he took my younger sister and me out to ride. I rode Dolly, and my father borrowed another pony from the rancher where Dolly lived for my sister to ride. Her pony probably belonged to the little girl who lived with the rancher. I felt a special kinship with that girl, although I doubt I could have put the kinship into words. Like me, since my mother left my father, she lived with a man unattached to her, a sort-of-stepfather, a man who slept with her mother even though they were not married. This was quite something, a big happening in our small, morally rigorous, and conservative Christian town. Everyone involved was tainted, like it or not, with or without choice. The fact that she was an innocent bystander, a child, made no difference.

The girl and her mother lived in the one large room over the rancher's office, in a rough structure that was not quite a house and not quite a barn. I saw the messy double bed where the girl's mother and the rancher slept. I never did understand where the girl slept. Yet even without clarity on many of the details, somehow I knew how precarious her situation was, living in that strange room with a circular metal staircase rising, as straight up as a circular staircase can rise, from the rancher's office to his bedroom. I knew it was all his. I knew everything rested on the girl and her mother not making the smallest mistake, while still remaining human and alive and desirable to the rancher. It is a tough line to walk, being human and without error. I knew about that too.

So we borrowed from that girl her precariously owned pony, her pony as long as she and her mother managed to make no mistakes, managed to stay with the rancher at his ranch, in his bedroom. And with my father following along on foot, my little sister and I started out on a little ride. We did not make it very far before my sister's pony, the pony of the girl who lived with the rancher, decided it was far enough and neatly and effectively gave a buck that sent my little sister flying off his back. I have the vaguest memory of my sister in a little heap on that dusty dry summer prairie ground. My father immediately insisted that she get back on the pony. If you get thrown, you get back on the horse, he said. That was the philosophy we grew up on, no matter that most moments of our young lives seemed to be moments of, metaphorically, getting thrown. Get back on the pony, my father said. My little sister, notoriously passive, if one can be invisible and notorious at once, shook her head, no. Perhaps the only time that she put her foot down as a child, she refused to get back on that pony. Get back on right now, my father told her forcefully. She did not and did not and did not get back on that pony. Remembering that summer day, I once again feel the fear that she was about to get hit, about to get hurt, hurt by my father. Still she refused.

Finally, remarkably, my father gave up. I think we were all a little stunned at my father's retreat. I had never seen him give up. And giving up to a small girl child, that was something. In my family, small children were meant to do as they were told. Small children, especially girls, were to be seen and not heard. They did not make demands or take up space. One did not bother about small children. And yet here was my father, acquiescing to the wishes of a small child.

My father opened the back of his car for my sister to climb in. Growing up, my little sister always seemed to be in the back of the car, the far back, where dogs and ski boots go. My older brother and I usually bullied her into sitting there. And as far as I remember, our parents never intervened. So she bent down, ducking her head, to climb into the back of the car. As she bent over she rested her weight on her arm and, just as suddenly, collapsed against the dirty carpet that covered the area where she so often sat. Like a grotesque cartoon arm, her arm did not merely bend at the elbow; halfway between her elbow and her wrist it bent again, making a second right angle, a second elbow of sorts, where there should have only been one.

As usual, my little sister did not complain of pain. She simply did not complain, ever, that I can remember. Yet this time, she put her foot down, this time she refused. I remember, for moments, not understanding why her arm bent like that, why my father appeared so startled, why he hurried me to return the two ponies to their corral. I do not remember the drive back. I do not remember my father apologizing to my little sister, or at least acknowledging that my sister was right, this time, she was right not to get back on the horse. What I remember is her refusal, that and the way her small face looked as she climbed into the car.

For my sister and me, our childhood was, at times, a nightmare. Annie and I, we each found a way, our own way, of surviving. We had to. And mine, my way, involved horses, being on horses and with horses, reading horses, dreaming horses, playing horses. Strange, looking back it is strange, it is unexpected to see after all these years that my father was the one who gave me the animals, he gave me the horses, that carried me out and far away.

Horse Crazy

Girls and the Lives of Horses

In 1983 John E. Schowalter, chief of child psychiatry and professor of pediatrics and psychiatry at Yale University, wrote about the phenomenon of American girls' passion for horses: "I have been struck by a relatively common but not much studied phenomenon, the 'horse-crazy' girl."[1] Schowalter noted that this passion existed as far back as the late nineteenth century. Still today, this prevalent phenomenon is, as Schowalter said thirty-five years ago, "not much studied." This is surprising given that girls' love of horses in the United States continues to be very common and fed by a plethora of popular culture books and toys.

Girls love horses, but why? What does this love say about what it means to be a girl? And what does it say about the meaning of horse lives? I explore these meanings, and this love, of girls with horses in the United States. I am interested in the girls' experience of the horse-girl relationship. I am also interested in the lives of horses and what horse lives reveal about their significance in human existence. The love of horses and the girl-horse relationship in some ways reproduce traditional gender norms. In other important ways, girls' experiences of riding horses and their love of horses offer a challenge to sexist ways of thinking about being female and to mainstream ideas about girlhood. Finally, I investigate the ways U.S. horses are a type of capital—animal capital—and produce profit that is both symbolic and material. These are interrelated forms of capital. Horses as symbolic capital normalize girls while horses also exist as more traditional economic capital offering the possibililty of material profit.

⤚ This is a book about love, and about the life-giving possibilities of love. As a girl I loved horses, and my horse—the relationship I had with him, the calm and sense of well-being (rare in my childhood) the strength I gained through being with him—helped me survive being a girl, allowed me to become an adult. In some ways, I was raised by nonhuman animals, by a small gray Siamese cat, a dusty brown Shetland pony, and a chestnut quarter horse.

While my relationship with my cat was not fetishized by consumer culture, looking back on my childhood, I see now that girls and horses were a thing, and they still are. We are sold girls and horses, and linked to that consumption is a popular culture of horsey girls in the United States, Great Britain, and other places.

Girls are many things, horses and fashion, thinness and dissatisfaction. I believe horsey culture offers girls something, a kind of freedom, that fashion does not. My earlier work explored the grip of social power. This book looks at the ways we shake power loose and make (a) life in spite of power. Horsey girls are girls who, to some perhaps small extent, resist mainstream culture's death grip of frail-girl, skinny-body, make-up-and-beauty demands. Horsey girls find a way to something else.

While some girls had fantasies of thinness and boys who will protect and keep them, men who will validate their existence, I had fantasies of horses. I dreamed of being with horses, raising horses, training horses, riding horses, and being myself a horse. At school when my body was alone—and merely a small girl—I was silent. On my horse, Snipaway, I became huge and powerful and beautiful. On my horse, I mattered in both senses of that word: in becoming someone with significance in the world and in becoming embodied, physical and real.

My family had little money for toys. Yet I did have and prized plastic Bryer horses and the small wooden stable where they lived. I read about horses as much as I could, although my reading material came to me by happenstance. (Oddly, for all the reading I did, I only discovered the public library as an adult.) I read around the edges of other people's lives, the books my mother and stepmother kept on their shelves, and those given to me by family members for Christmas or my birthday. The paucity of my horsey reading material, however, did not stop me from filling my mind with horses.

In spite of my deep love, the horses in my life died with so little fanfare, so little peace. We humans tend to keep our horses as long as they are useful to us and not much longer. A horse's life might be good for a time, but a horse's death is too often an ugly affair.

Perhaps I wanted to write this book only to honor my horse family, to honor the love I shared with them, the life that they gave me. Still today, when I turn my mind to peace, I shut my eyes and return to my horse. I am once again riding him through pine forest, the forest rising up from my little mountain town. Snow falls gently around us and all the world is quiet.[2]

This book explores the relationship between humans and nonhuman animals—between girls and horses—focusing on the United States. Many people understand that real love happens between girls and horses, between humans and other animals. Yet this love is also sometimes viewed suspiciously, even as childish. The adult who claims her dog is her best friend may be seen by her work colleagues and acquaintances as odd. *Horse Crazy* takes seriously human and animal relationships. It explores my own growing up with a horse and my own and other "horse-crazy" girls' experience of loving horses, while also analyzing popular culture's celebration and exploitation of girls and horses, investigating the history and lives of horses, and studying the ways girls' agency emerges through their connections with horses.

Some girls become "girls"—they take on the mainstream culture's demands to be "normal" and "feminine"—through horsey relationships. This happens in part through their consumption of horse stories, movies, and television shows, of which girls are often the main and intended audience, like the popular *My Little Pony* television series. Yet simultaneously, such girls defy the demands of normal "girlishness" through the actual experience of riding and being with horses. The focus in this book is on the world of middle- and working-class girls who largely ride for pleasure rather than the predominantly male world of racing or the elite and extremely expensive world of horse shows. In this world, the world of horseback riding simply for the love of it, horses open for girls the possibility of some freedom from the constraints of normative gender. This book also explores the realities of horse lives and deaths, too often brutal realities—brutal in spite of the love of girls—juxtaposing horse lives with the love of girls, horse lives as they happen beyond that girl love.

From a theoretical standpoint, I draw on Michel Foucault's concept of normalization, that is, the construction of the subject through various social powers. Foucault and other poststructuralist thinkers explore the meaning of life, girl life and horse life, and the ways power works on and through and around all of us. While the cultural meanings of horse-girl relationships, or what I call the symbolic capital produced by horses, can normalize and restrict girls, the horse-girl relationship also embodies Nikolas Rose's idea of a politics of vitalism, in which a form of life resists normalization, inspires experiments in living, and is, to use Rose's phrase, its "own telos."

Girls develop a complex agency through their relationships with horses. In much of their lives—in their families, in school, in religious institutions—girls are socialized as "normal"; they are normalized. Yet there are outs, ways that girls burst through the grip of normalization, challenging it and demanding a kind of freedom. I claim that in three respects, girls' love for horses enables them to mount such challenges. One, horse-crazy girls often develop counternormative combinations of self-assertion and caregiving. Two, these girls acquire an embodied connection to horses, and to themselves, through riding. Three, their love of horses allows them to, in some part, refuse the heteronormative social demand to prioritize relationships with and desire for boys above all else.

First, with regard to self-assertion, relationships with horses offer girls another way to be persons in the world. I contend that girls become something more with horses. This is what the women I spoke with told me: they described feeling bigger, stronger, freer, and more powerful. And they also described *being* more powerful, that is, more able to manage their lives as girls and, for many, as girls on the margins.

Such self-assertion, moreover, arises in tandem with the caregiving. Horse-crazy girls move beyond the stark duality of nurturing girl (as in the conservative thinking that girls are "naturally" caring and nurturing) versus self-assertive girl (as in mainstream liberal feminist thinking wherein girls should prioritize entering the public world of work over inhabiting the world of domestic caregiving). I show the political importance of the girl-horse relationship for its embodiment of a kind of girlhood that defies the categories in conventional debates about gender politics. Girl-horse love's combination of nurturing and self-assertion does not fit neatly into either conservative or liberal ideologies of gender. The both/and quality of girl-horse love suggests a way of thinking about gender that conforms neither with the ways it is discussed in the work of such important contemporary conservative writers as Ryan T. Anderson, nor as it is defined in the ongoing work of such liberal feminist communities as the National Organization for Women.

Second as for my argument that horse-crazy girls experience counternor-mativity in their embodied connection with horses: horseback riders work to attain physical connection, oneness, with the horses that they ride. As one woman I interviewed said about her experience riding, "I become one with the horse, and bond."[3] This is a starkly different experience of embodiment than mainstream U.S. culture demands of girls, wherein they must make themselves thin and frail, and even disassociate themselves from their bodies. Animal studies scholars Lynda Birke and Keri Brandt write about gender and body connection with horses: "The desire to achieve that oneness also enables a transcendence of the constraints implied by learning to perform femininity . . . learning to communicate bodily with horses permits women to experience their embodiment in more positive ways."[4] Girls and women who ride literally rein in and collaborate with a large, powerful animal, one that might intimidate but ultimately can help liberate them. This is a profound and unique form of empowered embodiment that is congruent with Rose's idea of vitalism, which I will explore in this book.[5]

Third, the friendships girls have with horses provide an alternative to the relationships that a heteronormative culture pushes girls to have with boys, and the girl-horse relationship empowers girls considerably more than the conventional girl-boy relationship does. Even in the fantasy horse games girls play, the girls are strong because in their imagining they are on horseback, or they are themselves horses. And the girls who have access to actual horses have an opportunity to become themselves, by which I mean they develop according to experiences valued for themselves, not according to norms in which they subordinate themselves to boys. They find a place where they have control and choice. They make decisions not only for themselves but for and with and on the horses too. In this relationship, girls are often the leaders. Helen, a former horse-crazy girl I interviewed who is now a horse-crazy woman, told me that when she rides, "I feel very independent, like I am free."[6] And the girl-horse relationship supports this feeling and state of being. Horses and girls are, in Donna J. Haraway's terms, "significant others."[7]

Horse Crazy contributes to the field of animal studies in its exploration of the significant bispecies relationship between girls and horses, and it addresses the important cultural phenomenon of horse-crazy girls. Over the past decade there has been a proliferation of writing on human relationships with other animals in this rapidly developing area of animal studies by environmentalists and animal-rights activists. Haraway's *When Species Meet* (2008) offers a helpful entry point to examine the girl-horse/human-animal relationship. Haraway's notion of "companion species" challenges conventional ways of thinking about humans and other animals as two sides of a binary split, with humans/men and rationality on one side, nature (and women), other animals, instincts, and things of the body on the other side. Haraway refuses this dualism and argues that we are all inextricably connected.[8] We are nature, and it is us. And as all things in life (and death) grow and change, forever becoming something else, we grow and change in relationship with all that is around us; we *become* in the midst of relationship, including relationship with nonhuman animals. Haraway writes, "Beings do not preexist their relatings. . . . There are no pre-constituted subjects and objects, and no single sources, unitary actors, or final ends." Haraway clarifies that our relationships—with humans and other animals—are always contingent and always changing or, as she writes, becoming. "In Judith Butler's terms," Haraway notes, "there are only 'contingent foundations'; bodies that matter are the result. A bestiary of agencies, kinds of relatings, and scores of time trump the imaginings of even the most baroque cosmologists." Haraway writes, "[T]hat is what *companion species* signifies."[9]

Being companion species means that human and horse become together. To explore companion species is to explore that being-in-relation, the collaborative becoming of woman and dog, of girl and horse. In this becoming and in the possibilities inherent in it, girls with horses find a kind of freedom.[10]

Girls in their relationship with horses experience new ways of being girls, ways of being that challenge and subvert normal gender identity. Elspeth Probyn's term for this being-in-relationship of girls with horses is to "be-long."[11] In this, the becoming of girls with horses includes but moves beyond the girls being empowered as *girls*. The girl-with-horse is a being unto itself that is more, indeed that is bigger, faster, more beautiful, safer, than just the girl or just the horse. This is not merely a matter of the girl being on top of the horse and being in control (and, I might add, "control" is a tenuous and mutual affair when it comes to riding horses). With a horse, and often one particular horse, the horsey girl becomes the girl-horse. In this transformation, qualities that inhere in the horse can also inhere in the girl. As one woman I interviewed said about her beloved childhood horse, "He was my beauty"—not in the sense that he was her beautiful possession, but in the sense that his beauty became hers too. Alone, she explained, she was not beautiful; and that is of course what girls are supposed to be in our dominant culture: beautiful, an object worth gazing upon. But when she was a girl-with-horse, she became beautiful and shared other qualities with him as well—active qualities like bravery and strength and speed.[12]

Physical contact, bodies touching bodies, plays a significant role in girl-horse relationships. Touching horses also plays an important role in healing, as practitioners of various forms of equine therapy understand quite well. In my first book, *Boundaries of Touch: Parenting and Adult-Child Intimacy* (2007), I explore both the impact, and our thinking about the impact, of physical contact between human adults and children. One biological response to touch I discuss in the book is the release of a hormone called oxytocin, which plays a critical role for humans and other mammals in feeling connected as well as in giving birth, lactation, and orgasm.[13] There is a growing literature on the biomedical impact on humans of contact with nonhuman animals, including the role of oxytocin. In part because contact with horses can cause the release of oxytocin in humans, horses and horseback riding are used as therapy for a wide range of conditions, including developmental, physical, and psychiatric disabilities.[14] Research indicates that contact with horses helps calm anxious humans, focuses and connects humans limited in their abilities to engage socially, and develops other physical capacities of humans with disability. Some (including several of the women I interviewed) argue that a primary benefit for humans being with horses (and other animals) is the increase in the level of oxytocin—indeed, both the humans and the horses seem to experience this increase of oxytocin in their systems—induced by being in the presence of horses, but more particularly through the physical contact of stroking, grooming, and riding horses.[15] The becoming of girls-with-horses happens in bodies, bodies in contact with bodies.[16]

The impact of all this on the horse remains to some extent unknown. Yet I do think there are impacts of the human-horse relationship that we can see, inscribed so to speak, in and on the horse's body. Horse bodies represent physical animal capital. Their very bodies both constitute wealth (as horse-meat, for example) and produce wealth (such as through their past agrarian labor). From the development of horse breeds, to branding, to the use of bits, to the growth of a particular muscular structure in training for a spe-cific horse showing event, humans have an impact on horses much as horses shape humans and human experiences. These are traces that one can see.

Horse Crazy Theory

Central to my theoretical framework are Foucault's ideas of normalization and biopower. Foucault developed the concept of normalization to explain one central way that power happens. The framework for the theory of nor-malization (and of biopolitics discussed below) can be found in Foucault's ideas about fundamental power structures in liberal society. Liberalism is professed to be an order of rights and egalitarian relations. However, Foucault calls into question the common thinking that modern liberal dem-ocratic society is characterized by a pure increase of human freedom as compared with earlier times. Foucault argues that we must focus our atten-tion not solely on the state but also on other forms of power. He argues that a critical characteristic of modern society is an array of social and political institutions or disciplines, such as families, schools, governments, and mili-taries, that participate in the formation of a type of human subject or "sub-jectivity." According to Foucault, these institutions, these disciplines, make liberalism possible. He argues that modern liberal society is characterized by the internalization of the expectations of these institutions, and that through this internalization, individual choice is constrained. This is the process of normalization. Thus, again, the disciplines of prisons, schools, hospitals, and other such institutions—which make liberalism possible—make up the inegalitarian and hierarchical relations of normalization.[17] Political theorist

Jacob Segal explains, "[T]he various 'disciplines' or institutions—such as schools, prisons, hospitals—[are] where individuals are socialized to act according to 'norms' to be healthy, to be law-abiding and to avoid the opposites of being sick and criminal."[18] About this Foucault writes, "The disciplines characterize, classify, specialize, they distribute along a scale around a norm, hierarchize individuals in relations to one another and, if necessary, disqualify and invalidate."[19]

For Foucault, this process means that in all societies, but with greater intensity in modern society, the way we come to make choices, the way we come to do what we do and think what we think, springs from our society. We make choices, have feelings, develop ideas about ourselves and the world through a social process of interaction. Through this process, some ways of acting, feeling, and thinking become that which constitute what is considered normal. Other ways of acting, feeling, and thinking become deviant. Foucault explains that this process, normalization, results from social forces, that is, social power that acts on us as individuals. As I wrote in 2012,

> Through normalization, individuals are disciplined to be "normal" in a dualistic framework that both springs from and reproduces social power.
>
> Normativity, although not an instrument of those in power according to Foucault, often supports the privilege of the more powerful in society. In the dualism, "normal" defines the supposed attributes—such as being "civilized"—of those in power, those who are predominantly white, male, American, citizens, and middle class. On the other side of this binary, "abnormal" defines the supposed characteristics of marginalized groups, those predominantly of color, female, un-American, undocumented, ethnic, and impoverished. In the dualism, the "abnormal" are understood, for example, as "savage."[20]

Yet these forces do not merely act on us from the outside. In this subjectification, we also internalize the influences, and they become a part of who we are.

For example, in the United States today, there is enormous pressure for girls and women to be thin.[21] Girls experience this compulsion to be thin nearly everywhere around them, in mass-mediated ideas of beauty, in the diet and exercise industries, in school with other girls, in mainstream health care institutions, and so on. Girls internalize these expectations, these obsessions with thinness, and pressure themselves. They monitor their eating practices and calorie intake, they worry that this or that article of clothing makes them "look fat," they compare themselves to others. They fill their minds and imaginations with anxious thoughts about their weight. This is a form of social power acting in and on—normalizing—girls.

Foucault's concept of normalization helps us see how seemingly innocent interactions between a girl and her mother as they shop for a new pair of pants—or between a girl and her horse as she holds her mare's heavy hoof between her legs and cleans it with a hoof pick—are involved in the power-laden construction of identity. In contrast to the normalizing demand for girl bodies to be thin, in caring for her horse, we see Foucault's claim that power can be productive of girl subjectivity in ways not merely oppressive. In this, a girl's inner experience of mundane activity, caregiving for her mare, is transformed into something vital. She is not merely a caregiver but giving care in the form of self-assertion as a horse-crazy girl. Her care is inexricably connected to her self-assertation in the world as a skilled horse person. In *Horse Crazy*, I explore the ways girls transform power to be creative, joyful, and life giving or, in the terms of Rose, vital. I explore this transformation through a concept I call "vital care."

Along with normalization, the other Foucauldian concepts I invoke in this book are biopower—the "technology of power centered on life"—and biopolitics—the ways in which our human life spans, crime rates, and overall public health are managed and controlled by larger forces of social power.[22] While normalization acts on individuals, biopolitics shape populations. Foucault explains that biopower bodes "nothing less than the entry of life into history, that is, the entry of phenomena peculiar to the life of the human species in the order of knowledge and power" (141–142). Biopolitics involve a cultural, social, and political perception "and address a plethora of human efforts to manage, control, and alter the vital human experience."[23] So a biopolitical counterpoint to the normalization of girls' obsession with thinness might be public health campaigns focusing on obesity and educating the public about "healthy eating practices." These campaigns act on populations working to manage eating, health, and body size. Foucault explains the links between the concepts of normalization and biopower. He writes,

> [W]e can say there is one element that will circulate between the disciplinary and the regulatory, which will also be applied to body and population alike, which will make it possible to control both the disciplinary order of the body and aleatory events that occur in the biological multiplicity. The element that circulates

between the two is the norm. The norm is something that can be applied to both a body one wishes to discipline and a population one wishes to regularize.[24]

Here Foucault separates power from the state and from intentionality. The "one" Foucault refers to above is a doctor or teacher or minister who does not intend to normalize. She does so because of a replicating form of discourse in which she herself is caught.

Norms that prescribe a particular body size regularize the bodies of humans, particularly women and girls, in the United States today. In her idea of "animal capital," social theorist Nicole Shukin urges us to cross the species barrier and also consider Foucault's concept of biopower in terms of nonhuman animals. She insists we think about other animal life when we theorize about "the technology of power centered on life."[25] She explains that "it is not enough to theorize biopower in relation to human life alone.... [T]he reproductive lives and labors of other species (sexually differentiated labors, let us not forget) also become a matter of biopolitical calculation."[26]

Animal Capital

For Shukin, the neglect of nonhuman animals reflects a limit in Foucault's theory. "The biopolitical analyses [Foucault] has inspired," Shukin writes, "are constrained by their reluctance to pursue power's effects beyond the production of human social and/or species life" (11). Following Shukin, who pushes us to think about the biopolitical production of both human and other animal life, I argue that horses become what Shukin calls animal capital, that is, a form of biopower. Few scholars have used the work of Foucault on biopower to think about nonhuman animal life. Shukin writes, "While theorists of biopower have interrogated the increasingly total subsumption of the social and biological life of the anthropos to market logics, little attention has been given to what I am calling animal capital" (7). For Shukin, animal lives produce both economic and symbolic forms of this capital, that is, animal capital. To explain the biopolitical uses of animals, Shukin explores the role of the beaver in Canadian history. Historically the beaver produced material capital in the form of skins for human consumption. Shukin explains that the "reproductive value of animals is by no means only biological." The beaver in Canadian history has produced more than the material resource of its skin: "If the beaver has furnished one species of animal capital for the nation as colonial pelt, it has furnished another as postcolonial brand. . . . [A]nimal signs and metaphors are also key symbolic resources of capital's reproduction" (12). Canada's official emblem since 1975, the beaver is a sign, a symbol of Canada, that works "as a tool of affective governance to involve Canadians in a project of national identity building" (3). Using the beaver as the national emblem "consolidated the economic and symbolic capital accumulated in the sign of the beaver over three centuries of Euro-Canadian traffic in North America, presenting it as a natural, self-evident sign of the nation." The sign of the beaver "stands in for an organic national unity that in actuality does not exist" and obscures a history of colonialism, white supremacy, and genocide (3).

Animal lives produce animal capital in two forms, the material (or economic) and the symbolic. Today, horse bodies produce capital in their production of leisure for segments of the population, for example, just as cow bodies produce food. Historically, horses worked on farms to help their human owners produce crops and other material goods. Not merely material, animal capital is also symbolic; it produces cultural meaning and it normalizes. Like (and often with) cows in the United States, contemporary horses create symbolic forms of capital; horses also have a starring role in a national story of origins about the righteous movement of white people across the continent to civilize (colonize) the "wild" land. Horse books, television shows, and film characters often support this national story.

Both in terms of the symbolic capital of horses in popular culture including western movies and, more recently, *My Little Pony*, and the material capital of living horse labor, Shukin's thinking about animal capital sheds light on the lives of U.S. horses and on their relationships with girls. Historically in the United States, with the shifting use of horses from productive work to leisure, increasingly horses were symbolic animal capital; they have lived, for example, in children's literature where they shape the meanings of girlhood, of working hard and of living correctly. With industrialization and the development of consumer culture, horses were mass-produced as toys, such as the My Little Pony plastic figures, to be consumed by children. Thus, as animal capital, horse bodies come in various forms—both actual horses (hired, for example, to act in westerns) and the plethora of plastic toy horses and horses made out of words in storybooks. These are forms of symbolic animal capital and, as such, forms of biopower.

Anna Sewell's 1877 novel, *Black Beauty*, comprises a signal moment in the production of symbolic horse capital. It spawned the pony book genre in children's literature that I discuss in chapter 3. Many such horse stories have emerged since, right up to the contemporary horse TV show *My Little Pony*. In *Boundaries of Touch*, I showed how popular literature, such as the self-help books genre, is used to sell us normalizing ideas about social phenomena such as gender. In *Horse Crazy*, the most popular stories about horses and girls—those that have sold well and have been read widely—have sold girls normalizing ways to be girls, I argue. For example, stories about pretty pink ponies like the extremely popular *My Little Pony* peddle a narrative in which being gendered as a girl means being cute and lovable. I will also show, as I discussed above, that actual girl-horse relationships challenge the very normalization that is inculcated by such stories.

Plastic toys first produced by Hasbro in 1982 as six pony figurines, My Little Pony has inspired numerous books, four television series, a film, countless plastic toys, and other products. And all these forms of My Little Pony have created both material animal capital (money) and symbolic capital as they model "normal" girlness for girls to internalize. These stories and the pony characters in them normalize girls to be pretty and sweet, cute and demure. At the same time, they also encourage tolerance and commitment to friendship. Horses—even when pink and plastic—offer a kind of challenge to normative gender and the bullying and relational aggression many U.S. girls experience. My Little Pony characters have sweet, cute, and demure names—such as Apple Blossom, Rainbow Dash, and Pinky Pie—that reinforce hegemonic femininity. Indeed, the ponies' names are remarkably similar to the names of pornography stars—such as Honey Cup, Stormy Day, and Annie Sprinkle—who among other possibilities can also be sexualized and sweet, cute and demure. To play with this similarity, one website developed a game where players guess whether a given name belongs to one of the My Little Pony characters or an actual pornography star. The website notes, "She has flowing hair, smooth skin, languid eyes, *and* she's completely naked. Are we discussing here a star of one of the approximately four hundred thousand single-, double-, and triple-X-rated films out there, or one of the approximately four hundred thousand different 'My Little Ponies' that flooded toy stores in the Eighties?" (I played the game and only answered correctly half the time.)[27]

The majority of American girls only own "horses" by consuming toys like My Little Pony and the fantasy stories about horses that saturate the market. Girls have horse-themed birthday parties, purchase plastic horse figures, and view horse movies and television including an animated feature-length *My Little Pony* film and four different animated *My Little Pony* television series.[28] Girls can play their own, make-believe My Little Pony games evoked by the brightly (distinctly nonhorse) colored toys, in pink, orange, purple, and green, and by the accompanying *My Little Pony* books and television shows, involving friendships between the ponies, their social events, and the grooming of the ponies to look sweet and pretty.

My Little Pony and other toy horses are beautifully packaged, abstracted from horse reality, ready for consumption. Here it is important to note that, in sharp contrast to actual horses, toy horses never age, defecate, dangerously kick, step on one's feet, or buck wildly in an effort to toss their clinging human rider off. The living animal does all these things, and regularly. Like all relationships, girl-horse relationships are not without problems. Spending time with horses may be a dream of many girls, but the lived reality is not so dreamlike. Being with horses means facing the possibility of injury, even serious injury.[29] Caring for horses involves extensive time and effort handling—removing, piling, sweeping, and shoveling—their manure.[30] And of course, horses, like all living things, like girls themselves, age, get sick, endure injury, die.

Many horse-crazy girls never actually own or even spend time with a horse. Yet some do. What happens to those horses as they and their human girls age? Katherine C. Grier's history, *Pets in America: A History* (2006),[31] explores the normative United States pet-owning culture in which many people treat their living and dead pets' bodies much like the bodies of their closest human relatives. For some humans, their "pets" *are* their closest relatives, as was true of me when I was a girl. Humans spend enormous amounts of money on their animal companions when they are alive and even after they die. Humans often cremate them or buy graves in pet cemeteries and bury them. They hold funerals and memorials for them. But whereas horse owners have many opportunities for consuming horse-related products and services for their living animals, the old age and death of horses are different from those of other companion animals. This is, in large part, because of their size. In contrast to supporting a cat or dog in old age, one cannot keep one's aging horse inside one's own household, and it is expensive to put an old horse out to pasture for her retirement. What happens to old horses? And how do humans handle the sizable problem of disposing of dead horse bodies?

In a 2012 article in the *Los Angeles Times*, journalist Michael Haederle noted that the then-economic crisis "weighs heavily on horses." Haederle wrote, "Across New Mexico, officials say, hungry horses are being turned loose on public and tribal land or left by the side of the road. Others languish out of sight in backyard stalls, like the six emaciated horses Albuquerque police discovered in June when they answered an unrelated call at an auto salvage business." Haederle wrote that the rise in unwanted horses "nationally is reflected in the number exported abroad for slaughter each year— about 138,000."[32]

Along with the problem of size, horse bodies offer the possibility of profit because they can be sold for meat. Foucault notes that the management of life is also the management of death. Likewise, in death, horse bodies are used for food—it is not normative for humans to eat horsemeat in the United States, but elsewhere it is—and rendered profitable in myriad other ways. In 2007 Congress effectively banned the slaughter of horses in the United States. Until then, United States horses were slaughtered here and then sent to western Europe and other places as human food: one study found that over a four-year period ending in 1990, 1,371,940 horses were sent to slaughter in the United States.[33] Since 2007, buyers have been shipping horses from the United States to slaughterhouses in Mexico and Canada to harvest their meat. And as I discuss in chapter 7, in spite of the taboo on humans eating horses in the United States, humans' pets *have* eaten horsemeat.

Dolly's Death

↬ When I visited my grandparents for two weeks in the summer in their small Wyoming town, we had an evening ritual. Not every evening, but often, my grandfather would drive my grandmother and me around his properties so that we could check up on things. We drove for miles on winding country roads, some dirt, some paved. We drove past my grandfather's farms, where corn and wheat were grown. We drove past his cattle. Part of his small empire included a cow-calf operation that we visited.

My grandmother sat in the front seat next to my grandfather. I
sat in the back. We all looked out the window as we drove, mostly in
silence. Sometimes my grandfather would point this or that out. The
corn looked good. The cows looked healthy. One year driving past a
pasture of cows grazing with their one-month-old babies, perhaps to
amuse himself, my grandfather gave me a calf. We drove into the pasture so that I could see her up close from the car. She was small and
red with white markings on her face. She had tiny hooves and a small
swooshing tail. She looked just like her mother, in miniature. I only
saw "my calf" that one time. Yet I thought of her for months, wondering where she was, what she was doing. I even thought of a brand for
her, a brand that would be mine alone. It involved the initials of my
name merged together into one small and connected design.

Always naïve and ridiculously trusting, it was only years later that
I finally realized what happened to "my calf." Around the same time,
as a young adult, I also realized what had happened to my childhood
Shetland pony. A decade before, I had outgrown her. You do not have
to be very big to outgrow a Shetland pony. When I grew too tall and
too heavy for her to carry me, she was already quite old. I was told
at the time that she had been put out to pasture near where we lived
in Laramie, retired to a life of pony-style leisure. Strangely, that same
year, on one of my childhood trips to visit my grandparents, I saw her
in one of the pens at my grandfather's sale barn and could not understand why she was there.

A large number of old, no-longer-useful-to-their-humans horses
and ponies end their lives with cows and other livestock at slaughterhouses. In the United States, humans normally do not, but our dogs
and cats do eat horseflesh. And the meat is also shipped to Europe
and other places where humans eat horse. My pony ended her life in a
slaughterhouse where she was transformed into someone's food.

Politeness and gender prohibited my asking questions of my
grandfather about the calf or my little pony. I did not understand, but
accepted fully, the mystery of male power.

Vitalism and Girls' Love of Horses

We can distinguish between the instrumental and noninstrumental uses of horses. On the North American continent, humans both ate horses brought by European colonizers and used horses for productive work. Then, starting in the early twentieth century and continuing today, horses began to be used for leisure and thus for largely noninstrumental purposes. The horse-crazy girls I study ride "for pleasure" (that is horse people's way of saying they ride for fun, not to race or compete in horse shows, not for work, and not for transportation). These girls have relationships with horses that are principally noninstrumental. Their lives with horses chiefly matter in the moment, for that moment, not for future gain, much like a human-to-human friendship. They love being with horses, and riding and caring for horses, for the pleasure of these activities and relationships. And more profoundly, they love horses. Love for another being is intrinsically noninstrumental. One does not love to get something from one's friend, but simply because one loves. About this, philosopher Michael Oakeshott writes, "The relationship of friends is dramatic, not utilitarian.... Loving is not 'doing good'; it is not a duty; it is emancipated from having to approve or to disapprove."[34]

Part of my interest in horse-crazy girls springs from a connection that I see with Rose's concept of "vitalism." Drawing from Foucault, Rose's vitalism resonates with the noninstrumentality of the girl-horse relationship. Vitalism for Rose grows out of his criticism of nonvital models of the "correct" life. He is critical of the conservative belief in a human essence, or essentialism, and the conservative belief in biologically determined gender roles as well as the liberal humanistic belief in human subjects and the never-ending possibility of their linear advancement. Essentialism proposes a way that all humans are, based on supposedly timeless biological human qualities. And humanism suggests a particular ongoing improvement in a way that, through proper future development, humans will become. In this humanistic framework, liberal feminist humanism argues that women will develop proper self-assertion when they are freed from sexism.

In contrast to both of these models, Rose's vitalism encourages experiments in living. To some extent this is what horse-crazy girls do, that is, they are not merely guided by a model of how to live; they ride beyond the bounds of models. In some sense, horse-crazy girls take up Foucault's suggestion "to make [their] lives 'a work of art.'"[35] By this, Rose clarifies, Foucault offers "an invitation to creativity and experimentation" in our living. This vitalism or "life politics" is, like many girls' experiences with horses, not about morality or a hidden kind of truth. It is not about subordinating oneself to a "regime of authority" or subordinating the present to a future goal. Horse-crazy girls love their horses, love to be with, care for, and ride them; they love to read and think about, and to play at, horses—and they do all these things for their own sake.

As pleasure riders, horse-crazy girls rarely have somewhere they must go, or something they must do; they ride to ride and care for the sake of caring. When I spent time with my pony, Dolly, at the age of eight, there was nothing that had to happen, nothing we had to do, nowhere in particular to go. From the Wyoming pasture where she lived with a small herd of horses, I caught her and groomed her for the love of her, for the love of her smell, the feel of her coat, the sound of her nicker. When I rode her off across the Wyoming plains, I rode for the love of her motion beneath my legs, the clop-a-clop movement, and the sound of her feet as they played out their pattern on the sage-and-wild-grass-covered prairie. I loved her and rode her for the enjoyment of these activities, the pleasure in them, and the present-moment physicality they entailed. The freedom here was distinct from trying to be a good girl or a beautiful girl, or trying to be anything. Instead, my pony and I explored the world as we found it, traveling alone together, far away from my little town and its demands.

Vitalism, Rose writes, "would operate under a different slogan" than that of social progress or self-improvement; instead, "each person's life should be its own telos" (282–283). In riding a horse I made my life what it was, not what it should be. In this vitalism "we should oppose all that which stands in the way of life being its own telos," Rose argues. "This would not be an anthropology or an essentialism of the human: there is no essence here serving as the basis for critique, and waiting to be realized." In riding I was not trying to enact myself as a typical girl working to be attractive to boys (what is the feminine thing to do? how should I act according to that standard?). Rose's vitalism would be "in favour of life, of the 'obstinate, stubborn and indomitable will to live,' of the conditions that make possible the challenge to existing modes of life and the creation of new modes of existence. . . . Such a political vitalism would certainly take sides: it would take the side of an active art of living" (283). Riding a horse as I did is a "new mode of existence" precisely because it was not given to me (or other girls) as a lesson in how to act. This will to live is not necessarily an adventure but a resistance to norms that restrict by identifying activities as abnormal. Thus horse-crazy girls enact a politics in the sense of taking a side against the norms that deny possibilities.

About this "undefined work of freedom," Foucault writes that it allows us to "separate out from the contingency that has made us what we are, the possibility of no longer being, doing, or thinking what we are, do, or think."[36] In part this is the freedom that springs, everywhere, from life itself, the freedom of never fully knowing what might happen next, never fully containing the possibilities of being—and of being, in the case of horse-crazy girls like me, with a horse. I never knew how or what my horse, and my relationship with him, would be, would happen, on any given day, on any given ride, at any given moment.

In spite of their commitment to and love for horses, their love of being with and around horses, to the extent horsey girls live for a moment in vitalism, it likely lasts only so long. Girls grow up to live in a world demanding gendered and raced lives of them, a world where profit often matters above everything else, above even life itself. Horses and girls age, and horse bodies must be managed, sometimes after their human girls have grown up and gone away. The body of horses used noninstrumentally for pleasure riding are sometimes brought back to instrumental use before death in their slaughter for human and pet food, and for glue and other such products. In a capitalist world, girls can only fend off the instrumental for so long.

Horse Crazy Methodology: Evidence of Horses and Girls

Horse Crazy is grounded in a combination of qualitative/ethnographic evidence, via in-depth interviews and spending time at stables, my own personal narrative writing, and social historical and popular cultural analysis.[37] In the latter, I study the consumption of horses in popular culture beginning with Sewell's 1877 novel. I examine popular works of pony book literature as well as the main nonfictional books for the horse-crazy girl audience, primary from the early twentieth century to the present. These include books coming from the United Kingdom and the United States, with a focus on the heyday of the pony book genre, the 1930s to the 1970s.[38] Finally, I examine the history and lives of United States leisure horses through social historical analysis and by studying the scholarly literature that addresses horse lives, deaths, and history.

I use personal narrative writing in *Horse Crazy*, often understood to be a relatively new sociological methodology.[39] In the personal narrative, I write about being a girl myself who loved, read about, and dreamed about horses; I owned a Shetland pony from 1975 to 1980, from the ages of eight to thirteen, and then owned a quarter horse from 1980, when he was a yearling, until his death in 2004. In this writing, I explore my own growing up in Wyoming and Montana, where I spent long days riding my horse alone in the Rocky Mountains. I signal the change in the text from traditional scholarly writing to personal narrative by margin (one is indented more than the other), alignment (one is justified, one is ragged right), and an icon.

Social scientific writers of personal narrative, or memoir, make both their own personal story and self-reflexivity about their story one of the frames (in my case, one among several) for the knowledge claims in their sociological analysis.[40] Personal narrative is another way of—another sociological methodology for—describing and interpreting our social world. It falls within a broader category that is described by sociologist Robert R. Alford and others as qualitative or interpretative.[41] In *Horse Crazy*, I intersperse my three primary frames—social historical research, cultural analysis of children's pony book literature, and my qualitative interview data—with the secondary frame of memoir writing about my own growing up as a horse-crazy girl. In my analysis, personal narrative will not replace more traditional sociological methodologies but will supplement them. In my book *The Parallel Lives of Women and Cows: Meat Markets* (2012), I used personal narrative to explore violence and trauma in my own experience. In *Horse Crazy*, I use personal narrative to explore the (my) personal experience of love—girl-horse love—and to enhance the discussion of girl-horse love that I develop through the in-depth interviews and other primary sources such as the pony book genre. Personal narrative is more and more common in sociology as well as in other disciplines like history and even professional fields such as social work.[42]

Who Are the Horse-Crazy Girls and Why Are They So White?

Primarily as the data source for chapters 5 and 6, I investigate U.S. girls' passion for horses via twenty-five open-ended, in-depth interviews with adult women who were horse crazy as girls (many of them remain so as women). I also interviewed one horseback-riding trainer, an elderly gay man (like horse-crazy girls, the horsey men I interviewed are nonnormative); the mother of an eleven-year-old horse-crazy girl with disability; one woman who owns and runs a stable that rescues horses and offers horseback riding lessons; the workers at an equine therapy stable; a pony book collector and expert; and three men in their twenties who identify as "bronies." Except for one of the bronies (who is from Portugal and lives there currently), the participants in my study were selected through snowball sampling from two different geographic areas: the western Rocky Mountain area where I grew up and the Northeast where I currently live.[43]

About half of the participants in my study experienced some form of discrimination and marginalization in childhood. Like me, a queer girl with disability, in my case, disability stemming from serious and ongoing childhood trauma,[44] some form of marginalization resulting from trauma or queer identity or disability is probably not unusual—indeed is likely normal—among horse-crazy girls. Interestingly, all the women identified as women, none identified openly as transgender or gender nonconforming. I spoke with one lesbian white woman in her early sixties who told me being passionate about horses gave her a place to belong in her early childhood in an urban area in the Midwest. At age six, she knew she was lesbian but did not feel safe telling anyone. She explained that she would have been very isolated in her heteronormative home and community if the horsey world— in which she could hang around stables and go horseback riding—had not given her a place to go, a place where she fit in. She argued that there were more queer girls among horse-crazy girls than among other groups of girls because horses allow for a nonnormative girl to be accepted and to belong. My sense is that girls with disability are another disproportionately represented group, and for a similar reason.

The women I spoke with overrepresent the white middle class, although one grew up working class, two grew up working poor, and three upper class.

One participant is African American, and two more identify as women of color. The rest identify as white. Of the twenty-five women, four openly identify as queer women or lesbian, and six have disability (all but one of those six have physical disability). Twelve of the twenty-five women enjoy multiple intersecting privileges with no stated disability, marginalization based on race, economic struggle, or queer identity; that is, two are white wealthy women, and ten are mainstream, white and middle class.

It will be important for future studies to explore horse experiences among people on the trans spectrum, those who are gender nonconforming, and all girls of color. U.S. communities of color, of course, have histories with horses. As the western United States was colonized, African Americans were among those who moved west seeking freedom from slavery and racism, land for farming and other opportunities, including work with cattle as cowboys (and, albeit lesser known, as cowgirls). The Federation of Black Cowboys explores and celebrates this history of African Americans in the West.[45] As discussed in chapter 2, many Native American groups also were and continue to be avid horse people.

In spite of these rich histories that diverse groups of people have with horses, I had little success disrupting the whiteness of my sample by looking for participants in two racially diverse areas in the United States, the Northeast in and around New York City, Philadelphia, and Boston; and the southwestern state of New Mexico (this did, however, give my sample some geographic diversity). To some extent the whiteness I encountered probably points to the profound segregation that continues to exist in the United States today, and the snowball technique that I used tended to reproduce that segregated whiteness. Snowball sampling entails asking around and making contact with participants in a relatively informal manner. As one gathers participants, they help connect the researcher with more participants, that is, people they know who share the relevant characteristic—in my study's case, a girlhood passion for horses. Yet because the United States remains a very racially and economically segregated society—which I explore in my coauthored book, *Seeing White: An Introduction to White Privilege and Race* (2011)—people who are white often only know other people who are white, and therefore starting with one or two white people leads to a largely white snowball sample.[46] I no longer know personally many people who do, or did once, horseback ride. The few horsewomen I do know are white, and the people who sent me to former horse-crazy girls sent me to white horse-crazy girls. Did white riders tell me about other white riders because white people tend to only know other white people? Or is the horseback-riding world dominated by white girls and women?

I asked the participants in my study if they knew (or still know) women of color who rode as girls or who ride today. Almost all of my participants, including Carrie, the one African American woman I interviewed, said no.[47] One white woman had a vague memory of, as she said, "one Asian girl" riding for a time at her childhood stable. Another woman thought that there was an African American family who came to their stable for a time. No one was able to give me any names. White people also dominate the horse books I read, both those from the pony book genre for girls and the popular books on horses oriented to adult women.

In two of a few horse books that I found in which people of color were involved, one person was a Native American man, GaWaNi Pony Boy, who had edited a two-book series on women and horses, *Of Women and Horses: Essays by Various Horse Women* (2000) and *Of Women and Horses: More Expressions of the Magical Bond* (2005). In the first of these books, he compiled twenty-two essays written by women about horses.[48] Only *one* of those women was of color, and she was a princess in Jordan and not from the United States.

Even in the case of Carrie, who had a diverse community of family and friends, the world of horses was white. A woman in her early forties, Carrie said about her girlhood riding: "I was probably the only Black person out there at the stables . . . everyone was white." Carrie, who grew up in a white neighborhood, mused, "So much of your childhood experiences depends on your parents and the access that they provide you with. I grew up in a community with lots of access to horses and a dad that supported it. Would I have been just as horse crazy if I did not grow up in a white neighborhood?" Carrie explained, "Horses was what I talked about with white girls. With Black girls, horses never entered the conversation. For girls of color, there is no seed there, they do not even think about it."[49]

The experience of my horse-crazy and white thirteen-year-old daughter mirrors this. Now in middle school, Lena went to a predominantly African American elementary school in Harlem. Her closest friends were African American, Latinx, and white. Lena played regularly with all these children, but she only played horses with two other horse-crazy friends, both of whom were also white. When I asked if her friends of color were interested in horses, she said that no, only the two white girls expressed interest in horses.

In studying predominantly white girls, I study the role of race in human-horse culture. Aside from the limits of snowball sampling, my experience suggests that the world of horsey girls in the United States actually is dominated by white girls. As with other predominantly white groups, in my interviews, the white participants never raised whiteness as an issue until I asked about it. (White people tend to be oblivious about their own race and only notice the race/ethnicity of groups of color.)[50] The link between horse-craziness and whiteness seemed to be normative and taken for granted. In part the whiteness of horse culture probably springs from the greater wealth of white people in the United States, which allows them more access to the (expensive) world of horses. Yet the economics of horses does not explain the phenomenon fully. Lots of passionately horse-crazy white girls cannot afford horses and still experience this infatuation. I wonder why so many horse-crazy girls are white both in the popular imagination and in the experiences of the women I interviewed. Beyond the economic issues, how is whiteness produced and reproduced by this cultural phenomenon? If being horse crazy offers some freedom and power to girls, why is that freedom, for the most part, only offered to white girls? And what boundaries might be placed around their whiteness and the privilege inherent in it?

My study of horse-crazy girls, like my book on ways of thinking about touching children focuses on the mainstream white middle class. White middle-class culture is normative in the United States and therefore interesting because it often legitimizes the interests of elite, including white and middle-class, groups. Social class is often, although not always, a factor in who has access to horses.[51] Sometimes, in selected places and time periods, poorer girls have owned and ridden horses. In my experience growing up in Wyoming and Montana in the 1970s, poor and working-class girls might have horses or access to them because, at that time, both land and grass were more readily available. As the cost of land and hay goes up in Montana and Wyoming, the cross-class ownership of horses declines. In my childhood in those two states, land was relatively cheap. One could have a horse or two, several dogs, and a plethora of cats that for the most part took care of themselves, outside, on one's land.

This is likely to be more unusual today as gentrification has changed the social landscape of the towns where I grew up. Yet in other less-desirable-to-elites places in the western United States, poorer people still have horses. For example, best-selling author and horse person Michael Korda describes his experience of visiting a small Texas town, Archer City, and attending their annual rodeo.

> The air was richly scented with popcorn, barbeque, and horse and cow manure, and it was astonishing how many horses were present, tied to the stunted trees or to trailers. The horse has long since retreated from urban life in the East, but in the West it still remains a visible part of small town and city life. I had, in fact, just come from Amarillo, where I had given a speech to the managers of Hasting's, a large southwestern book and record chain, and I was surprised to discover that at breakfast time half the vehicles parked outside fast-food places and diners seemed to consist of pickup trucks towing an open trailer with a horse standing in it, already saddled and bridled, ready to ride.
>
> There's something odd, to an easterner, about the sight of a whole bunch of horses chewing away at their hay in the parking lot of a Burger King, but in Amarillo it didn't raise an eyebrow, and on rodeo night in Archer City (compared to which Amarillo might as well be Paris) the horse was omnipresent.[52]

Most people in the United States do not live in small, relatively isolated towns like Archer City, or even somewhat larger cities like Amarillo. But much like in my childhood, there are still such pockets, places where horses are more widely accessible.

Nonetheless, outside of those pockets, in most parts of the United States today, low-income girls do not have access to actual horses. So in this way horsey culture reinforces white middle-class cultural norms. In my study I question the ways predominantly white and middle-class horsey girls both support and challenge normative culture.

My twenty-five in-depth interviews provide the primary data for chapters 5 and 6 and inform the entire manuscript. For chapters 5 and 6, I believe twenty-five in-depth interviews is sufficient data to develop a particular line of experience of horsey girls in the white middle class, and to argue that this horsey girl experience disrupts the normative white female-gendered binary of self-assertion versus care. I use a qualitative approach because I am less interested in generalizing to the entire population and instead hope to reach a deeper understanding of how the experiences of the women I interview disrupt normative gender, sexuality, and able-bodiedness and reinforce normative whiteness. Without a random sample, I cannot generalize from my data to the larger population of horse-crazy girls. My findings merely suggest a possible outcome for a broader group of horse-crazy girls and women. Finally, all the women that I spoke with relied on their memories of childhood, their memories of loving horses and of being horsey girls, and so the experiences they report—like my own—are mediated by memory and time.

Literature on Girls and Horses

There are a few popular books, and only one scholarly volume, addressing girls and women and their love of horses. Among the popular, commercial books, Melissa Holbrook Pierson's *Dark Horses and Black Beauties: Animals, Women, a Passion* (2000) explores women's and girls' relationships with horses. The description on the back notes the need for her popular book (and for my scholarly study): "In a phenomenon too prevalent to be mere chance, little girls all over the Western world wake one day to find themselves completely taken over by the love of all things equine."[53] In *Dark Horses and Black Beauties*, Pierson touches on various horse-related topics, including women's horse experiences, sidesaddles, and her own love of horses. A chapter called "Horse's Mouth" consists of a series of one- to three-sentence-long quotes by women and girls about horses, with no attribution. In one a woman claims, "I could not be happier than when I'm kicking around in the horse manure, smelling like a barn." Pierson's manuscript wanders with little structure or argument through a range of horse-related topics. It is a sweet and gentle, albeit nonscholarly read.

More recently, another popular press published a nonscholarly book by Susanna Forrest, *If Wishes Were Horses: A Memoir of Equine Obsession* (2012), about her own childhood passion for horses. In her lively and engaging writing style, Forrest describes her own experiences with horses and also samples others' experiences with horses over a broad sweep of time from the Bronze Age to the present. This book is a fun read and offers accounts of both Forrest's and, in a nonsystematic way, others' encounters with horses.[54] Yet unlike *Horse Crazy*, *If Wishes Were Horses* describes a variety of horse-human relationships and does not focus on girls, nor does it offer a systematic study or analysis of these relationships.

Several books, both scholarly and popular, have been written in the growing field of animal studies on dogs, dogs' relationships with humans, and dog lives. For example, in her powerful investigation of dog-human relationships, Haraway asks: "Whom and what do I touch when I touch my dog?" and "How is 'becoming with' [my dog] a practice of becoming worldly?"[55] Haraway claims, "Animals are everywhere full partners in worlding, in becoming with. Human and nonhuman animals are companion species, messmates at table, eating together, whether we know how to eat well or not."[56]

Haraway's important questions beg further scholarly examination in terms of human-horse relationships. A few scholars address this topic in book form. These include *Gender and Equestrian Sport: Riding Around the World* (2013), edited by Miriam Adelman and Jorge Knijnik, which addresses gender and the sport of horseback riding. This edited volume offers a global look at the gendered cultures surrounding and springing from horse and human sporting practices.[57] A scholarly book edited by Dona Lee Davis and Anita Maurstad, *The Meaning of Horses: Biosocial Encounters* (2016), examines human and horse relationships globally and across historical time periods.[58] In fascinating scholarly articles, sports and gender studies scholars like Lynda Birke, Kerri Brandt, and Katherine Dashper have explored the relationships of horses with humans, particularly adult women who are athletic partners with their horses.[59]

Few writers to date have examined the profound and long-standing relationship of human girls and horses, particularly from a scholarly perspective. *Horse Crazy* fills a gap in its focus on U.S. girls and their relationships with horses, and is unique in its investigation of the lives of horses in this social and historical context.

Like dogs (and cats), the girls who love them often consider horses pets, and yet unlike dogs and cats, there is a limit to the cuddly intimacy a girl can share with her horse. Horses usually cannot come in the house or sleep in the girl's bed, although one woman I spoke with, when she was a girl, did lie down next to her horse in his stall and sleep there.[60] In his book about "horse people," ignoring the experience of intimacy of many horse-crazy girls, Korda writes,

> It's hard for most people to develop any kind of intimacy with an animal that weighs a thousand pounds more than you do, can accelerate from a full stop to thirty miles an hour without breaking into a sweat, and jumps cleanly over fences and ditches that you could hardly even climb over or across on all fours, and do

all of this (and more) with you on its back. You can't pick it up and cuddle with it, like a kitten, or curl up in front of the fire with it, like a dog.[61]

Korda is of course correct that many intimacies shared between humans and household pets, like dogs and cats, cannot be shared with horses. And yet he is wrong about the reality of intimacy, at least from the perspective of girls who love horses. As I discuss in chapter 6, many if not most horse-crazy girls do experience a profound intimacy with their horse companions. Numerous former horse-crazy girls told me that their horse was their "best friend."

Girls, even predominantly white girls, fall within a category holding limited social power in the United States and other places. The contrast between that limited power and the desire and capacity to develop profound intimacy with an animal who "weighs a thousand pounds more" than the individual girl is striking.

Riding Dolly

When I was a child, alone was a safe place to go. And I was alone anyhow, alone with reading, disappearing into books, by myself in another world. Alone I would ride my pony, Dolly. She and I would spend a whole day riding, away, always away.

After my mother or my father had left me at the ranch for the day, I would take Dolly's bridle and head for the corral where she was kept with lots of other horses. It often took a very long time to catch Dolly. As I told you, she was smart. With me running behind her, she would race and dodge between the other horses, zipping away from me. Catching Dolly was an ordeal. Plenty of times, I thought it was never going to happen. And then, as though she sensed she had pushed me to the point of despair, she would suddenly let herself be caught. How the day went was pretty much up to Dolly.

Once caught, I would put her bridle on and head out to ride on the ranchland. Everywhere you looked you saw the plains. Some people think the plains are ugly, empty and desolate. But I know otherwise. I can tell you that the plains are beautiful, empty and beautiful. The plains are like the sky. They speak of forever. So, as the sky stretches beyond the edge of everything, the plains mirror the sky. They too reach for always. The plains offered me their endlessness. And there, with my pony, I was safe.

The only limit was time. I had to be back, ready to leave, when whichever parent was coming to get me. So, off we would go, riding away, riding across endlessness.

Chapter Overview of *Horse Crazy*

Following the introduction, each chapter in *Horse Crazy* moves the book forward in historical time. In chapter 2, I explore the history of horse bodies, horse bodies before the time of me, of Dolly, and of my horse, Snipaway. I briefly examine the history of horses in the United States, where they came from and how they got here.

Whereas a million years ago, horselike species evolved in the Americas, most left, migrated to other continents, and became extinct in the Americas around ten thousand years ago. Historians argue that the modern horse first came to the Americas with Spanish explorers in the 1500s. Horses migrated here much like cows, their partner farm animals, with colonizing humans. Horses worked in the colonizers' interest and, soon thereafter, in the interest of indigenous humans, Native Americans.

Adrian Franklin's *Animals and Modern Cultures: A Sociology of Human-Animal Relations in Modernity* (1999) examines the shifting nature of human relationships with other animals over time.[62] One such change in human-horse relationships involves the important shift in the primary use of horses from productive labor to leisure and sport. In the United States, and in other places too, horses have not always been the domain of girls. Once horses were associated with men, male power, and masculinity.[63] Before industrialization, horses were routine parts of human life, so ordinary that Gail Cunningham argues, "For pre-industrial societies, indeed probably up to the First World War, the horse was such a commonplace and essential part of everyday life as to be virtually invisible to modern eyes. It blends into the period furnishings in much the same way as steam trains or open fires."[64]

What I demonstrate about cows in *The Parallel Lives of Women and Cows* is also true of horses. They too produce profit. Historically, their labor produced the necessary resources of agrarian life. With industrialization in

Europe and the United States, horses moved from their productive, working role to one of producing "leisure and sport," increasingly for women and girls. Today, as gender studies scholar Katherine Dashper writes, "among leisure riders, horse riding is a predominantly female activity."[65]

Moving from this horse history, in chapter 3 I explore the consumption of horses in popular culture. I focus on horse-crazy girl literature, from *Black Beauty* in the late 1800s to the twentieth-century pony book genre. Children's literature scholars describe the zenith of the pony book genre as running from the 1930s to the 1970s. In terms of that time period, in chapter 3 I ask, What does the consumption of storybook horses—fantasy horses—mean for girls in the United States? On one hand, of course, pretend horses produce material profit from the sale of books. Yet they also produce symbolic capital, normalizing the political, economic, and raced reality in which children live in the United States and the United Kingdom. Further, U.S. children's horse literature reinforces the sexism of the larger culture, making girls and women invisible or relegating them to passive roles serving and caring for boys and men. In sharp contrast, as I discuss in chapter 3, British pony books offer girls a powerful challenge to normative gender roles even as early as the 1930s.

In chapter 4, I briefly consider my own horse-crazy history, picking up in the 1970s, when much of the pony book genre leaves off. In 1970, at age three, I moved with my family from Denver, Colorado, to Laramie, Wyoming. In 1980 my mother found work in Bozeman, Montana. We moved to Bozeman and I went to junior high (middle school) and high school there. In chapter 4, I consider and contextualize the recent history of this part of the country, its literal and metaphorical fences, and the courage that horses gave me, a small and scared girl. My horse brought me agency and a kind of freedom—to wander in the mountains, he and I, to be, through him, strong and fast, to feel safe as I rode. This freedom was neither perfect nor pure. But in contrast to the violence in my family and to the conservative white community in my small town, my horse offered me possibilities of freedom, of having power. Like all possibility, this possibility of power and freedom was not limitless; fences ran through the forests of my childhood, and in so many ways my capacities were cut short by violence.

In chapter 5, I investigate the ways horse-crazy girls push back against normative ideas about how girls should be, as in the conservative caregiving model and the liberal ideal of self-assertion in the world. The U.S. conservative writer and public figure George Gilder wrote a still-influential book during my childhood. It came out originally in 1973 with the title *Sexual Suicide,* and in 1986 it came out again with the title *Men and Marriage,* arguing that the proper role of girls and women is that of caregivers. This book continues to influence conservative debates today, as in the work of contemporary conservative Ryan T. Anderson, for example. Contemporaneously with Gilder, second-wave liberal feminists such as Betty Friedan argued and still today argue that girls should assert themselves in the public world over and above the private world of care. My book intervenes into these late twentieth- and early twenty-first-century ideological debates, debates that continue today. In chapter 5 of *Horse Crazy,* I make a clear argument about girls and their horses that rebuffs the ideological binary framing of gender by both liberals and conservatives.[66] I develop the concept of "vital care" in which care and self-assertion are combined, not opposed, in the relationship of horses and girls.

In chapter 6, I return to the experiences and words of horse-crazy girls, including my own. I investigate the meaning of horses and the role of this profound love in the lives of twenty-five women who were crazy about horses as children and told me about their passion. Ultimately, I believe horse-girl connections matter to girls both because they are deep and intimate relationships and because they give girls power, power girls might not otherwise have. In this chapter I explore girl-horse becoming and the ways that being-with-horses allows girls to become, perhaps in contrast to many other areas of their lives. I argue that horsey girls defy heteronormative demands in their relationships with horses. These girls find, with their horse companions, a relationship that frees them from the social insistence that girls tie themselves to boys. Nonconformists, queer girls, and girls with disability find a place to belong in their horse relationships.

In my concluding chapter, I briefly investigate the lives and deaths of horses in the United States today, including horse death in slaughterhouses and the horse rescue movement. I consider the story of Clever Hans, a horse who seemed to have advanced mathematical and other skills, and wonder how and what Hans really knew. I show how the various ways horses are treated reflects how power is involved in the very way humans conceive of and "construct" the meaning of other animals.

We live in a moment where many U.S. families love certain nonhuman animals as much, if not more, than their familial humans. The chosen animals rose to favor for social and historical reasons that go beyond (or around) questions of intelligence and sentience. Extremely smart and clean animals like pigs usually end their short lives obese and in a slaughterhouse. Too often, their deaths are brutal. On the other hand, dogs—neither as smart nor as clean as pigs—reign in human homes. Pigs we eat, dogs we do not. Horses, which like dogs are not normally eaten by humans in the United States, are also beloved. In contrast to dogs, horses do not necessarily remain beloved throughout their whole life span. My own much-adored childhood pony died in a slaughterhouse. In this final chapter, I explore horse lives. I examine how horses live and die and, in their death, what horse lives mean to contemporary U.S. humans. Be they girl or horse, often the lives that matter are lives that produce something for power. Even so, horse-crazy girls challenge this very instrumentality in their love and vital care of horses.

U.S. Horse History from Colonization to Recreation

Working for Men, Playing with Girls

Michel Foucault leads one to ask, What is a horse anyway? Is it something to be turned into meat as horses were, for example, by some indigenous groups in what became the United States? Is a horse a living tool to be used for productive work as it was for farmers until industrialization changed the shape of agrarian labor? Or is a horse a creature with its own reason for being, as animal rights activists argue today? Foucault explains that biopower forms these meanings about what life is, and whose life is valuable, about whose life matters, and whose does not.[1] While normalization works on (and in) individuals, biopower forms populations, populations in this case of horses. Foucault writes, "[I]t is over life, throughout its unfolding, that power establishes its dominion."[2]

In chapter 1, drawing from Foucault, I discuss Nicole Shukin's argument about how horse lives matter as animal capital. Shukin argues, "The 'question of the animal' exerts pressure on theorists of biopower and capital to engage not only with the ideological and affective function of animal signs but with material institutions and technologies of speciesism."[3] Shukin explains that animal capital is produced through both symbolic and material "logics of power" (5). In the latter, horse bodies, living and dead, produce wealth. In the former, horses are a form of representation, symbolism, such as the image of a running mustang that transforms into a moving car in an automobile advertisement on television. The wild horse running symbolizes freedom and beauty; and when the horse becomes the car, the car gains these animal signs. It too symbolizes freedom and beauty, a being of the wild. The mustang in the car advertisement produces symbolic animal capital; it works to sell the car and to sell emotional experience now associated with the car. Yet mustangs' material bodies also produce material animal capital in the meat they become when sent to slaughter.

Symbolic animal capital often occludes history. In the advertisement, the wild horse no longer comes from a history of colonization, no longer springs from the "cultural and ecological genocides of the settler-colonial nation form mediating capital's expansion" (4). Nor do we see the twentieth-century human violence against mustangs, the tens of thousands rounded up and slaughtered for meat. In the advertisement, we view the running mustang as a politically neutral and ahistorical animal symbol. It carries an "ideological and affective function" with no sense of the history of mustangs in this country.

"[A]nimal and capital are increasingly produced," Shukin argues, "as a semiotic and material closed loop, such that the meaning and matter of the one feeds seamlessly back into the meaning and matter of the other. In the nauseating recursivity of this logic, capital becomes animal, and animals become capital." It seems that all of life, mustang life, the symbolic meanings of mustangs and the material bodies of mustangs, have been subsumed. For horses and for most humans too, Shukin writes, "the balance of power seems, ominously, to be all on the side of capital." Yet, she says, "it is crucial to also recognize the amplified vulnerability of capitalism" in biopolitical times (16).

Shukin offers the all-too-recent historical example of capital rendering leftover cow bodies into food to feed cows, who themselves would soon be turned into meat, and whatever cow material was left at the end of the process of slaughter and meat production would in turn be rendered into food to feed *other* cows. In this case the loop made a perfect, closed circle. Yet from that "closed loop of animal capital" came life's own push in the form of disease, mad cow disease. Now those raising and fattening cattle in the United States are no longer allowed to feed them cow. Shukin writes, "Indeed, novel diseases erupting out of the closed loop of animal capital—mad cow disease, avian influenza—are one material sign of how the immanent terrain of market becomes susceptible, paradoxically, to the pandemic potential of 'nature'"

(16). Horse lives, our human lives, all lives are not merely, or only, shaped by forces of power. As Foucault states, "It is not that life has been totally integrated into techniques that govern and administer it." Life, Foucault clarifies, "constantly escapes them."[4]

Horses as we know them today did not spring into being outside of human intention. We humans and horses together came to be beings that exist for and with each other. Horses are simultaneously animal capital and members of human and nonhuman families. Human beings create the meaning of horses in our relationships with them. In chapter 2, with a focus on the United States, I investigate horse history and the changing "nature" of horse lives over our shared past. I briefly describe horse evolution, their role in colonization in the United States, and their use by Native Americans. Humans brought horses to the Americas. Following the arrival of Europeans and their horses in the late fifteenth century, white conquest spread through the Americas. In what became the United States, white colonizers, with horses, understood themselves as civilizing or domesticating the frontier. Humans used horses as material animal capital both to colonize and to challenge colonization. We used them to work, we ate them, and we fed them to other animals. As discussed above, horses produce capital that is material, such as the production of food in their work on farms, and symbolic, such as the role of horses in the western movie genre.[5] Humans made life with horses and used horses as food, used them to produce food, and used them as symbolic animal capital to entertain human life. As the use of horses shifted away from production of material goods on farms and transportation toward recreation, their role in the production of symbolic capital increased via performances of conquest by entertainers like Buffalo Bill and in the new visual culture of film. Today in our service economy, horses generate leisure and entertainment, forms of animal capital that can be symbolic (the association of horses with cowboys and masculinity in movies), and material (tourists pay for horseback rides on dude ranches).

Decades after the "domestication" of the frontier, horses were domesticated in the popular imagination. With industrialization in the first half of the twentieth century, horses went from being understood as productive working animals for men to animals associated with leisure activities for women. About this Katherine Dashper writes, "Once a vital partner to humans in agriculture, warfare and transport, the modern horse is now predominantly a partner in human sport and leisure." She explains, "Another outcome of the change in use of the horse from a work animal to a leisure animal has been the feminization of horse riding and the horse industry."[6] In other words, in the shift from labor animals to leisure animals, horses also shifted from being understood as animals belonging to the world of men to being associated with women and, increasingly in the twentieth century, with girls.[7]

All that history led up to and made possible the contemporary passion of girls for horses. In this chapter, I consider the shift from the primarily male use of horses to their increasing use by women and girls.[8]

Horse Origin Stories: Horse Evolution

Horse and human animals have a story that predates our current entanglements with and in power. Mammals have been on earth for two hundred million years, and horses for many of those. We primates also claim a long presence on earth. Interestingly, the earliest known horse and the earliest known true primate or euprimate fossil come from the same place, a region called Polecat Bench in Wyoming, not so far from where I grew up riding a small member of the species *Equus*, my Shetland pony, Dolly.

Called *eohippus* or "dawn horse," the first horse evolved in North America fifty-six million years ago.[9] This early horse stood from ten to twenty inches high, with an "arched back, short neck, short face, short, flexible legs, and a long tail." Its front feet had four toes and its back feet only three, and there were remnants of past toes on both its front and back feet. *Eohippus* had molars for grinding on the sides of its mouth. The first tiny horse changed, and changed again, over millions of years, adapting to the "shifting geography and climate by way of teeth and leg bones and size. Some branches became extinct, and others sent forth bigger and faster new lines."[10] *Eohippus* lived for an impressive twenty million years, and from it came the *Orohippus* genus and three species. These species spread over much of the earth. Moving in the opposite direction of early humans, some of the horses went north and crossed the Bering land bridge to Asia and beyond. Some stayed in North America and eventually, only four million years ago, evolved to become *Equus*, our horse of today.

Between *eohippus* and *Equus* were millions of years and millions of planetary changes. Early horses did something often recommended to me in my childhood: they rolled with the punches. They adapted and adjusted, again and again, to massive environmental changes. Paleontologist Matthew Mihlbachler, in Wendy Williams's history, *The Horse: The Epic History of Our Noble Companion* (2015), explains, "Horses are unique.... Something happened to them that allowed them to adapt to whatever was thrown at them. Whatever it was that happened to them, it allowed them to track their changing environments so closely that we can use their fossilized teeth to track the history of climate change." Mihlbachler used a notable number of old horse teeth, seven thousand, stored at the American Museum of Natural History in New York City, to study horse evolution. About this, Williams writes, "[C]older temperatures, plant shifts, dietary changes, changes in silica content, and changes in horse teeth all correlated. It was as if horses and grasses were waging a fairly constant war.... Interestingly, other animals were not able to respond this way."[11]

Sixteen million years after the arrival of the dawn horse, North America and Greenland split from Europe, and five million years after that came *Mesohippus,* which, journalist Deanne Stillman writes, represented a "significant advance in horse evolution." *Mesohippus* stood about two feet high. Stillman writes, "[I]ts brain had grown larger, and the horse now had a total of six grinding teeth, with sharp crests on each tooth to help it survive on new forms of vegetation."[12]

Soon *Miohippus* followed *Mesohippus,* and these two species lived together in the Miocene Epoch, like *eohippus* in what is now my childhood home, Wyoming, the place where my father was born and raised, and where my grandfather had his sale barn and cattle business. The lives of my family rested on the history, the evolution, of horses. From *Mesohippus* came *Mercyhippus,* whose central toe was big, round, and hoofish. *Mercyhippus* could run, and run fast, often faster than its predators such as the wolf, which has hung in there until our time, and the saber-toothed tiger, which has not. From *Mercyhippus* came nineteen new horse species, and eventually the genus *Dinohippus*. And four million years ago from *Dinohippus* came *Equus,* ready and waiting to be loved by horse-crazy girls today, four million years later (40).

Equus stood at 13.2 hands, the unit now used to measure horses, standardized at four inches per hand. Stillman writes about *Equus,* "It had a long neck, long legs, and a long muzzle; its mane was short and stood upright, its ears were medium-size, and it had stripes on its legs and back. It looked very much like a donkey" (40). *Equus* split off into twelve different species, including *Equus caballus* or "the true horse." Some of the horses remained in the American West. Others migrated from North America to Asia, Europe, and Africa, where some evolved into zebras. Three subspecies came of one branch of this family tree, *Equus ferus*. These three include the ones in the Eurasian steppes that evolved into the currently endangered *Equus ferus przewalskii* or Przewalski's horse. In Europe and western Asia came the now (only recently) extinct *Equus ferus ferus* or tarpan. The last known tarpan died in 1909. And the third is our domestic horse, *Equus ferus caballus*.[13]

The true horse was, and the domestic animal we ride today remains, a prey animal. To survive, it had speed, able to cover thirty miles per hour or more. It also had sharp eyesight and excellent hearing. It had huge "satellite eyes," writes Stillman, "bigger than a whale's or an elephant's, and just as haunting," on the side of its head, offering a wide range of lateral vision, about 340 degrees.[14] The horse's sight is superb, both by day and night: "The ability to constantly scan for threats, even in the dark, helped the horse to survive." Describing a characteristic that those of us who ride today are familiar with, Stillman explains, "Any visual disturbance on the horizon would trigger flight—birds that were suddenly on the wing, or a waterfall." True horses, like our domestic horses today, had large ears that constantly moved, shifting to face forward and sideways and back, allowing it to pick up faraway sounds of potential danger. "The early rumbles of an earthquake, thunder in the distance, the rustle of leaves—all these sounds and many more would set it off, sometimes causing it to run for miles" (41).

Many horses left their place of origin in the North American West, migrating all over the world. Most people agree that those who remained died out about twelve thousand years ago. During the Pleistocene Epoch, from 2.6 million to 11,700 years ago, sheets of ice moved across the continents. During this time many species of mammals went extinct. Some believe that the ice and global cooling caused the extinctions; others argue that around the end of the Pleistocene, humans wiped out many species by overhunting. Still others hypothesize that disease wiped out countless species. About these different explanations, the University of California Museum of Paleontology notes on its website, "The issue remains unsolved; perhaps the real cause of the Pleistocene extinction was a combination of these factors."[15] Despite uncertainty as to why it happened, most people agree that *"Equus* seems to have disappeared from its homeland during the Ice Age."

Humans have found fossil evidence of pre-Columbus horses in North America; yet the majority agree that these fossils are from the Pleistocene. Most scholars believe true horses died out twelve thousand years ago on this continent, and domestic horses evolved from horses that migrated back to the Americas with humans. They returned as animal capital, carrying the colonizers from Europe five hundred years ago.

Horses Return to the Americas Carrying Colonization

In 1492 the Spanish explorers, the conquistadors, came to the Americas. They came and they kept coming. Historian Stan Hoig writes in *Came Men on Horses* (2013), "The Conquistador Period lasted essentially from Columbus in 1492 past Oñate in 1598, providing more than a full century in which generations, and world conditions with them, changed."[16] Horses as animal capital were central to the change. In a book edited by two Native Americans—whose very names speak to the importance of horses in their cultures, George P. Horse Capture and Emil Her Many Horses of the Smithsonian Institute—Herman J. Viola writes, "America's Native peoples have little for which to thank Christopher Columbus except the horse."[17] After their long absence, he returned horses to the Americas. On his second voyage in 1493, he brought as many as twenty-five Andalusian horses, and like their colonizing humans, the horses kept coming. Horses labored for colonization as material capital and helped the first expeditions of Spanish colonizers colonize the Americas, look for gold, explore and take over land, and kill and enslave Native peoples.

In the beginning, Native Americans were scared of the horses that came carrying white men on their backs. Viola explains, "They had never seen an animal that could carry a person. They called the horses 'sky dogs,' believing that they were monsters or messengers from the heavens. The first Hopi to see horses paved their way with ceremonial blankets." One indigenous man, Saukamaupee, a Cree Indian living with the Piegan in Canada, described to a fur trader the first time he saw a horse. He encountered the animal during a battle in approximately 1730, after horses had made their way north. The dead animal had been hit by an arrow in its stomach. "'Numbers of us went to see him,' Saukamaupee recalled, 'and we all admired him. He put us in mind of a stag that had lost his horns, and we did not know what name to give him. But as he was a slave to man, like the dog, which carried our things, he was named the Big Dog'" (9). Eventually, the similarity to elk led the Piegan to name horses "elk dogs" or *ponokomita*, still the Piegan word for horses.

The desire to have horses quickly replaced Native people's fear. The colonizers worked to keep Native Americans from gaining horse animal capital, "knowing that horses would give Native Americans a powerful tool for protecting their land from invasion" (7). Spanish law at that time required military men to ride uncastrated male horses, stallions. This meant, Viola writes, that of conquistador Francisco Coronado's 558 horses, 556 were stallions, only two were mares (female horses), and he had no geldings (castrated males). Unlike today's cats and dogs, when humans "fix" horses, they only castrate or geld the males, making them geldings and unable to reproduce. Mares are almost always left intact and able to reproduce. Leaving male horses ungelded, leaving them stallions, presents problems in that stallions are wilder than geldings and prone to fighting other stallions. Stallions were and continue to be considered a more masculine horse, a horse for a "real man" to ride. Besides the wildness of stallions, having a colonizing cavalry riding only stallions in a place where there are no other horses means that one cannot produce, or breed, more horses. As long as this rather impractical policy was in place, the conquistadors had to keep bringing new horses over on boats.

Hoig describes these men with their masculine horses, the early conquistadors, as having "a wide reputation for cruelty and brutality." Hoig writes, "These first expeditions embarked from Europe largely to explore, discover, and conquer land and seek gold but not principally to colonize or Christianize." They wanted wealth and land for Spain and "fame and position for themselves, and they suffered little restraint from the state or the church as to how they got them."[18] Later generations, perhaps equally cruel in their results, focused on different goals—colonizing and Christianizing the humans whom the Spanish "discovered." As more of the continent was colonized, both human lives and the daily lives of horses, their work and their living conditions, shifted and changed.

Native Americans and Horses

The colonizers, on horseback, stole land and life from the Native Americans they encountered. Native Americans stole horses from the colonizers to make their own herds and develop their own horse cultures.[19] Shifting the origins of and responsibility for the existence of wild horses to indigenous people, Viola claims that mustangs came from those horses taken by Native Americans. Because the Spanish originally brought so few mares, they limited their own capacity for breeding horses or for those horses that got free to breed. Yet over time, they both brought more mares from Spain, and of course half of the foals born in the Americas were fillies (female infant and young horses). Viola explains that the "Indians acquired their horses from Spanish herds in New Mexico. . . . The bulk they obtained as a result of the Pueblo Uprising of 1680" (8).

As the Spanish colonizers gained power and land, they moved into what is now New Mexico in the United States. They built "a large colony in Santa Fe, the heartland of the Pueblo Indians." Viola describes the Pueblo people as "placid" and enduring. They lived under Spanish domination for one hundred years before deciding it was time to rid their land of the Spaniards. With the guidance of Popé, "a Tewa religious leader from the San Juan Pueblo," the indigenous people expelled the colonizers from Santa Fe "with remarkable ease." They killed "some five hundred Spaniards" and forced another thousand to flee to the south. In their rush to escape, the Spanish left behind lots of livestock, including hundreds of horses. The Pueblo people traded some of the horses to other Native American tribes. And according to Viola, "From New Spain, the horse population expanded rapidly across North America, moving north and east along established trading networks that existed between the various Indian tribes" (8). From these came wild horses, mustangs, and the horses acquired by other indigenous groups throughout what became the western United States. Viola explains that by the late eighteenth century, "[V]irtually every tribe of the Far West was mounted or at least had access to horses (some of the mountain tribes ate rather than rode theirs)" (7).

Native people recognized the value of horses, and they quickly became "an integral part of the culture of many western tribes." Viola clarifies that the Kiowa and Comanche of the southern plains, the Arapaho, Crow, Cheyenne, and Sioux of the northern plains of my childhood, and the northwestern Nez Perce and Blackfoot Indian cultures quickly incorporated horses as central and important. Horses were used for battle, hunting, moving communities, and, in some cases, as food. "Young men would risk life and limb to enter the villages of enemy tribes in order to capture a prized horse staked near its owner's tipi. Capturing an enemy's horse was a coup, a great achievement meriting praise and honor from family and friends. Plains oral histories abound with stories of lucky and luckless young men who made horse capturing an art" (9–10).

Viola elucidates that for many Plains Indian tribes, horses represented generosity as well as bravery and freedom. When a young man acquired enemy horses, he would often "give his prize to a widow or other unfortunate member of the community, thereby manifesting his generosity as well as his bravery." Because of other changes happening rapidly around them, horses remained central to Native life for only a short time; on the Plains, for example, this period ended in the 1870s. There were increasing numbers of white people taking up land and killing buffalo, leaving too few and too little land for the Plains people. The U.S. government worked to turn Plains Indians into farmers. Albeit perhaps no longer central to their livelihood, horses remain, Viola argues, "a fundamental part of their culture" (10).

The National Agricultural Statistics Service, an agency of the United States Department of Agriculture, indicates that many Native American groups maintain large numbers of horses. According to one National Agricultural Statistics Service study in 2002, Native Americans own at least 115,464 horses. About this, in her work on U.S. horse populations, Emily R. Kilby writes, "Yet because reservation horses are often handled as communal property rather than individually owned and because large herds on Plains and Western reservations are often managed as range animals, that enumeration may be very approximate." In Montana alone, at least 8,230 of the approximately 129,997 horses live on reservations.[20]

Viola explains that many Plains Indians still practice giving away horses as a demonstration of the generosity so important in their cultures. He writes that this is often done at a "powwow ceremony known as 'the giveaway.'" Viola describes the powwows as "tribal gatherings much like family parties, where friends and relatives meet once a year to renew old friendships, dance, and carry on traditions of their past." The yearly Crow Fair on the Crow

Reservation, located in southeastern Montana, a couple of hours' drive east from Bozeman where I lived with my horse Snipaway, is an important example of a powwow. One year at the fair, in 1991, six horses were given away by different Crow families.

When Viola asked a Crow friend if horses still mattered in the community, the friend expressed surprise at the question. The friend's language indicated that for him, horses were associated with men; he explained that "a Crow man would no more want to be seen riding a sorry-looking horse than he would want to have disobedient children." "And," he said, "a good friend, a good clan uncle, a good son-in-law deserves a good horse. Last year, my three daughters came to the house for Christmas dinner, and I told their husbands to look under the Christmas tree, where there was an empty bridle for each of them. 'In the spring,' I told them, 'go to my pasture and pick out the horse you want from my herd. It is my gift to you for being such good husbands to my daughters.'"[21]

Horse Capital and Horse Labor: Horses Gendered Male

For centuries in North America, horses were working animals who belonged to the world of men, and more broadly they served in a world controlled by men. In the early U.S. nation-building, horses were often associated with the frontier. They played a role on both "sides," supporting both the Native Americans, who were normatively understood to be "wild," and the supposedly first builders of white "civilization," the cowboys. In colonial times and well into the early twentieth century, horses were accessible to, and needed for survival by, many people. This is not to say that women never rode, but that horses were generally understood as animals gendered male and belonging in the realm of men.

European men rode horses to colonize the Americas. Pioneer men, white and of color, drove and rode horses as they moved west, sometimes, but not necessarily, with women and children. Native and other men hunted with horses. Cowboys rode horses as they handled cattle. Men of many ethnicities rode horses to war. Men used horses to steal horses and other livestock. Men used horses to travel. From their return to what became the United States in the 1500s through the 1800s, horses often lived with their humans in male societies, semi-segregated from women. Such societies included colonizers, sheep herders, cattle ranchers, and cowboys. Horses in these contexts largely produced material capital in colonizing land and resources, through farming and ranching, and in transporting goods and humans.

Popular western novels and movies, past and contemporary, reflect this gendered-male use of horses and the culture surrounding them. In popular culture, horses became symbolic animal capital associated with male bravery and white "civilization." Will James, the western writer, born in 1892 and originally from Quebec, dreamed of being a cowboy. (He adopted the name Will James, having originally been given the decidedly less cowboy-sounding name Joseph Ernest Nephtali Dufault.) James wrote and illustrated twenty-four books about the western United States and the lives of cowboys, and he claims in his preface to one novel, *Home Ranch*, originally published in 1935, "to know something about cows, herds of 'em, and cow horses and the folks that's in the country they range in."[22]

The men in *Home Ranch* prefer being on a horse's back to being anywhere else. They do the (always gendered male) work of cowboys and can be out on the range for months at a time, on horseback, and in the sole company of other men. One of the few females in the novel, the ranch owner's daughter, June, is worrisome because she, being a girl, likes horseback riding *too much*. June was "married to saddle leather and horses and sort of made her home in the stable and corrals." Her parents struggle to redirect her energies towards ladylike activities, like getting a formal education and meeting a "nice young man of good family and high standing and then marrying that kind." Ultimately June's wishes prevail, and she is allowed to stay home away from the ostensibly civilized company of elite, urban, and white people. Although still required to do women's work in the home, she did get to spend significant leisure time on horseback. The parents lost that battle with their daughter. Yet on the positive side, the parents were successful in getting June to "quit saying 'Goldern' and 'dadgum it' and such words."[23]

Some cowboys were men who had fled the world of heteronormativity, marriage to women and all that it meant.[24] Their central relationships were with horses and other men. In his famous Pulitzer Prize–winning novel *Lonesome Dove* (1985), Larry McMurtry writes of such a society of men. *Lonesome Dove* addresses a group of men who had been Texas Rangers together and remained together after their work as rangers was done. At the beginning of the novel, set in 1876, the men were running a small livery business called the Hat Creek Cattle Company and Livery Emporium in a tiny Texas town McMurtry named Lonesome Dove, near the Mexican border. McMurtry depicts a world made of men who are deeply connected and committed to one another and to their horses.

When McMurtry's character Captain Woodrow F. Call decides to steal horses and a herd of cattle from Mexico and to drive the herd to Montana, all five in the company (four men and one teenage boy) go along. It is practically assumed that they will. The men do not prioritize relationships with women over those with their male comrades. All are single. Only one, Captain Augustus "Gus" McCrae, has even been married—twice in his case, and both times only briefly because his wives quickly died. McMurtry describes the experience of Pea Eye Parker: "He had never known what to think about women, and still didn't, but so far as actions went he was content to take his cue from the Captain, whose cue was plain. The Captain left them strictly alone."[25] Gus enjoys teasing Pea by suggesting, repeatedly, that Pea should marry a widow named Mary Cole who lives nearby. McMurtry offers Pea's perspective:

> To Pea it was all just a troublesome puzzle. He could not remember how the subject had come up in the first place, since he had never said a word about wanting to marry. Whatever else it meant, it meant leaving the Captain, and Pea did not plan to do that. . . . He had lived with men his whole life, rangering and working; during his whole adult life he couldn't recollect spending ten minutes alone with a woman. He was better acquainted with Gus's pigs than he was with Mary Cole, and more comfortable with them too. (139)

Gus's pigs aside, horses were the true animal companions of the men. Many of the cowboys in the novel did almost everything from the back of a horse. In sharp contrast, women rarely rode horseback. When they did it was usually a new and unusual experience for them. McMurtry differentiated women from men by depicting walking for the cowboys as an activity to be avoided. McMurtry describes one cowboy, Soupy Jones, in this way. "He was brave, but lazy, a fine cardplayer, and by all odds the best horseman any of them had ever known. His love of being horseback was so strong that he could seldom be induced to dismount, except to sleep or eat" (211).

Horses had been central to the working lives of many men in the United States, but around the turn of the twentieth century, they slowly became less important. As industrialization happened, people increasingly used trains and cars for transportation and machines for farming. In the first half of the twentieth century, horses as material capital ceased to be central in actual work producing more material capital. Simultaneously, horses increasingly produced symbolic capital as they came to be imagined in starring roles, with men, in popular culture. Westerns, one of the first and biggest motion picture genres, starred horses with (mostly white) men, men who played cowboys and men who played Indians.

Westerns were a script for a larger-than-life story happening in the minds of white people across the United States. In this script horses played alongside cows in starring roles. Horses and cows embody iconic symbols of Americanness, symbols that produce capital much like the "material production of capital through their bodily matter." Both the material bodies of horses (and cows) and the symbol of horses (and cows), "the sign, the representation," produce capital. Like the cows I explore in an earlier book, horses "play a pivotal role in a central (and binary) story of white American origin, that is, the white male conquest of the American West." In this story's version of colonization, horses help bring "civilization" to and domesticate the "savage" wilderness.[26]

Buffalo Bill's Civilization

Buffalo Bill introduced the West into the world of visual popular culture. He made the first world-famous western spectacle, almost a movie, before we had movies. Buffalo Bill's horses produced symbolic animal capital through his popular cultural depiction of western history and his celebration of white colonization and conquest.

All the tall and other tales told about Buffalo Bill notwithstanding, one thing seems clear: Buffalo Bill was an extraordinary equestrian. Before he became an early American celebrity, he was also a celebrated buffalo hunter. Whereas he might not have killed as many as the legends claim, he did kill a lot of buffalo in his day. Stillman writes, about Buffalo Bill, that riding his horse named Brigham, "he wiped out buffalo by the hundreds." Over one eighteen-month period, "he boasted that he had killed 4,280 buffalo."[27]

Along with killing innumerable buffalo, Buffalo Bill took part in battles meant to subdue, through any means necessary, Native American

communities in what became the western United States. Perhaps the brutality depicted in the tales about Buffalo Bill was accurate. Yet his private "suc-
cesses" (as white people understood the ruthless treatment of indigenous
peoples) were probably not so grand. One tall tale asserts that Buffalo Bill
avenged his friend George Armstrong Custer "just hours after the massacre."
He supposedly retaliated for Custer's death at the Battle of the Little Bighorn
by scalping a Native American man named Yellow Hair. It was said, perhaps only by white people, that Buffalo Bill awed Native Americans. Some
claimed that Buffalo Bill was the only white person, "the only *wasichu*," the
Lakota respected. He was also fabled to be the fastest Pony Express rider,
"tearing through Indian Territory and dodging arrows all the way." About
his magical image, Stillman calls Buffalo Bill a "one-man frontier trinity." She
writes, "In Buffalo Bill the three totems of the American wilderness came
together and now live forever—man, buffalo, and horse" (129).

Racist, and brutal to indigenous people and buffalo alike, Buffalo Bill
could really ride a horse. And unlike some famous equestrians, Buffalo
Bill acknowledged his horse partners and seemed to care deeply for them.
Stillman writes that Buffalo Bill "had a deep kinship with the animals he rode."
Over the course of his life, twenty-two horses were particularly important
to him, "although, strangely, he had no such feelings for the mighty buffalo
from whom he derived his claim to fame" (129).

After his first career actually working in the western United States on
horseback, allegedly for the Pony Express, fighting Native Americans, and
definitively killing lots of buffalo, Buffalo Bill started his second career as
a celebrity. This new work was the work of the actor, the work of the show,
and through this work, Buffalo Bill's horses produced symbolic animal capital. On May 19, 1883, at the age of thirty-seven, Buffalo Bill launched what
Stillman called his "equine extravaganza," the "Wild West, WF Cody and WF
Carver's Rocky Mountain and Prairie Exhibition." It was a huge hit. Versions
of it traveled around the United States. There was even a show in Madison
Square Garden, though by then the volatile Carver, named in the original
title, was no longer involved.[28] Eventually Buffalo Bill's Wild West show made
its way across the Atlantic to Europe, where it toured eight different times.

With Buffalo Bill traveled dozens of Native American and white people,
and around 250 horses, mules, and other animals. Many of the humans and
many of the horses alike were famous. They included people like indigenous

leader Black Elk and cowboy Buck Taylor.[29] The show was as successful in Europe as it had been in the United States and, writes Stillman, "reached greater acclaim in repeat trips across the Atlantic, even as the thing it portrayed was nearly gone" (152). The West as show, with horses as stars, would be long remembered.

Watching Horses

In *Animal Capital: Rendering Life in Biopolitical Times* (2009), Shukin explores the concept of rendering. She addresses the interesting double entendre of the word. Rendering, she notes, "signifies both the mimetic act of making a copy, that is, reproducing or interpreting an object in linguistic, painterly, musical, filmic, or other media . . . *and* the industrial boiling down and recycling of animal remains." She argues that this "double sense" of the term *rendering* "provides a particularly apt rubric for beginning to more concretely historicize animal capital's modes of production."[30] Biopower, Shukin explains, "operates through the power to hegemonize both the meaning and matter of life," both symbol and material. And horses are rendered in both senses. They are living beings who come to all kinds of bodily ends.

Horses have also been at center stage, at the heart so to speak, of the moving image since humans developed moving images. "The first recorded moving image," Stillman writes, "could have been anything—a herd of antelope, a dancer, crashing surf—but as it happens, it was a horse."[31] Wealthy financier and horse enthusiast Leland Stanford hired photographer Eadweard Muybridge to photograph a horse in motion in an attempt to settle a bet. Stanford believed horses fly, ever so briefly, when they run. In other words, he argued that there is a point while galloping when all four of the horse's hooves are in the air. Supposedly Stanford had money to waste, and he bet others, who denied the possibility of all hooves being off the ground at any given point, twenty-five thousand dollars that they were. To win the bet, Stanford spent fifty thousand dollars using Muybridge's photography and, at quite a financial loss, showed that he was correct.[32]

Stillman describes the project:

> On a June morning in 1878, racing fans and reporters assembled at Stanford's estate to watch the experiment unfold. Muybridge had constructed an elaborate rig—a forerunner of movie cameras. From a shed on one side of the track, a dozen

large cameras bulged through an opening. . . . The trotting horse Abe Edgington took the track, pulling a two-wheeled sulky driven by one of Stanford's trainers. There were twelve wires underneath the track at twenty-one-inch intervals, each connected to a different camera. As the sulky wheels ran across the wires, the shutters were tripped. (197–198)

When Muybridge brought forth the results, all the world could see that, for a moment, all of the horse was in the air. Muybridge went on, in 1879, to invent and patent the zoopraxiscope, the first moving-picture projector, and horses continued to star in the show.

Thomas Edison also invented a movie projector, the kinetoscope, with the help of his employee, William Kennedy Laurie Dickson, and patented it in 1897.[33] The first movie show, using the kinetoscope, was exhibited at the Columbian World Expo in Chicago in 1893. And as Stillman illuminates, "It was another first that had to do with the horse. Called *The Blacksmith Scene*, the movie lasted less than a minute and portrayed two men at an anvil hammering a horseshoe as a third looked on."[34] After the fair closed in 1894, Edison started making semidocumentary westerns, including one called *Bucking Broncho*, featuring a bucking mustang and a "real" cowboy. In 1903 Edison released what some consider to be the first feature-length western (fictional) film, *The Great Train Robbery*, twelve minutes long, starring horses, trains, bad guys, and good guys (200–201). As symbolic capital, horses were central to the western genre, telling stories of white conquest, colonization, and race(ism) in the United States.

Mustangs

Like that produced by Buffalo Bill, his horses, and his show, and by the western movies that followed, symbolic capital has also been produced by mustangs. They played and continue to play a role in American mythology. Mustangs are wild horses that have come from domesticated stock. Some of the domesticated horses brought to the Americas as tools of the colonizers got free, and some stayed free. Over time other domesticated horses, descendants of those brought with colonization, joined them. They and their ancestors became the mustangs that still roam the western United States today. Mustangs are not a breed of horse but a blend of numerous breeds, descending from horses that "escaped from or were released by Spanish explorers,

Native Americans and other ranchers, miners and soldiers."[35] About mustangs, Stillman writes, "At the end of the nineteenth century, there were two million wild horses ranging across seventeen states, from California to Missouri, Texas to Montana." They were hunted for sport and because some ranchers believed they "ate too much grass." They were captured to be sold to slaughterhouses and to be used for riding. Consequently, mustang numbers have dwindled.[36] Stillman writes that between 2000 and 2008 alone, "75,000 wild horses [were] taken from the land." Many of those were sent to slaughterhouses. And now, more wild horses are "in government custody than on the range."[37]

Oddly, mustangs exist in the popular imagination at two ends of a binary split. On one hand, glorified, mustangs represent freedom and something understood to be quintessentially American. Stillman lays claim to this depiction as she demotes, "with all due respect," the official United States emblem, the eagle: "[I]t is really the wild horse, the four-legged with the flying mane and tail, the beautiful, big-hearted steed who loves freedom so much that when captured he dies of a broken heart, the ever-defiant mustang that is our true representative, coursing through our blood as he carries the eternal message of America."[38]

On the other hand, in sharp contrast to Stillman's patriotic depiction of mustangs, many in the West understood and continue to understand mustangs to be vermin and pests. Stillman offers this perspective from an early twentieth-century *Cattleman* magazine: "They eat too much grass, these horses drink too much from streams which else would sustain peaceful and profitable herds and flocks of cattle and sheep. There have grown to be too many of them" (238). Defining them as pests, one could justify hunting mustangs, and doing so brutally both for sport *and* for a profit.

Turning the work of killing into sport was common in the western rural world where I grew up. For example, the boys of my childhood hunted groundhogs, also considered vermin and pests. This youthful hunting was both sport and training for western boys. Through the killing of groundhogs, the boys learned to handle a gun, to shoot and to hunt. I remember some boys earning a dollar for each dead animal they produced. Like many horse-crazy girls, I loved animals and had tearful exchanges with my older brothers as I tried and failed to persuade them not to hunt the groundhogs.

The groundhogs built intricate mazes running for long distances under the surface of the land. Here and there one of the entries to the maze would open as a hole in the earth. Semi-hidden holes are a problem for livestock. Horses and cattle would sometimes step in one and break a leg. A broken leg in that time, and for most horses and cattle still today, represented a death sentence and thus a huge loss for the rancher.

Cattle ranchers like my grandfather Aldous Clarke in eastern Wyoming, and sheepmen like my great-grandfather Tulesis Cisero Halley in western Nebraska, saw public land as theirs and believed it should be put to profitable use, that is, use such that it made *them* a profit. Groundhogs threatened that profit. And so, at least according to most ranchers, did the wild horses. The ranchers argued that (unlike groundhogs) mustangs were not even indigenous to the area. They said that wild horses did not belong in the western United States. The mustangs were "varmints," garbage left behind by other humans. In this line of thought, the cattle lobby launched one public relations campaign in the 1970s, "asserting that wild horses weren't really wild but feral newcomers to this country ('varmints'), and therefore, protecting them would be the same as protecting alley cats or invasive weeds. Moreover, as a non-native 'foreigner,' the mustang was a threat to the limited food and water supply on the range."[39] These conservative westerners claimed wild horses used resources that should have gone to profitable animals, in other words, their own cows and sheep.

Welfare for Ranchers (Not for Mustangs, Treehuggers, or Other Varmints)

Offering a powerful example of biopolitics and the management of life— horse and cow and sheep life—in 1934 the federal government began to regulate livestock grazing through the Taylor Grazing Act. This act came about in response to the demands of the U.S. livestock industry, and it divided the West into portions, each of which could contain a set number of cows or sheep. To use one of the portions or allotments, ranchers had to have a permit. The fees for the permits were and remain remarkably low. Stillman writes that they were "pennies on the head in 1934, and today about $1.39 per cow." This practice has "led to what many rangeland observers call 'welfare ranching,' a subsidized industry in which stockmen receive a government handout in the form of cheap land."[40] This was a handout that otherwise conservative westerners appreciated. Mike and Diane, who generously cared for my horse Snipaway for me, despised treehuggers and anyone else they believed to be on government support. Ranchers were one of few exceptions to their anti-government-support rule.

The conservative stockmen and the government agreed that ranchers deserved the support they received. In this thinking, almost no one else should get government support, and that included the vermin mustangs. Stockmen and the federal government stood together on the mustang issue. Stillman quotes a grazing service spokesman who said in August 1939, "A wild horse consumes forage needed by domestic livestock, brings in no return, and serves no useful purpose" (245).

Today, 50 percent of the remaining mustangs live in Nevada, where 67 percent of the state is public (federally owned) land. Hunting mustangs in Nevada is a century-old tradition. As noted above, in 1897 approximately two million wild horses lived in seventeen western states, with the majority in Nevada.[41] That year Nevada made it legal to kill wild horses. Akin to gold fever, the term used for those who flocked to California during the Gold Rush in 1849, people in the western United States, in the early twentieth century, had "mustang fever."

Those with a case of the fever, those who hunted the mustangs, were called "mustangers." Mustangers (and stockmen) believed they were taking advantage of a natural resource in Nevada and simultaneously doing a "public" service (for the private businesses of ranchers like my grandfather). Mustang fever spread as another Nevadan natural resource, silver, began to disappear. "Nevada turned its attention to wild horses," Stillman writes, "a readily accessible treasure in seemingly endless supply."[42] Wild horses "could be rendered into products such as pet food, glue, clothing, and meat" (240). Even wearing mustang hides as coats became fashionable. As discussed earlier, in the United States, horses were not a common food for humans, but mustang meat was fed to pets. And there was a real demand for horsemeat in Europe, where humans did (and still do) eat it.

In response to the call for mustang products, more and more men hunted the horses. Not only lucrative, hunting mustangs was an exciting sport. The *Popular Science Monthly* celebrated the profitable diversion in a 1925 headline, "How a Cowboy-Aviator Hunts: The World's Most Thrilling Sport Found in Ridding Western Grazing Land of a Million Outlaw Animals—Adventures of a Famous Buckaroo."[43] That buckaroo, Charles "Pete" Barnum of South Dakota, traveled to Nevada around 1899 and became the "most celebrated mustanger." Barnum shipped approximately seven thousand horses to stock-yards for rendering. Stillman adds, "Considering that about 25 percent were killed in the process before they even got to the stockyards, that means that he had actually rounded up about nine thousand horses" (240). His ruthless-ness matched that of Buffalo Bill. Stillman exposes Barnum's brutality as it is described in an article written by western writer Rufus Steele. In his admir-ing profile of Barnum, Steele quoted Barnum describing the excitement of mustanging. Barnum explains, "I have ridden neck and neck with these game old stallions. . . . I have beaten them across the nose with my quirt until their faces were drenched with blood, only to have them slacken sufficiently to dodge behind my horse and thence to continue on their contrary way."[44]

Horse Crazy: The Courage of Wild Horse Annie

An early horse-crazy girl in the United States, Velma Johnston (1912–1977), stood in the way of male violence against mustangs. The violent roundups of mustangs continued without limit until Johnston, who was from Nevada, got in their way. Like other horse-crazy girls to come, she was profoundly brave. And similar to several of the women I interviewed, Johnston had dis-ability. She had polio as a child and spent months confined at a sanatorium in an upper-body cast. "When the doctors took the cast off, the polio was arrested but [Johnston's] face had stuck to the plaster, and she was perma-nently disfigured." She also could no longer move her neck.[45] Johnston felt shy and uncomfortable around other humans. She was self-conscious about her appearance. With horses, she felt safe and connected. Horses were her friends.

Johnston's family was intimately tied to the history of Nevada and its wild horses. Her paternal grandfather ran a silver mine in the 1870s. When the sil-ver ran out, her grandfather took his family and headed to California. On the way, they ran out of food and had no resources with which to purchase more. Johnston's then-infant father was breastfeeding, but as the food ran out so did his mother's breastmilk. One of their horses, a formerly wild mustang mare, had a nursing foal. Johnston's grandfather saved the infant by milking the mare and feeding her milk to the baby boy. The story was "passed down through the generations: how a little boy in the desert was saved by a wild horse."[46]

Johnston came to be known as Wild Horse Annie and, starting in 1950, dedicated her life to protecting wild horses in Nevada and the western United States. Wild Horse Annie was honored by a famous children's book writer, Marguerite Henry (also discussed in chapter 3), who wrote more than a dozen novels about horses that horse-crazy girls like me grew up reading and rereading. Henry dedicated *Mustang: Wild Spirit of the West* (1966) to "'Wild Horse Annie' in whose moccasins I have been walking these many moons." Henry tells the story of Johnston (aka Annie) and her fight to save and protect the mustang.

Annie took on the battle one day when she was driving to work, daydreaming, and suddenly noticed a cattle truck in front of her that was full of mustangs. The horses were in terrible condition, many with open and bleeding wounds, packed in together. Some appeared to be dying but were held upright by the bodies around them. In her children's book, Henry writes about what Annie saw that day. "The truck was jammed, crammed, packed with mustangs, more dead than alive! Tatters of flesh hung loose on their necks. Blood trickled from their nostrils. They had the look and stench of death. All that kept them on their feet was the way they were wedged in."[47] Annie was stunned and confused. Whose horses were these, and where were they being taken? Why were they in such awful condition? What had happened to them?

Annie was meant to show up at the office where she worked as a secretary. Instead, deeply concerned about the animals in front of her, she followed the truck, driving a couple of hours out of her way until it reached its destination, a local slaughterhouse. Henry describes the experience for her child readers from Annie's perspective: "I looked at my gauge; the tank was half full. I looked at my watch. The office would be at its busiest now. Everyone would be wondering about me. As I followed the truck on and on, the gentle morning sunshine gave way to merciless heat. Blood and sweat crusted on the horses' bodies. Heads bobbed nervously, then drooped low, and lower."[48] In the adult account of the story, Stillman clarifies the horses were "suffering from buckshot wounds." Stillman describes them: "There was a stallion whose eyes had been shot out and a badly trampled colt. Some of the horses were bleeding from their hooves, which were worn down from being chased across hard rocks."[49]

In the version intended for children, Henry holds back some of the details. Yet she offers a realistically brutal depiction. Henry's 1966 children's story stands in stark contrast to the absence of writing about slaughterhouse deaths today. She writes,

> Two brawny men were lowering the tailgate of the truck. To my horror I saw that some of the horses were hobbled, hindfoot to forefoot! Now their feet were jerked out from under them, and on their sides they were pulled like cold carcasses across the tailgate and into the plant. Only their heaving bodies showed they were still breathing.
>
> I knew now why they had not been killed. They had to be brought in alive or their flesh would have rotted in the sun. But at last death would come. It might not be gentle, but surely it would be swift. And then their meat would be ground and stuffed into cans.[50]

Annie soon found out not only how brutal but also how extensive were the mustang roundups. Mustangs had become big business. With lots of money to be made, and applauded by the ranchers who wanted the horses off the public grazing land, mustangers began hiring private planes to chase down the mustangs and run them ragged, at once gathering and making them docile. In Nevada alone, mustangers slaughtered one hundred thousand mustangs in the eight years following the Second World War.[51]

Because the mustang hunts were disturbing to some in the eyes of the public, Stillman notes, "The hunts were only whispered about" and at times "boasted about in certain bars" (252). Annie started writing letters to local newspapers in the hope of finding others upset by the mustanging. And people did slowly reach out to her, some with "terrible stories," others with tips about current or future hunts.

One night, Annie pursued a tip with her husband, Charlie. They found a makeshift corral holding four hundred mustangs waiting to be taken to slaughter. Annie began photographing what she saw. In an interview with *Desert* magazine, Annie described the mustangs, "milling around in the dry dust, hysterical with fear." She said, "Their hoofs and mouths were bleeding.... They emitted strange tortured cries."[52] The men keeping the horses overnight saw the flash from Annie's nighttime photographs and came driving right at her in their car, shouting at her. Then they veered away from her and came driving back, this time right at Charlie who took out his gun and aimed; at that point the men drove away.

Annie developed her film at home that night and took her photographs to the county commissioner's office first thing in the morning. She showed the photographs to the first bureaucrat to arrive. He found them compelling and returned with Annie to where the mustangs were still corralled, accused the men "of cruelty to animals, and ordered them to release the mustangs." Stillman describes the results of this small triumph. "As word of the horses' release spread across Storey County, the range war against the horse exploded, and it now had a human target. Annie received death threats, and began responding to knocks on her door with a rifle in her left hand. But she didn't hide—in fact, she and Charlie . . . often met in the neighborhood tavern, along with other locals, to talk about the situation" (253–254).

Others heard about and got involved in Annie's struggle to protect the remaining mustangs running wild in the western United States. Henry's book about Annie came out in 1966 and helped inspire a letter-writing campaign by child readers, "the pencil brigade, a far-flung grassroots action waged by schoolchildren." Stillman explains that Gregory Gude received the book for Christmas, and after reading it, "the eleven-year-old son of Maryland congressman Gilbert Gude" started writing letters to "his father's colleagues." Gregory wrote, "I think we need a law to protect our wild mustangs before they are all killed." Others joined Gregory, including Joan Bolsinger, "a fourth-grade teacher at Eastwood Elementary School in Rosebud, Oregon, who told her students about the vanishing wild horses of the West and suggested that they could help." Bolsinger's students wrote "letter after letter in support of a bill cosponsored by Oregon senator Mark Hatfield and Washington senator Henry Jackson, who had spearheaded some of the great wilderness legislation of the era" (261). Bolsinger and her class were quickly joined by children writing letters from every state.

The vast majority of the two million mustangs living wild at the turn of the twentieth century have been wiped out. There are less than 35,000 mustangs roaming free in the United States today and only 23,000, at most, on public land.[53] To some extent, these mustangs live, and live relatively unrestricted lives, due to the bill supported by Wild Horse Annie and a letter-writing social movement of children from across the United States.[54] The bill, the Wild and Free Roaming Horses and Burros Act of 1971, passed. President Richard M. Nixon signed the bill into law in December 1971. Sweeping wild horses into a romantically savage past complete with Native Americans, colonial forces, and indomitable spirits, Nixon explained his position in terms of symbolic animal capital:

In the past seventy years, civilization and economics have brought the wild horse to 99 percent extinction. They are a living link with the conquistadors, through the heroic times of the western Indians and pioneers to our own day. . . . More than that, they merit protection as a matter of ecological right—as anyone knows who has stood awed at the indomitable spirit and sheer energy of a mustang running free.[55]

The Work of Leisure: Horses Gendered Female

Over time horses moved from the productive, instrumental, frontier space dominated by men to the noninstrumental, domestic, settled, and "civilized" world of predominantly (white) women and the family. In particular, after the nation industrialized in the nineteenth and early twentieth centuries, both ways of thinking about and actually using horses changed. From animals meant for what was understood to be male work in farms, ranches, wars, and transportation of humans and human goods, they shifted to beings designated-for-female leisure work. (I use the term "leisure work" because what might be leisure for women and girls was still work for the horses.) With industrialization and the growth of factories and urban spaces as centers of production, stables, farms, and ranches largely ceased to be (male) places of horse-involved production. Instead, stables became increasingly female and domesticated places, largely white, for fun and "spare time."

One woman I interviewed, Fiona, said about her experience, "There have definitely always been more girls and women in the sport of horseback riding than men."[56] This was corroborated by other women I interviewed. Helen, for example, said, "I think society views horses as predominantly a female hobby."[57] It is important to note that in each gendered realm, horse bodies were productive in ways both symbolic (for example, in western movies) and material, including as physical products such as pet food, glue, and horsemeat for human consumption in Europe.

As horse productivity decreased, the expense of keeping them increased. In this way children paralleled horses. With industrialization, children ceased to be productive members of their families; they ceased to be tiny adult workers. With this change, the no-longer-productive children became children who needed attention and resources to develop into productive adults. As children became expensive, people had fewer and fewer of them and family sizes shrank.[58] As horses became expensive, and the land they needed to live filled up and increased in cost, fewer and fewer people had access to horses. As they did less productive work, both children and horses were increasingly understood to be luxuries. Gail Cunningham writes, "And because of the expense and space required to maintain horses, equestrianism is a comparatively specialized activity in the way that tennis, running or football are not."[59]

Pushed out first by trains and then by cars and farm machinery, horses moved from being an everyday part of life to being focal points of children's—increasingly girls'—fantasies. No longer commonplace in reality, horses haunted girls' dreams. These dream animals in the Americas descend from domestic stock. In spite of descending from domesticated animals, horses, like nature (and like white women, and all women and men of color), have been understood to be "wild." As historian Patricia Nelson Limerick illuminates, the history of the American West is a history of conquest.[60] Horses were animals to be conquered, animals one must "break" to make them useful.

In another parallel to horses, ideologies of and the use of "nature" and the land also shifted. Today, in contrast to that earlier normative belief in conquering "nature" (and horses), many people in the United States push to appreciate "nature" without harming or changing it. An idea that became popular among equestrians in the 1980s was that horses ought to be "gentled," that one should work *with* the horse—as in "horse whispering" or "natural horsemanship"—instead of "breaking" or conquering it so that it gives in to humans and human demands. "Gentling" is a prevalent practice today among horse people.

These changes and their implications continue. To some extent, the common ideas about both nature and horses have moved increasingly from something to be *used by* (male) humans for production to something to be *enjoyed with* humans (predominantly white females, in the case of horses) in leisure.

Riding While Sexual

As to female enjoyment, one worry mainstream society had, which continues to bubble up as a concern about girls and women who ride, involves female sexuality. It has been commonly believed that girls and women are sexually aroused, even to the point of orgasm, by riding horses. Sidesaddles handled this potential indecency as they kept women's legs closed. Yet they were significantly more difficult and dangerous to use. Sidesaddles, like corsets, constrained women's bodies as well as their riding. Radclyffe Hall's character Stephen, in her famous 1928 novel, *The Well of Loneliness*, refused to ride sidesaddle as a girl, and this deeply upset her mother due to the impropriety of it.[61] Conversely, Rachel P. Maines briefly explores the use of horseback riding to cure women's hysteria for the very reason that women were believed to be stimulated to orgasm while riding. At the time, around the turn of the twentieth century, orgasm was one medical response to—and proposed cure of—the epidemic of hysteria (a central misogynist "disorder" of that time) in Europe and the United States.[62]

A male horseback-riding trainer named Gary whom I interviewed disclosed that one of his young students had told her parents, and they told him, that she sometimes had and enjoyed orgasms when she rode.[63] And scholar of children's literature Nicholas Tucker does find "sexual overtones" between girls and their horses in the pony book literature, including a girl torso "moving rhythmically as he [her horse] moved" and girls who are "in love" with their horses.[64] To the extent that human love, intimacy, and sexuality slip into each other, surely girls have sexual feelings about their horses and experience sexuality while riding. This mainstream concern with girls and women being sexual on horseback reflects a broader concern with girls and women experiencing sexuality at all. The anxiety about their sexual experiences while riding reduces the horse-girl relationship to a mere biological (sexual) response. While sexual arousal might be one pleasant effect of riding for some, none of the former horse-crazy girls I spoke with focused on this as a reason for horseback riding or even a regular part of their riding experience. My sense is that like many normative concerns about women's sexuality, this concern springs from anxiety that women have sexuality and are sexual beings, more than from the embodied experience of arousal being at the center of women's riding encounters.

Human Evolution: From Men Breaking to
Women Whispering with Horses

Horses in the United States today exist as leisure animals associated with women and girls. With their role in human leisure and association with girls and women, the training of horses has changed, in general becoming gentler.

As vegetarians and prey to meat eaters, horses evolved to be and remain herd animals. Even today as companion animals, horses use constant vigilance to protect themselves. Anything could be a threat, and as riders know, horses will often treat surprises, such as a new brightly colored horse blanket, or a piece of trash on the side of the road that was not there yesterday, as dangerous and shy away from such terrifying encounters. Most horses remain, as Michael Korda explains, "ready at any moment to make the mad dash for safety on which survival depends." Horses evolved to rely on other horses to maintain continual vigilance. "As a herd animal," Korda writes, "the horse craves and needs the company of other horses—there is safety as well as companionship in numbers. Even the most restless of horses is likely to stand quietly in its field so long as it can see, however far away, other horses, but left on its own, it may start running until it loses a shoe or injures itself."[65]

As I discuss in chapter 7 in regard to a horse named Clever Hans, horse alertness exceeds the human capacity to pay attention. Korda writes, "Horses pay attention, in ways and to a degree that we can hardly even imagine." Horses might seem peaceful, quietly grazing, but they are perpetually aware. They evolved to be with other horses and "in constant communication with each other, their ears flicking back and forth as they listen for any sounds" and watch for any signs of danger.[66] While riding or grooming or watching horses, humans might not be paying close attention to them. In contrast, "[I]t's almost impossible for a horse not to pay strict attention to its rider, or to the people who work around it in the barn." Korda explains, "The fact that it's eating, or dozing, or appears to be ignoring your presence doesn't mean that its senses aren't fully focused on you, or that your feelings about the horse, and to some degree your intentions toward it, haven't been communicated" (104).

From this attentiveness comes the capacity for profound connection. A goal of many riders in the past and still today has been to be one being with your horse. Because horses are so attentive, it can seem that your horse is reading your mind, that the horse responds to your wish before you have a chance to indicate the wish to the horse, or perhaps before you are fully conscious of your own desire. Korda claims that horses listen "with an acuteness that no animal that talks can approach" (104).

In sharp contrast to the gentle, quiet, and astute listening of horses, in the normative western United States, and other places too, particularly in horses' history of working productively for men, many humans have trained horses in a manner that is anything but gentle. In my childhood in Wyoming and Montana, and still today in some places, people "break" horses when they train them. As a child, I knew that breaking a horse meant that one imposed one's will on the horse so that the horse eventually gave up its own will and submitted fully to the (adult) human's wishes and desires; the horse's experience in this relationship to adult humans was, not incidentally, similar to the experience of being a child in my family. As a child, I learned that a poorly broken horse was a horse that did not give itself fully to fulfilling human dictates. A poorly broken, poorly trained horse had a "will of its own."

The now-famous horse trainer Monty Roberts describes this method in his autobiographical book, *The Man Who Listens to Horses* (1996). Animal studies scholar Lynda Birke claims that Roberts is "one of the best known" practitioners of natural horsemanship. Roberts, born in 1935, writes about growing up in California with a father who was a horse trainer and western riding instructor, whose "methods of dealing with horses were what [he] would describe as conventional—but that is to say, cruel." Roberts adds, "The standard way of breaking in horses in those days was a method that is popular even today."[67] His father would take six horses and tie each to a post thirty feet from the next horse.

> Next, my father stood in the middle of the corral with a heavy tarpaulin or weighted sack attached to the end of a rope. He threw the sack over the horses' back and around their legs, moving from one to the other.
>
> When the sack dropped on their haunches and around their rear legs, the horses panicked. Their eyes rolled and they kicked, reared and pulled back against their restraints as though their lives depended on it—because in their eyes, it did. Who could tell them that this wasn't the end of everything? Fear is in their nature, and they were driven wild with it and plunged back and forth and sideways on the ends of the ropes, fighting for their lives. Their necks and heads swelled up and frequently they injured themselves. It was—and remains—a desperately cruel sight. (22)

After eight to ten days, Roberts describes the "blood tracks" on the horses' pasterns "from where the ropes had worn through the skin." As the process continued, the horses faced more violence for any expression of will. When Roberts's father began to ride the horses, he "kicked them in the belly" and "tried to raise some fight in them if he could. If they moved, they were whipped." Over a period of three weeks, the horses fought less and less. Roberts writes, "Their relationship with their human masters was now defined—they were working out of fear, not out of willingness" (22).

Roberts expresses a disdain for cruelty to horses that is a common theme in girl-oriented horse literature. From *Black Beauty* in 1877 through contemporary horsey girl stories, writers frame cruelty as morally wrong, something that good riders do not rely on. Roberts offers an interesting secondary reason for abstaining from physically punitive methods, and that is that horses work for and with humans better when trained without cruelty. He writes, "To destroy the willingness in a horse is a plainly daft, unforgivable thing—it's among the dominant characteristics of the horse, and if it's nurtured it can grow into the most solid and rewarding aspect of their working lives. Of the horses I've held dear in my life, I've enjoyed most their willingness to try for me, over and over again" (22).

From an attempt to work with the horse, in relationship together, and to listen more carefully came a new movement in the western United States, or at least a new movement for white, middle-class horse people, particularly for women as horses have moved into the world of leisure. For over fifty years this movement has challenged mainstream ways of training horses and has developed and grown. As a participant in my study commented, men lead the movement, but primarily women follow and use the new techniques. This development parallels how changes in child-rearing practices came about in the twentieth century: male doctors told female parents—mothers—what to do, and the mothers followed the male advice and did what the men told them (see my analysis in *Boundaries of Touch*). Just as women still do the majority of the labor of parenting in the United States, so women do the majority of recreational horseback riding, yet the advice of women in horse training, as in parenting, is still not taken as seriously as that of men. All of the famous horse whisperers are men. As a woman I interviewed described, when you go to the trainings, the horse-whispering instructors are men and the crowd of people, who are there to learn how to train their horses, are women. Indeed, Birke notes about the practice's name that it "is a particularly sexist term, given the majority of the riders are women, and there is a significant majority of women in 'natural horse*man*ship.'"[68]

Birke attempts to define the term, explaining that different people mean different things by "natural horsemanship." She writes, "There are many practitioners with differing styles and points of view advertising as 'natural horsemen/women.'" Nonetheless, she clarifies, "[A]ll emphasize understanding why horses do what they do and approaching them with sensitivity." Birke writes that practitioners of natural horsemanship "desire to understand horses and interact with them in natural ways; that is, draw on what is seen to be the animal's instinctive behavior pattern and on what people perceive as equine behavior in the wild" (220).

As discussed above, "horse whisperers," men such as Roberts, Ray Hunt, Tom Dorrance, and Hunt and Dorrance's younger follower, Buck Brannaman, offer us a new way to train horses, indeed a new way to think about our relationships with them.[69] As much as anything else, this new way is defined by a "clear demarcation from what are seen as conventional approaches" and the belief that those "traditional methods involved a kind of cruelty that is now outmoded."[70]

Like Roberts, Hunt was all too familiar with the type of horse training called breaking horses. He too had the experience that "violence and aggression can successfully 'break' these animals. . . . [B]roken horses can be ridden." Yet as journalist Meg Daley Olmert explains, Hunt "has come to see that those methods, based on anxiety rather than trust, at best produce only a limited partnership." Daley Olmert writes, "Ray [Hunt] now offers the horse a better deal."[71]

Daley Olmert claims, "Whether on a horse or walking toward one, Ray [Hunt] can read its body and its eyes, and know what it's thinking and feeling. His powers of observation are a gift from a time when the tireless scrutiny of animals meant survival." Over many, many years spent observing horses closely, Hunt learned that "horses have an overwhelming need to belong. A horse is a desperately social creature willing to sacrifice its freedom to be part of a herd." Hunt works with this "powerful bonding instinct to create a herd of two—himself and the horse" (85).

Like Hunt, Roberts claims to know how to pay extremely close attention to horses so as to be able to communicate fluently with them. In a sense, he speaks their language, a language of movement, touch, and sound that Roberts describes as "primitive, precise and easy-to-read." About this language he claims, "Once it's learned, it allows a new understanding between man [*sic*] and horse. But there's nothing weird about it and it isn't exclusive to me—just recently I had my farrier achieving similar results in a few minutes."[72]

Roberts describes a workshop he gave for the queen of England. She had heard about his training methods and was intrigued. The queen reached out to him and invited him to demonstrate his work with one of her horses in England. The horse was a filly (a young female horse), an "adolescent, skittish and wide-eyed with fear." Roberts writes, "I recognized a creature more scared than I was and needing my assistance." Normally a calm person, Roberts experienced anxiety as he started to perform in front of the queen. Yet upon seeing the scared young horse, he immediately calmed down and focused on interacting with her. Roberts claims that this "young, untouched filly behaved exactly as [he] predicted." He writes, "Without my putting any kind of rope or harness on her, she was following me around the ring within seven minutes of our starting work together. If I turned and walked in a circle, she did too, her nose just a foot or two from my shoulder. Where I went, she followed. In her predicament, she trusted me. I was her comfort" (10–11).

Runaway Ponies and Other Stories of My Grandmother

❧ As a child, I was unaware of natural horsemanship. Indeed, I had only a few horseback riding lessons and no other training before my father gave me my pony, Dolly. Equipped with a pony, I was expected to figure out how to ride—by riding. Some of what I learned came from the stories I read and those I was told from time to time by my grandmother. I took the stories under advisement, but I never let them influence my decision to ride. Just like I was going to breathe, go to school, and sleep at night with my cat Thomasina, I was going to ride.

It was when I went to visit my grandmother, my father's mother, during the summer that she and I would discuss things. Sometimes she would tell me about our family history. She would tell me stories, stories that were true, stories of our family. Maybe because I was little, maybe because my grandmother was old and held so many memories

inside of her, I never managed to completely understand who was
who in her stories. I would ask, who was that again, Gram, and she
would patiently explain one more time. But still, it would be unclear to
me. When she referred to Uncle Tom, did she mean my uncle Tom, my
father's uncle Tom, or her uncle Tom? Even though I do not understand the relative placement of the characters, I still remember many
of the stories. So at least some of my grandmother's memories live
on with me. Hopefully it will not make our shared relatives uncomfortable that, while they are remembered, it may not always be in the
proper role or time.

There were two terrible horse accidents in the family. Two relatives
died because of a horse, my grandmother told me. One terrible horse
accident happened to someone who was either my grandmother's
brother, her uncle, or maybe her cousin. Whoever he was, my grandmother held a horse responsible for his terrible death. When the
accident happened, this relative was riding in a carriage of some sort.
I think his father and brothers were with him. The carriage placed the
story far away from me. I had never been in a carriage. In this story,
the horse spooked and ran away with the relative. The relative fell out
of the carriage, and not only did he fall out, he fell under. And the
carriage ran over him, killing him. My grandmother told me his father
and brothers saw the whole thing. They were never the same. I didn't
know them before or after, so this did not mean much to me.

The other horse story my grandmother told me over and over. Some
people tell stories over and over on a regular basis. Maybe because
their head is so cluttered they cannot remember that they have already
told this particular story to this particular person. Or maybe it is
out of a certain desperation, a wanting, needing, to be heard. Maybe
they believe they have hit upon a story that will allow them, finally, to
drink fully of another human being's attention. So they tell the story,
and then again, and again, all the while hoping. Well, this was not
my grandmother. My grandmother was not one of those people who
repeated stories. Maybe she was desperate, but she never showed it. All
she showed was dignity—dignity and distance.

The story was a simple story. It had no magic to it. In the story a
cousin, who could not have been my cousin because this cousin lived

in the days before cars, was not careful when riding a pony. Due to carelessness, the cousin, who was a little boy, got his foot caught in the stirrup of the pony's saddle. As the story goes, something spooked the pony and she ran away with the little boy cousin. At this part of the story I empathized with the little cousin. I too had a pony. And she ran away with me on a regular basis. One time with me clinging to her back, she raced off through a grove of trees. There is a reason why everyone says Shetland ponies are clever. That time she raced off through a grove of trees, she clearly had thought through her plan with care. She raced, dodging trees, until she approached a branch that was just the right height. It was perfect for a small pony to race under, but not so high that I could squeeze under with her. Dolly was both very little and very smart.

The next part of my grandmother's story was the warning. I had thus far received only one or two concussions, a broken thumb, and a perfect imprint of horse's teeth across one side of my face. I was thrilled when the doctor said that unfortunately the teeth marks were so deep they would scar me for life. I was thrilled, but my grandmother was not. She called my father's house several times to make sure everything possible was being done. There is nothing more we can do, and yes, she has had her tetanus shots, my father would say once again. Anyhow, the poor little cousin was not so lucky. When the pony ran away with him, he fell off with his foot still caught in one of the stirrups. The pony only ran harder. She ran and ran until she had dragged that little cousin to death. At this part of the story my grandmother would look at me significantly. *Did I get it?* her look would say. I was not sure if I did.

Was my grandmother simply telling me to be careful when I went riding? I would explain, but Gram, I don't ride with a saddle anyhow. I always rode bareback. She didn't have to worry about my feet getting caught in the stirrups. Was my grandmother hoping I would stop riding all together? Was her story a don't-mess-with-horses-they're-too-dangerous story? One thing was for certain, I was not going to stop riding horses. Not even for my grandmother. Maybe her story was a warning about life. Maybe she was telling me that life is dangerous.

You never know what lurks around the corner. You never know when a small mistake like carelessly letting your foot slip in your stirrup will cost you your life.

My grandmother never told me what to do. She never told me that I should not love horseback riding, that I should wear dresses, that I needed to lose or gain weight. My grandmother was simply not bossy. She was not demanding. She was too distant, too elegant for that. She only told me one repeated story, her warning story. And then she looked at me to see if I understood.

3

Dreaming of Horses

The Pony Book Genre and Other Horse Stories in the Mid-Twentieth Century

Former horse-crazy girl and avid reader Jenny explained that in response to her obsession with horses, her parents did not buy her a horse or expensive horseback-riding lessons. Instead, she said, they "bought me lots of books. I read the classics. *National Velvet*, *Black Beauty*, the Black Stallion books . . . Marguerite Henry! I read all of those! Do you remember how, with those Scholastic books, you'd get those flyers and you could order books from school? I would find every horse book in those."[1]

Like Jenny, many little girls own horses, just not the live kind. And like her, many of the women I spoke with expressed passion for children's horse books. In an interview, pony book collector and expert Jane Badger explained to me,

> Pony books allow girls to identify with characters who have fulfilled the reader's dream of horses. Most children who read pony books will never have a pony of their own, and quite possibly not have lessons, or anything much to do with a real horse. Reading about people who have achieved the dream allows the reader to enter into a world they have little other chance of experiencing. The love of horses seems to strike whether or not you have any access to a real, live horse. Pony books are often pure wish-fulfillment.[2]

When asked if she read children's horse books, one woman I interviewed, Helen, responded, "Yes, yes, yes!"[3] Another woman, Fiona, said that still today, "I have an awful lot of horse books, both fictional and nonfictional." As a child, she "would regularly read them."[4] Speaking from his experience as the former editor in chief of the commercial publishing house Simon & Schuster, Michael Korda explains, "Few kids these days, however horse-struck, are likely to have that kind of [close] relationship with a horse unless they live in the country." Instead, girls pretend to have horses, play at being horses, and, like Jenny, read horses. And it is girls, not boys, who obsess. Korda writes, "These days, of course, it's mostly girls that are horse-struck. Boys can take horses or leave them, but with girls it's as if the teenage Elizabeth Taylor in *National Velvet* were part of their gene pool."[5]

What does the consumption of horses in stories mean for girls? In this chapter I explore the children's stories about ponies and horses in popular culture and in particular the pony book genre in children's literature in the twentieth century. I claim that fantasy horses in pony book stories are a form of symbolic animal capital. These storybook horses produce profit, meaning, and affect around social categories like gender, race, and class. In particular, the books offer girls normative stories of mainstream, white, middle-class people. Like the example of the mustang used to sell a car at the beginning of chapter 2, storybook horses and ponies also sell things, or rather they sell ideas and feelings. They sell ways of feeling and thinking about being (white, middle-class) girls.

Pony books offer story situations where individual, and always white, girls face adversity and, through hard work, ultimately triumph. Often in the story a girl does not have and desperately wants a horse. This individual girl faces her problems—not being able to afford a horse, not knowing how to ride, or loneliness—and through her hard work and individual initiative succeeds at resolving them. In some ways the girl pulls herself up by her own bootstraps and is a model individual in a capitalist world order. The fictional girl with her pony also does what girls are supposed to do: she cares for others. In the case of these stories, she cares for horses.[6] On the other hand, the girl with her horse in the story challenges normative cultural demands for girls by her hard physical and often dirty work, by facing danger, by being outdoors and of the world rather than inside the home.

While they reinforce a capitalist work ethic and individualism, the stories also challenge mainstream ways of thinking. Those from the United Kingdom in particular frequently defy normativity when it comes to gender.

The pony book genre often supports fantasies of freedom and strength for girls and offers a place for girls to imagine themselves as the heroes of their own visions, hopes, and dreams. Even in the early and mid-twentieth century, these storybook horse-crazy girls do not dream of boys saving them; they dream of horses and horses that they, the girls themselves, save. In part, girlhood in the stories embodies my notion of vital care (discussed further in chapter 5). Many of the girls in the stories self-assert to materialize their dreams. They are strong and heroic like normative boys in mainstream culture, but their dreams are less about capitalistic material gains or instrumental ends than normative boys' dreams. Rather, these girls assert themselves and work hard so as to have a profound connection with another being.

The pony book genre was largely from the United Kingdom as the writers were principally from and wrote them in Great Britain. They were nearly all written by girls and women and focused on girl readers. I concentrate on the central period of the genre, the 1930s to the 1970s.[7] More pony books were written after the 1970s; that forty-year period was merely the genre's heyday. Today's horse-crazy girls still read the books written during that prime period, as Korda has said. To ensure that I explored books that were relevant both when they were published and today, I focused on pony and horse books that fell into at least two of the following categories: those addressed by contemporary scholars of the genre; those that have been recently republished as electronic books; those that the women I interviewed brought up; and those that I myself had read as a child.

The Hero of Her Own Story

About the meaning of the fantasy of owning a pony, and children's pony book literature, Korda writes:

> [U]ndoubtedly a certain innocence seems to attach itself to the whole idea of owning a pony, as if the pony were a way of prolonging childhood dreams and fantasies. Surely it's no accident that one of the few books that never rates anything less than a misty-eyed five-star review from its readers on the Amazon .com website is *Misty of Chincoteague*, with *My Friend Flicka* (admittedly the latter is about a boy and his pony, but most of the readers seem to be girls) a close second.[8]

Indeed, extending childhood is a consistent pony book theme; girl characters like Jean in Christine Pullein-Thompson's Phantom Horse series wish that their childhood could go on "forever" and mourn that they have "to grow up, go out into the world, work and be educated, worry over gas bills and the washing-up and whether the floor's clean."[9]

Beyond Korda's suggestion that the stories prolong childhood dreams and a period of relative vulnerability, I argue that for girls pony books are a place of empowerment.[10] Scholar Alison Haymonds writes, "Horses empower girls in pony books. A horse gives a girl a sense of her own identity, self-respect, control, and an almost mystical understanding of nature."[11] Unfortunately, the pony books' challenge to normativity ends with gender, as they largely reproduce a white middle-class worldview.

Haymonds describes the pony book genre as comprising stories typically "in a British setting, generally rural, with a young hero, nearly always female, whose relationship with her pony is central to the action" (54). And Haymonds identifies the surprising absence of scholarly literature about the girl-centered pony book genre.[12] Given the plethora of twentieth-century pony books, it is striking to have so little written on them. It is a lack of attention paralleled in the absence of scholarly literature on horse-crazy girls and perhaps springs from the fact that topics involving girls, girl characters in books, girl readers, and girls who are passionate about horses, historically and today, garner less notice than topics involving boys. Yet as Haymonds claims, it is strange that even "feminist critics seem to have ignored the pony book while embracing other forms of popular fiction for girls."[13]

British pony books from the dawn of the genre in the 1930s and on have had a healthy focus on girls, albeit always only white girls. In part, these stories probably interest their girl readers because they contain active, heroic girl characters. Diverging from most twentieth-century children's literature in the United Kingdom and the United States, girls make up a significant number of the characters—and they are vigorous and lively—in British pony books.[14] Girls often play a central role in the stories, and while boys might be central too, it is usually not without girls. Yet the stories depict the world as adamantly white. With very rare exceptions, all humans are white. While it is almost exclusively white children that find themselves reflected in the stories, and heroically so, it is the rare pony book that has a white male instead of white female hero.[15] I have yet to find a hero of color.

Even when they play a role in the stories, boys do not dominate the novels. Badger explains that those authors who depict boy characters, like Moyra Charlton, Eleanor Helme, and Marjorie Mary Oliver, "all wrote stories that involved girls and boys equally" (20). In sharp contrast to the British stories, in the United States boys dominate in most popular children's books about horses, including in Mary O'Hara's *My Friend Flicka* (1940), Walter Farley's *The Black Stallion* (1941) and his Black Stallion series, and Marguerite Henry's *Misty of Chincoteague* (1947) and her Misty series.[16] As a girl, I read and reread these three books and anything by these authors that I could get my hands on. In the few boxes of childhood things that I had and kept are several books by O'Hara, Farley, and Henry. All three—*My Friend Flicka*, *The Black Stallion*, and *Misty of Chincoteague*—involve the catching, taming, and training of a wild horse, and in all three boys are the heroic actors. Haymonds writes, "It is significant that American horse stories that were popular during much the same period as the British pony book have tended to be 'rites of passage' books for boys rather than girls." She elaborates, "The coming of age of young males is still one of the key themes of American literature, films, and popular culture, and this also was true of the earlier and influential horse stories."[17]

In the memoir she wrote about her sisters and herself, the popular pony book author Josephine Pullein-Thompson writes about the lack of heroic girls in other children's literature: "In so many children's classics, the girls' roles—truthfully mirroring their times—were dreadfully inferior. Jo March in *Little Women* was a great improvement."[18] Regarding this, Josephine Pullein-Thompson's obituary states:

> In the equestrian novels that she, her mother Joanna Cannan and her younger twin sisters Diana and Christine, wrote—nearly 200 between them—riding horses was also the way that girls could show that they were just as good as boys, if not better. Their heroines relished mucking out stables and the freedom of galloping away across the countryside, and the pluckiest were able to turn bedraggled nags into rosette-winning champions, later returning home to celebrate with a truly "supersonic tea."[19]

In the books, girls with ponies make decisions, they make things happen, they challenge problems and help those who need help. Unlike girls in many other stories, and in contrast to the experiences of many real girls in actual life, pony book girls are actors and not objects. Nicholas Tucker, a scholar of children's literature, writes about the pony book genre, "[Y]oung girl readers are offered the chance to revolt, at least in the imagination, against the passive femininity they may feel they are expected to start acquiring."[20]

In the 1950s, pony books had their heyday insofar as many of them were produced in that decade. In her book on the genre, *Heroines on Horseback: The Pony Book in Children's Fiction* (2013), Badger explains, "In the 1950s the United Kingdom was slowly emerging from the privations of the Second World War. Rationing at last came to an end, there was little unemployment, and life seemed good." She continues, "The pony book, with its portrayal of an arcadian Britain, chimed perfectly with the interests of the population beginning to have more leisure time and looking to a better world. In the late 1940s and 1950s it seemed that if someone with a horsy background could lift a pen they could get a pony book published."[21]

Scholar Liz Thiel writes about Ruby Ferguson's pony book stories from that time period and claims they present "a social critique of postwar Britain that explores concepts of girlhood, exposes the potency of gender ideology and ultimately invites redefinition of the female role."[22] Like Ferguson's books, many books from the pony book genre present a strong critique of and challenge to gendered social norms. "In pony books," Haymonds writes, "the girls were no longer passive, they mounted the Great Steed and took responsibility for their own destiny. It was a symbolic gesture when they bought their first pony with their hard-earned money, for they were the ones who owned and possessed after centuries of being the possessed."[23]

A central theme of many pony books was "strong and independent girls working out their own destinies."[24] Again and again in the pony book literature, girls, that is the girl characters in the stories, live lives that they choose. "Above all," Haymonds explains, in this genre the girl becomes "the hero of her own story."[25]

Black Beauty

As Haymonds and others note, *Black Beauty* became a model for pony books.[26] The novel, written by the English author Anna Sewell, was in its time, and continues to be, an extremely popular book, often read and reread by horse-crazy girls.[27] Josephine Pullein-Thompson writes, "As soon as I could read, I had devoured *Black Beauty* eight times, sobbing over Ginger and the hardness of human life."[28]

Sewell struggled with walking due to an injury to her ankle. She needed horses to move about and, Badger writes, was "horrified by the ill treatment she saw meted out to horses." She wrote *Black Beauty* hoping to persuade humans to treat them with kindness.[29] Sewell wrote her book at a time that horses were common, as cars are today, in the United States and the United Kingdom. One does not normally pay attention to cars, nor did one in Sewell's time regularly pay attention to horses. *Black Beauty* called attention to these everyday animals. It came out in 1877 and told the life story of a beautiful black horse from the horse's perspective. It is considered one of the earliest examples of popular children's fiction about horses. Sewell wrote *Black Beauty* as a plea to treat horses well and, scholars like Gina M. Dorré argue, a plea to treat women well too.[30] Understood to be closer to animality themselves, women were, like nonhuman animals, both believed to need, and actually be in need of, protection from men.

Women of Sewell's day—those mostly similar to her in being white and middle to upper class—spearheaded the British and U.S. movements to protect children and nonhuman animals from the violence of men as well as from overwork and the cruel dictates of elite fashion.[31] In part, *Black Beauty* and other pony books offer children moral lessons about how to treat other animals and, more broadly, about proper manners, values, and how to live. They also teach children who they are as children and where they fit in the social order.[32]

Sewell's fictional horse, Black Beauty, narrates that he was born to a gentle and well-behaved mare on a farm, with other horses around, and a human owner who protected and cared well for his horses. Early in the book, Sewell makes a statement that speaks to social class, and in particular elite manners, and teaches a capitalist work ethic. Sometimes, Black Beauty explains, the other colts in his meadow "had rather rough play, for they would frequently bite and kick as well as gallop." Black Beauty's mother, Pet, said to him that unlike the six other "cart-horse colts" in the meadow with him, who had "not learned manners," Black Beauty was "well-bred and well born." She clarifies, "Your father has a great name in these parts, and your grandfather won the cup two years at the Newmarket races." Pet describes Black Beauty's grandmother, who, like a good (human) female, "had the sweetest temper of any horse I ever knew." She continues, "I think you have never seen me kick or bite. I hope you will grow up gentle and good, and never learn bad ways; do your work with a good will, lift your feet up when you trot, and never bite or kick even in play."[33]

Black Beauty carefully lives his life by these rules. Even when treated badly by humans, he struggles throughout his life to work hard and with a "good will." One of the few female characters in the book, a chestnut mare named Ginger, does not maintain, at all times, a good will or sweet temper. When Black Beauty first meets Ginger, we are told, "Ginger has a bad habit of biting and snapping; that is why they call her Ginger" (14). Ginger explains to Black Beauty that her bad temper came from never having anyone be kind to her.

Through Ginger, Sewell advocates kindness. Her story about "breaking in" Ginger challenges the all-too-common violence used in training horses. Sewell's Ginger uses the term discussed in chapter 2 and used still, one hundred years after Sewell wrote the book, in my childhood in the 1970s, "breaking the horse." About her training, Ginger explains that this was a "bad time" for her and describes her experience: "One dragged me along by the halter, another flogging behind. . . . They did not give me a chance to know what they wanted." The man who first rode her, Samson, had "no gentleness in him." He had "only hardness, a hard voice, a hard eye, a hard hand," and Ginger says, "I felt from the first that what he wanted was to wear all of the spirit out of me, and just make me into a quiet, humble, obedient piece of horseflesh" (24).

Ginger offers an example of what comes from mistreating a horse or, perhaps, a human female. While according to the novel she is problematic in her bad temper, one might also argue that Ginger is more than a bad horse. To some extent, she is also a hero in *Black Beauty*. Ginger resists the unjust treatment and being turned into an "obedient piece of horseflesh." She experiences and challenges the violence of the powerful—who in the novel, as in the lived experience of most girls, are almost all male—and refuses, through nearly all the novel, until just before her death, to give in. Ginger might be seen as a model of resistance for girls, particularly horse-crazy girls, who resist normative culture and the objectification of girls through their very passion for horses.[34]

Reading Horses: The Pony Book Genre

It took about half a century after the publication and enormous success of *Black Beauty* for the pony book genre to appear in the United Kingdom. "This is not surprising," Badger writes about the prepony book years, "The well-brought-up Victorian or Edwardian girl would never, ever have ridden anywhere without some form of chaperonage, making dashing adventure a little tricky."[35] The emergence of the new girl-centered genre reflects changes in "women's position in society" and in the world of horses too. About pony books arriving as a reflection of and response to changes in the lives of women and girls, Haymonds explains, "In the 1930s, 1940s, and 1950s, when the genre evolved and flourished, adolescent girls were becoming more independent, better educated, and had higher expectations of choosing their own career and lifestyle."[36] Further, positions as grooms caring for horses "opened up to women when they began to take the place of grooms during and after the First World War."[37]

Simultaneously, as discussed in chapter 2, with industrialization the role of horses in human lives had changed, and would continue to do so, in the United States and the United Kingdom. With increased use of machinery for the heavy labor that had been done by horses (and humans), horses moved from being working animals to being leisure animals. Before the war, to the extent that riding had been a leisure activity, it was so for elites. This too changed. Badger writes about the United Kingdom, "Riding as a leisure activity filtered down the social hierarchy during the 1920s" (10). In the United States too, as horses were used less for work and as the middle class grew, more and more middle-class people rode for fun, relaxation, sport, and exercise. A survey done by the United States Department of Agriculture indicates that between 1900 and 1940 the number of horses and mules used in agriculture and transportation went down by almost half, from nearly 22,000,000 to just under 14,000,000. By 1960 the survey reveals only 3,089,000 such working horses and mules. In reverse order, around the middle of the twentieth century, the numbers of horses "filling significant recreational roles" were growing. In her book chapter on "The Demographics of the U.S. Equine Population," starting with the mid-twentieth century, Emily R. Kilby writes, "Since then, the trend in equine numbers has been steadily upward." Kilby claims that by 2003 in the United States, the number of horses filling "recreational roles" was around 9,600,000.[38]

As horseback riding increasingly became a leisure activity in the early twentieth century (as discussed in chapter 2), more and more U.S. and British girls began to see horses as theirs to dream about, to ride, to own and groom. In the United Kingdom, the new pony book genre represented this change, and for some people this story, the pony book story, became iconic. The horse (or the pony) lived as symbolic capital in these books. The stories used horses and ponies to say something about the "nature" of human life with horses or, rather, the supposed nature of little girl life with horses. In a relatively short period of time, this story became a story thought to be for all times, forever and always. Korda quotes a contemporary woman, Louise, whose two little girls are horse crazy. She says, "[A] little girl and a pony, that's a story that never changes, isn't it?" "And never will," replies Korda.[39]

About the genre, Badger explains, "The pony book is not the same thing as the animal story: this had had a firm place in children's literature since the 1700s." The pony book genre had a different focus from animal stories. "Nonetheless, it was out of these early [animal] stories that the pony book developed. Although human beings appeared in these stories, it was the animal that told its own story."[40] Badger believes the earliest such narrator of a pony book was Dick in *The Memoirs of Dick, the Little Poney* in 1800.

Both equine characters, Dick and Black Beauty, greatly influenced the pony book genre and in particular one type, the equine autobiography. Badger writes,

> Horse after horse, pony after pony, each told its own life story. Most of these stories followed a remarkably similar progression: a wise first owner, the standard by which all succeeding homes are judged; a decent enough second owner, followed by a downward spiral until, by a massive stroke of luck, the pony is rescued by its original owner, even though it's tottering, scrawny, down on its luck and virtually unrecognizable. (11–12)

Like Black Beauty, the pony autobiographers usually argued that humans should care for and prioritize their pony's well-being. The question of care—putting others before oneself and caring for them well as the way to be a good and successful person in the world—held and continues to hold special importance for girls. Indeed, perhaps because horses and other animals were increasingly understood as being deserving of good care, theirs became a legitimate world for girls to enter. In spite of the dirt, manure, and danger, in spite of the need for strength and physical courage, all understood to be decidedly unfeminine, U.S. and British girls, in part, legitimized their love for horses through the feminine activity of caring for them. Perhaps there is something to Haymonds's questionable claim that caring is an "aspect of horses that girls enjoy more than boys," if for no other reason than caregiving has been a ticket into the barn.[41]

In contrast, the villains in the stories were humans "who ride only because it is smart, and who care not one jot for their animals' welfare, and those who think only of what they want, not what the pony wants." In one pony autobiography, *Moorland Mousie* (1929), author Muriel Wace, using the pen name Golden Gorse, wrote, "'It's quite clear your pony doesn't care for too much petting,' said Mr X. . . . 'Some ponies are like that, and if you are wise children you will understand.'" The pony hero, Moorland Mousie, said about these uncaring children, "But they didn't want to understand. The truth is that they patted me to please themselves because I felt warm and silky and alive. I do not call that kindness. How can it be kindness to us if we do not enjoy it?"[42] Normative pressures did and continue to demand that girls be kind, that they put others, including ponies, before themselves, and that they be skilled in caregiving. In terms of the ethic of care, being horse crazy or, in the United Kingdom, "pony mad," was no big leap for girls to make.

Along with the mandate to care for, and put first, one's pony, there were a number of other themes in the standard twentieth-century pony books. As symbolic animal capital, the ponies carried the themes through the story as though they—pony and idea alike—existed outside of any specific culture or historical time. Some themes involved characteristics over which the child characters (and the child readers) had no control. For example, in a perhaps mild challenge to elites, children who were rich—even though they did not choose to be rich as they were born into wealth—tended to be morally bad. Supporting an individualistic and capitalist work ethic, bad children were portrayed as not having earned what they had. Good children worked hard for their ponies and their horseback-riding skills. Contemporary pony book author Stacey Gregg describes the genre, like Korda and Louise above, as a story for all peoples, everywhere:

Classic pony fiction tends to tread a well-worn bridle path. The themes are universal. There's invariably a clash of both class and money, with our poor but worthy heroine versus the snooty rich girl who is heartless, spoilt and cruel. Then there are the ponies down on their luck that need rescuing, stables that are threatened with closure, runaway horses, frightful adults trying to ruin the fun and, at the end of it all, the glittering chance to ride to glory at the gymkhana.[43]

Another theme involved city children; in the logic of the pony book, these children tended to be unhealthy because they came from the city. Being in the country was healthy, and being in the city was not. Country children and middle-class, working-class, and poor children usually exhibited good behavior, teaching the reader and perhaps even the "bad" city children (and of course the rich children) how one should behave and, in particular, behave around horses.[44] Country versus city *adults* followed suit.

In Christine Pullein-Thompson's Phantom Horse series, the children, Jean and her brother Angus, have an unlikable aunt, Nina, who despises the country; it "bores her stiff." In a pinch when their parents have to fly off to Nigeria and have no one to stay with Jean and Angus, they get Aunt Nina to come. The children dread her visit. "She wore strange hats and false eyelashes and talked endlessly about embassy parties."[45] Further, as a city woman, Aunt Nina is problematic in her firm commitment to normative femininity.

Aunt Nina is concerned over Jean's lack of dresses and her failure to brush her hair more regularly. Pullein-Thompson frames Aunt Nina and her normative concern as problematic. "'Don't you brush your hair at night?' she asked. 'Look, it's all tangled, and your pyjamas are missing a button. Tomorrow I shall buy you a nightie, something really feminine to take away with you, and a pair of fluffy bedroom slippers.' She looked inside my clothes cupboard. 'You've hardly any dresses, either,' she continued. 'And nothing pretty'" (17). Aunt Nina, with her hegemonic femininity, even insists Jean wear a skirt and jumper on her upcoming trip to Ireland. Jean "felt ridiculous in them" (30). Making clear her opinion about Aunt Nina's fashion choices, Pullein-Thompson has Jean and Angus compare Aunt Nina to another relative when they arrive in Ireland. Angus says, "I'm so glad we came, aren't you? And Cousin Mary's nice, isn't she? Not like Aunt Nina. She won't buy you frilly nighties" (39).

Here we see the challenge horsey girls in pony books offer to normative ideals of girlhood. In this, pony books did far more than teach children to behave well and care for their horses. Haymonds writes about pony book heroes like Jean, "The female hero, who is resolutely uninterested in traditionally feminine tasks such as housework, fashion, and make-up, derives deep satisfaction from rising early to muck out and groom her pony, plan its diet and clean its tack."[46]

Though unusual in its ominous sexual undertones, pony book author Dorian Williams goes so far as to depict what life was like for girl grooms in a world dominated by men. Williams's character, Wendy, in his 1962 book, *Wendy Wins Her Spurs*, has a male employer named Mr. Whittle who keeps "trying to get her alone" and "is obviously resentful when her friend visits and shares her room, and at one point comes into her room after she has gone to bed."[47]

Some pony books also taught children about the realities of life with animals. Like humans, nonhuman animals get sick, get hurt, suffer, and die. Horses' life spans tend to be around twenty-five years, while most humans of course live much longer. So a human lifetime filled with horses is also a lifetime filled with many horse deaths. Like Marguerite Henry in her book about mustangs (discussed in chapter 2), Diana Pullein-Thompson was another author who worked to make her books realistic in this way. In an interview, she said, "Death is something you meet all too often when you are living and working with animals and, above all, I tried to be a realist."[48] In one of her books, for example, Pullein-Thompson describes a pony named Seaspray who caught tetanus. "Seaspray was there standing in the far corner, but she was scarcely recognizable; her dear grey face was pinched and drawn; her eyes were sunken, her nostrils dilated and her mouth closed; her soft grey nose was poked out; her back was hollowed and her tail raised. She stood with heaving flanks, outstretched limbs and with such an expression of terror, as I had never seen on any animal's face before."[49]

Not all authors were like Diana Pullein-Thompson. Some pony books "skim the surface of life and provide comforting puddings of reads."[50] Either way, realistic or comfort reading, one thing most pony books offered was the fantasy of an ideal, perfect friendship, that between the girl and her horse. Horses offered horse-crazy girls alternative fantasies to those of being boy crazy, being princesses waiting for princes, or being brides on wedding days.

Agency and Dreaming of Horses: Girls Writing for Girls

One of the most interesting things about the early British pony books is that horse-crazy girls themselves wrote many of the books while still girls. The Pullein-Thompson sisters—Josephine, born in 1923, and the twins, Christine and Diana, born in 1925—all three "badly bitten by the horse bug," grew up to be prolific and well-known pony book writers.[51] And they started writing as children, as girls. In 1941, at the ages of eighteen and sixteen, they published a jointly authored article, their first, in *Riding* magazine.[52] Together they wrote a second story, published in *Riding* in 1942. After that they coauthored a novel called *It Began with Picotee*. It took four years to be published, but they completed the book in 1942. Diana started her first solo pony book at the age of sixteen, *I Wanted a Pony*. It came out several years later in 1946.

Surprisingly, there exist many such child authors in the genre. At the age of fifteen, pony book writer Shirley Faulkner-Horne published her first book, which was nonfiction. Two years later in 1938, at seventeen, she published her first work of fiction, *Bred in the Bone*.[53] Strikingly, Sheila Chapman wrote all four of her pony books between the ages of twelve and fifteen. Gillian Baxter wrote her first pony book at the age of fifteen. Starting very young, Moyra Charlton wrote her first book, *Tally Ho* (1930), when she was only eleven. And Badger explains that at the age of fifteen, Charlton "wrote what is probably the earliest adventure involving children and ponies, *The Midnight Steeplechase* (1932)" (15). Badger writes, "*The Midnight Steeplechase* was really pioneering stuff, more remarkable perhaps because of the youth of its author; the book is a surprisingly mature piece of work." Her work was so sophisticated that when her books were published "there was speculation in the press that she had been helped by her parents, but she stoutly maintained that she had not; her first book was presented to them as a fait accompli" (16–17). These "pony mad" British girl authors stand as a challenge to ways in which mid-twentieth-century girls faced gendered restrictions on their lives, capacities, and choices. Badger muses, "Perhaps Charlton wrote what she herself wanted to read. . . . There is a certain neatness in a child producing one of the earliest examples of a genre intended for children." These girl authors had the power to speak, indeed to speak in part about the very restrictions they faced as girls, via published stories for other children like them.

While some of the pony book genre came from the United States, most of it came from the United Kingdom. And it is striking that the girl author phenomenon seemed to happen only there and not in the United States. Aside from their gender and age, these British pony-book-author girls did carry privileges in terms of their race and social class. All were white and predominantly Anglo-Saxon. Whereas they often wrote about middle- and working-class children, all the girl authors came from the middle to upper class. Indeed, most of the authors, adult and child alike, were elite, middle to upper class, and white. And while some readers might have been girls of color, only white girls saw themselves, their whiteness, reflected in the books until the end of the twentieth century.

Erotic Horses and Horse Love

British writer Enid Bagnold offered an early and forceful challenge to normative gender and "made the first step into portraying the visceral longings girls have for ponies," in what became a famous novel (1935) and film (1944), *National Velvet*.[54] Bagnold's horse-crazy girl character, Velvet, wants horses, wants to ride not as a side activity but as a way of life. In a distinct challenge to heteronormativity, Velvet does not dream of marriage or desire children. Indeed, she says, "I don't ever want children. Only horses."[55]

In the *National Velvet* story, Bagnold tells what became a standard theme in pony books. Badger writes, "Velvet loves horses but does not have one; acquires one (actually several); overcomes adversity and wins a race; then settles into a calm procession of gymhana [*sic*] summers." Velvet spends all her available time thinking of, dreaming of, playing at horses. In the novel, this horse-crazy girl describes her deep yearning:

> "I tell myself stories about horses," she went on, desperately fishing at her shy desires. "Then I can dream about them. Now I dream about them every night. I want to be a famous rider, I should like to carry dispatches, I should like to get a first at Olympia, I should like to ride in a great race, I should like to have so many horses that I could walk down between the two rows of loose boxes and ride what I chose. I would have them all under fifteen hands, I like chestnuts best, but bays are lovely too."[56]

Instead of being boy crazy, horsey girl characters like Velvet direct their passion to horses. As discussed briefly in chapter 2, some of the pony book relationships between girls and horses even have, as Tucker writes, "unmistakable sexual overtones." These are, Tucker claims, "well suited to the emotional needs of female readers not yet at full sexual maturity themselves, but still curious to experiment, in the safety and privacy of the imagination, with related feelings in this area."[57] Tucker describes a pony book by Monica Dickens: "In *The Horses of Follyfoot*, for example, during one particularly 'creamy' canter on her horse Robin, the young heroine Dora felt 'glued to the saddle, her torso moving rhythmically as he moved.' After such an intimate experience, she finds 'she is in love' with her horse." Tucker concludes, "[T]here are many readers of the same sex fully able to sympathise with these strong feelings" (163).

Interestingly, Walter Farley's boy characters *also* seem to have (homo) erotic connections with their stallions (the horses are nearly all intact—not gelded; stallions and Farley's human characters are nearly all male). For example, Alec in the Black Stallion series regularly becomes one being with his horse, and feels "nothing but the surge of great muscles between his legs."[58] Farley's character Steve also "felt a part of his horse," Flame. Farley writes, "Steve moved with his horse, glorying in the surge of powerful muscles beneath his legs. No longer did he feel that the stallion was separate from him, that he was riding Flame.... It was as though he and the horse were one. He was Flame!" Farley continues, "He let the stallion run, his tight fingers about the mane long since relaxed, as was his body. He continued clucking softly, his head close to the sleek neck. And beneath his knees he felt the restrained power within Flame."[59]

Farley's character Alec even shares a special language with the Black Stallion, made up of murmurs and soft sounds. When Cornwell, a journalist interviewing Alec, listened to Alec speak with his horse, Cornwell "wrote nothing. It was a language neither he nor his readers would understand." Cornwell realizes that the language belongs to Alec and the stallion alone. Almost as if describing an intimate exchange between human lovers, Farley describes this special language: "Most of it had been murmurings and touches, soft and gentle, and quick movements of the eye." While Cornwell did not understand, "the Black had understood everything. Cornwell was certain of that."[60]

Despite these parallel descriptions of boys and girls having something approaching erotic intimacy with their horses in these books, the old mainstream idea—that horse-crazy girls play out their desire for a penis through their love of and desire for horses—does not have its counterpart in commentary about books that feature horse-crazy boys: nothing that I have seen mentions the horse-crazy boy's erotic desire for a horse (or for a penis).

Finding Her Wild Horse in the United States: Christine Pullein-Thompson and the Phantom Stallion Series

About the Pullein-Thompson sisters, Badger argues:

> To any reader of pony books in the 1960s and 1970s, the Pullein-Thompsons were a key part of their reading experience. This was not only due to the sheer number of books but also to their accessibility, and to the sisters' knack of producing books that stood re-reading. The pony-mad reader knew that with them she was getting good, solid instruction. If you wanted to understand why the backward seat was bad, they would tell you. If you wanted to understand how to ride sympathetically and well, they would tell you that too. If what you wanted was straightforward adventure, Christine provided plenty of that.[61]

Of the three sisters, Christine Pullein-Thompson wrote the most books. Indeed, I briefly address her work here, in part, because she wrote the most pony books of any British author to date, and in fact, "worldwide she has no equal." Yet her writing also offers a quintessential example of stories, written by a horse-crazy girl who started writing as a girl, that challenge gender norms and give girls worlds where they are strong and brave and free.

Christine Pullein-Thompson died in 2005, and over the course of her writing career, "she produced pony stories covering pretty well every aspect of the genre, from tales of a wild horse to holiday adventure, rescue stories and hunting."[62] Christine Pullein-Thompson is particularly interesting for the purposes of this study not only because she was so prolific but also because she lived and wrote for a period of time in the United States, and some of her stories are set there.

Her Phantom Horse series included six novels about Jean and her horse, Phantom. Jean is horse crazy and devoted to her best friend, her horse Phantom, with whom she has many exciting adventures. In the stories, Jean saves her older brother, Angus, more than once, outwits adult male criminals, and rescues her horse and her brother's too when they are stolen. She is a brave, smart, strong, and passionate girl.

While Christine Pullein-Thompson wrote pony books from the 1940s until 1999, the first of the Phantom Horse series, aptly named *Phantom Horse*, came out in 1955, when there was a flood of books in the genre.[63] The last of the six, *Wait for Me Phantom Horse*, came out in 1985, so the series spanned some of the most important decades of the pony book genre.

In the first book of the series, Jean catches and tames the horse, Phantom, that carries her through the rest of the series. The book begins with Jean and her mother, father, and Angus moving to the United States from England for her father's work. Before the move, Jean is very upset at the thought of leaving her home and ponies. "I felt a lump rising in my throat. I didn't want to live in America. What would happen to Moonlight and Mermaid. . . . We discussed America for ages and all the time I had an empty feeling in the pit of my stomach."[64] Yet when Jean's mother tells her that she will be "lent ponies and there's a paddock and what Americans call a barn," Jean explains that she "suddenly felt much happier" (7).

The night of her arrival at her new home, in a fictional rural area about two hours' drive west of Washington, D.C., Jean learns about the wild palomino living nearby in the mountains that locals want to capture and kill. She is told by the daughter of a family friend, Wendy, "He's a thoroughbred with a touch of Arab in him, and he's a palomino because of his colour. He's the most beautiful horse you've ever seen, and whoever catches him can have him: that's the deal." Exhausted from the flight from England, Jean quickly wakes up. "Suddenly I didn't feel sleepy any more. If only Angus and I could catch him, I thought. If only . . ." (10–11).

Before the first book ends, after several exciting adventures on horseback, Jean does finally find, catch, and tame the wild palomino that she names Phantom. Fulfilling the horse-crazy girl dream, Jean and Phantom have an extraordinarily special connection. Jean is the only human that Phantom will allow to handle, much less ride, him.

Jean and Phantom do not stay in the United States for long. Yet the wild horse Jean found there makes "everything seem possible" for her back home in England. In the second novel, Jean brings Phantom home to England and jumps with him in a show near her village. Jean and Phantom win the competition; with her beloved horse, Jean feels that she can do anything. Jean reminisces about riding Phantom in the ring and winning: "[N]othing mattered but the feel of the turf beneath us and Phantom's effortless canter which felt as though it could last forever, through countless rings, round Badminton, through days and days of hunting, for half my life at least." She thought, "Everything seemed possible now."[65]

Wild Horses, Boy Heroes, and Children's Horse Literature in the United States

In British pony books, girls were left with the hope that "everything seemed possible." Girls transform "neglected, wild or unmanageable ponies" into "sleek, shining horses leaping to success in the top jumping class, fitting mounts for heroes."[66] Also wild, in popular children's horse stories in the United States, capturing and taming an actually feral horse—and not a pony that behaves wildly—has been a central theme since the early days of the U.S. genre. Yet in contrast to the British girl hero, in the United States, the stories' heroes are not girls but boys. In their effort to tame the wild animal, boys become men. In our binary culture with its basic mind-body dualism, nature, colonized people, and women are associated with the body, white men with the mind. In the binary frame of the stories, rational white boys capture and tame the wild (animal) horse.

Haymonds clarifies the difference between U.S. and British children's literature about horses: "It is significant that American horse stories that were popular during much the same period as the British pony books have tended to be 'rites of passage' books for boys rather than girls." She continues, "While the American genre is inextricably bound up with the story of the Wild West, where the horse is part of a wider and wilder landscape, and often the means of livelihood, the British pony story is placed firmly in a rural, domestic setting and enclosed stableyard, with riding perceived as a leisure or sporting pursuit."[67]

The idea of encountering the wild outside of oneself—the wild horse— and civilizing it as the way to become one's own developed, mature person resonates with the quintessentially American frontier thesis of historian Frederick Jackson Turner. Turner believed what made (white male) Americans "American" is the history of encountering and conquering the wild (Native American) frontier. In his famous and racist talk at the 1893 World's Fair, the Columbian Exposition in Chicago, "The Significance of the Frontier in American History," Turner argued that as colonizers moved westward, and thus pushed westward the frontier that divided them from land as yet unconquered—that is, through the violence of conquest—the colonizers became American. Turner said,

> Thus American development has exhibited not merely advance along a single line, but a return to primitive conditions on a continually advancing frontier line, and a new development for that area. American social development has been continually beginning over again on the frontier. This perennial rebirth, this fluidity of American life, this expansion westward with its new opportunities, its continuous touch with the simplicity of primitive society, furnish the forces dominating American character.[68]

The frontier represented the line between who "we" once were "and what we have and will become."[69] According to Turner, this frontier existed at the "outer edge of the wave—the meeting point between savagery and civilization."[70]

As I wrote in *The Parallel Lives of Women and Cows*, "For Turner, being from the United States, being (white) 'American' was a becoming that happened through this encounter of civilized man—of course—with the wild and uncivilized edge that exists on the other side of 'us.' Perhaps more than anything else, mainstream Americans become through this myth making, imagining ourselves into being through stories, fantasies about what others are and we are not" (27).

Cowboys and Native Americans, with their accompanying horses and cows, played central roles in many twentieth-century stories of Americanness. Cowboys were white and male, brave and stoic. They were the good guys. Indians in the stories ranged from being savage and bad (the "bad guys"), at worst, to being elements of the natural, animal world at best. About this I wrote, "Mainstream ideas about masculinity were at the core of this fantasy. Indeed, in this framework, civilization's ever-changing 'outer edge' birthed masculinity through its violent movement of so-called progress." Quintessentially masculine, the fantasy cowboys on their horses, with their cows, pushed the edge of the frontier west and further west. "In this thinking, masculinity came from, was born out of conquest, the masculine became masculine through conquering, subduing, controlling, entering Others."[71] Underlying the stories was the belief that the human "others," the Indians, and the animal others, the mustangs and wolves and other wild creatures, like the wild frontier itself, had to be civilized or wiped out. As children in the rural western United States, we played at this story, we played "cowboys and Indians."

Yet as *girls* in the play, the options were limited. We could pretend to keep house and wait for the cowboys to come home. Or we could watch the battles and wait for them to end. The active alternative that I remember was to give up on human characters and be horses. As horses *we* ran wild, we acted, we took part in drama, and we were free.

My Friend Flicka (1940) by Mary O'Hara

My Friend Flicka is set on a ranch outside of my childhood town, Laramie, Wyoming. It was the basis for a film that came out in 1943 in which the central boy character, Ken, was played by the well-known actor Roddy McDowall. As in both *The Black Stallion* and *Misty of Chincoteague*, a heroic boy captures and tames a wild horse. All three stories tell of a (white) boy transformed, a boy becoming a man through his encounter with and catching, befriending, and training of a wild horse. Unlike the fairy-tale quality of the Black Stallion series and of *Misty of Chincoteague* and other books by Marguerite Henry, O'Hara's novel *My Friend Flicka* is imbued with a gentle sense of sadness. Ken's father, Captain Rob McLaughlin, finds Ken frustrating and even a disappointment. At one point early in the story, Rob says to Ken's mother, Nell, "I'm beginning to think he's just dumb." Ken is aware of Rob's feelings about him; O'Hara describes one encounter between them in the following excerpt: "Ken was afraid to look at his father. His blazing blue eyes were hard to meet. They glared at you out of the long dark face with its jutting chin. Often Ken felt his own eyes reeling back from an encounter, and he would turn away or look down."[72] Nell is regularly anxious and "troubled," in part because the family is struggling financially with their ranch, and in part because of Rob's relationship with Ken.

Ten-year-old Ken is dreamy and forgetful and does very badly in school. When the story opens, he has just returned home to the ranch for summer vacation after his fifth-grade year at school, perhaps at the elementary school I attended, Beitel in Laramie. Ken has failed fifth grade and his father is furious. "Just as a matter of curiosity," Captain McLaughlin sarcastically asks his son, "how do you go about it to get a *zero* in an examination? Forty in history? Seventeen in arithmetic! But a *zero!*" (13).

The captain is an authoritarian who reminds me of male parenting in my own childhood. His family and workers defer to him in nearly all matters. His two sons, Howard and Ken, hang on his words, wait for his dictates, and obey his commands. On the other end of the gender binary, Nell, the gentle mother, is the only one who dares stand up to Rob. When she does, the boys "[look] at her in astonishment." O'Hara writes, "There was a soft look about her fawn-colored hair and smooth, unlined face, but nothing soft about the determined look with which she faced her husband. How could she be so fearless in the face of their father's anger and shouting!" (17).

Ken's dream in life is to have and train a colt of his own. At first his father says Ken "doesn't deserve it" because of his failing grades and many foibles. Yet Nell, fulfilling the "a mother knows" stereotype, convinces Rob that they cannot wait to give Ken a horse of his own. Ken, Nell argues, needs the horse *now*. To Rob's position that they wait until Ken deserves a horse, Nell says, "But Rob, he never will." Rob responds, "Why won't he? Howard did." And Nell explains, "Ken's different. He's so far behind now, it's hopeless. If you wait until he catches up, and really has it coming to him, he just won't get one at all" (59).

Nell argues that being responsible for his own colt will help Ken grow up and "be more of a man" (61). Nell convinces Rob that taming something wild will make a man out of Ken. Eventually, Rob consents. Nell and Rob's thinking is reminiscent of Turner's, whose man (always a man, always white) on the edge of the frontier becomes American through his encounter with "the wild."

Ken is allowed to pick out a colt of his own to care for, raise, and train. When Rob tells him at breakfast, Ken has only just involved himself in another mishap; the day before he had "stampeded the mares." He hesitated to join his family for the morning meal, "he felt so out of things." Yet in contrast to Ken's expectations, Rob tells him that he is going to give Ken the colt he so desperately wanted. Very excited, Ken jumps out of his chair when his father tells him:

> "I'll give it to you a week from today.... Between now and then you can look them over and make your choice."
>
> "I can have any yearling colt on the ranch that I want?" asked Ken.
>
> His father nodded calmly, pushed his chair back and took out his pipe. (74–75)

At first Ken is clear that the horse he picks must be male. Rob asks him, "Horse or filly?" (Here, as the word "man" sweepingly represents both human males and all of humanity, the word "horse" represents both male horses and all horses.) At his father's question, Ken paused. "This stopped him. His eyes lost focus as mental images crowded. Rocket was a mare. But there was Banner. And the Albino, mustang hero. There emerged from the confusion a definite sense of the superiority of the male." When Ken responds, he is clear: the horse will be young and the horse will be male. "I'll take a horse colt." In this clarity, Ken's new horse is making him a man already: "His voice was final and authoritative. An imperceptible glance passed between Nell and her husband" (75).

Ken's father explains to him that for failing all his examinations and having to retake his grade in school, what Ken deserves "is a good hiding." Rob tells Ken, "I don't want you to think I'm letting you off. I'm not. I haven't gone soft." Instead, Rob clarifies that he believes while Ken trains the yearling, the yearling will also train Ken. Rob wants the horse, he explains, to "make a man out of you."

Ultimately Ken realizes that if he picks a male horse, a colt, the horse will have to be gelded and Ken cannot bear that thought. "He was thinking of his own colt—a year from now—when they would be gelding it—he saw it suddenly as clearly as if it was there before him, a bright golden sorrel, like Banner—he saw the blood running down its legs. Sharp pains ran through him and sobs strangled him" (75). Unlike the Spanish conquistadors, most humans, in the 1940s in Wyoming, and in most places today too, geld all their male horses. It is, however, a bit less brutal today than it was in the 1940s. Due to this brutality, gentle Ken ends up picking a filly, Flicka. Perhaps, in the terms of the story, Ken is not man enough to face gelding his colt.

The Black Stallion Series (1941) by Walter Farley

In sharp contrast to the British pony books of the same time period, many of the early pony books from the United States, albeit read by girls, often featured a world that was all male, or nearly so, and all white. For example, in Walter Farley's twenty-one *Black Stallion* books, written from 1941 to 1989, nearly everyone, from horse to human, was male. Only one of the books starred a filly, *The Black Stallion's Filly* (1952), and she is tellingly named Black Minx. She is ridden and trained by boys and men in the novel's usual all-male world. Only one of the books has a primary human female character, *The Black Stallion and the Girl* (1971). This girl visits Alec Ramsey, the central human character in the series, at his horse farm, and she is the only female—human, horse, or otherwise—in the whole story. Outside of these two, mares, fillies, women, and girls rarely appeared in the stories. Where a female human appeared, she was relegated to a minor and traditionally female role, in the shadows of the story. In contrast to his father, Alec Ramsey's mother, for example, was rarely discussed. When she did appear, she either cooked, cried, or worried. She seemed to have no wishes, no dreams, no plans, no skills outside of caring for her son and his father, and the worrying and planning that care entailed.[73]

A white middle-class boy from Queens, New York, Alec plays the heroic role in the Black Stallion series. In the first book of the series—the basis for a film produced by Francis Ford Coppola that came out in 1979—Alec travels by ship to visit a missionary uncle in India, where he learns to ride horseback. During the return, the ship, called the *Drake*, meets a storm and crashes. Alec is saved from drowning by a wild horse being transported on the ship, the Black Stallion, who swims to an island with the boy clinging to him. Using the word "wild" three times in the sentence to make sure we get the picture, Farley describes the Black Stallion as "the wildest of all wild creatures, a stallion born wild."[74]

Wild, the Black Stallion is beyond human control, and so is the one person of color we meet in the novel (aside from a brief encounter with a "crowd of Arabs"). Farley repeatedly refers to this person, the stallion's handler on the *Drake*, as "the dark-skinned man." When the ship hits a storm, is struck by lightning, and "almost cut in half," the dark-skinned man cannot find his life jacket, and he frantically rushes up to the captain, "waving his arms and babbling hysterically." It is clear that the ship is sinking. When Farley's character of color sees that Alec has a life jacket, the man tries to "tear the life jacket from" Alec's back. "Alec struggled, but he was no match for the half-crazed man." (Here we read Farley's other epithet for his character of color.) The ship's captain protects Alec from the "half-crazed" and "dark-skinned man." Foiled in his attempt to steal a life jacket, he opts for another wild action, to jump off the *Drake* into an already full lifeboat. Missing the lifeboat, he falls into the water "screaming," and we learn that he "never rose to the surface" (182–189).

Alec eventually falls into the water himself. The Black Stallion then saves Alec from drowning by pulling him to an island. The two find a way to survive together, and Alec slowly tames (civilizes) the wild horse. In his taming of the Black, Alec exhibits qualities traditionally associated with girls, not boys, and in this challenges gender norms. Alec is gentle and moves slowly with the Black, as Farley often refers to the horse. When the book came out, the white male horse whisperers (discussed briefly in chapter 2) were yet to arrive on the popular U.S. horse scene. Nonetheless, Alec speaks softly with, literally whispers to, the Black. Perhaps his gentleness and his commitment to the relationship helped make Alec a character with whom girls could identify. The Black develops a profound connection to Alec and, over the course of the many novels, we learn, only to Alec. For other humans, the Black remains wild, although in this racist frame, not as wild or as stupid as the "dark-skinned man." The Black Stallion keeps his wits about him and survives. And, unlike the one character of color, the (brave and noble) Black saves someone else, Alec. In contrast, the (savage) person of color tries to save himself by putting another person at risk when he attempts to steal Alec's life jacket.

In reading *The Black Stallion*, some horse-crazy girls identified with Alec in their horse fantasies. If they wanted to be with horses, the U.S. novels offered them no active horsey girl characters. So when reading this country's horse literature, girls growing up anytime during the 1970s had only boy characters to identify with as they tamed the wild stallions. Jenny told me, "With *The Black Stallion* I didn't even miss a beat identifying with Alec." When I asked, "You identified with him, you didn't fall in love with him?" Jenny repeated, "I identified with him." She said, "The biggest suspense for me was breaking the stallion. Getting past the wildness in the Black or in one of the other horses later down the line. You know there had to be victory, whether it's winning a race or something else. So I totally identified with Alec in that."[75]

Misty of Chincoteague (1947) by Marguerite Henry

As Badger explains, the work of Marguerite Henry does not fall within the "strict definition of a pony book."[76] In contrast to British authors, and like the other two important U.S. authors of children's horse books above, O'Hara and Farley, Henry writes about wild horses. Her work was, as was O'Hara's, very popular in the United Kingdom. A former horse-crazy girl, now horse-crazy woman, that I interviewed, Helen, expressed passion about Henry's work and explained that she had read all of Henry's books. Even today as an adult, Helen said, "Marguerite Henry is my favorite author."[77] Henry's highly successful *Misty of Chincoteague* came out in 1947 and told the story of a wild mare, the Phantom, and her foal Misty. It was the first novel in a popular horse book series by Henry, a runner-up for the annual Newbery Medal from the American Library Association in 1949, and the basis for a movie that came out in 1961. After completing an earlier book, *Justin Morgan Had a Horse* (1945), Henry had hoped to get either Wesley Dennis or Will James (discussed in chapter 2) as her illustrator. When she discovered that James was dead, she sent her work and request for illustration to Dennis, and he agreed. Over more than twenty years, Dennis illustrated nearly twenty of Henry's books, including *Misty*. He became the creator of visual fodder for the dreams and imaginings of horse-crazy girls for decades.

Misty tells the story of an actual event, the yearly "Pony Penning" in Chincoteague, Virginia, in late July. Chincoteague has been holding the event annually since the 1700s, with the first published description of it dated 1835. The city rounds up wild ponies living on a nearby island, Assateague, and drives them across the water, the Assateague Channel, to Chincoteague, which is also an island. The foals are sold at an auction and the adult ponies are sent swimming back to Assateague for another year. The auction benefits the volunteer fire department of Chincoteague. The trimming of the foals from the pony herd keeps the herd within the 150-pony limit allowed to live on the Chincoteague National Wildlife Refuge on Assateague Island.[78]

As discussed above, in sharp contrast to twentieth-century British pony books, those from the United States, until late in the century, tend to restrict their girl characters, both in the sense of having few in number and making the girl characters relatively inactive, if there are any girls in the stories at all. In *Misty*, two children, Maureen and her brother Paul, who live with their grandparents in Chincoteague, dream of catching and owning a wild mare called the Phantom. The Phantom lives with the herd on Assateague Island. Paul is now just old enough to take part in the pony penning event. His sister Maureen, as a girl, is not allowed to participate, and says to her brother, "Wish girls could go along on the roundup; maybe she wouldn't bolt away from another girl." Paul responds with a dismissive snort.[79]

This year he believes they have a chance at owning the Phantom because he is going to join the roundup and is determined to catch the Phantom himself. Like the boys in other mid-twentieth-century U.S. horse stories, Paul has agency in the world and knows he has it. He understands himself to be capable and behaves accordingly. Maureen matters in the story too, but usually from the position of watching and supporting the actions of her brother.

The children spend the ensuing months planning and preparing for their imagined future owning of the Phantom. When the penning day arrives, Paul is ready, catches the Phantom as planned, and becomes a man, all in one fell swoop. Paul finds the Phantom with her newborn foal, a filly that Paul immediately names Misty. Paul drives the pair to where the other roundup men are waiting, to the men's great surprise. "Mouths gaped in disbelief. Eyes rounded. For a few seconds no one spoke at all. Then a shout that was half wonder and half admiration went up from the men. Paul Beebe was bringing in *the Phantom and a colt!* . . . 'Beats all!' [Paul] heard someone say. 'For two years we been trying to round up the Phantom and along comes a spindling youngster to show us up.'" Henry continues, "The men accepted Paul as one of them now—a real roundup man."[80]

While British pony book girl characters like Jean (discussed above) are active and at the center of their stories, in Jean's case catching her own wild horse and even rescuing her brother, Maureen, like other girl characters in U.S. horse stories until the 1980s, watches from a distance. For the pony penning, through all the excitement, Maureen's girlness limits her to the role of observer, and she is left behind in Chincoteague. Henry describes Maureen's helpless anxiety: "She felt gaspy, like a fish flapping about on dry land." In contrast, Paul has another exciting opportunity to prove himself, to be a man. When the roundup men drive the ponies into the water to cross back to Chincoteague, the Phantom tries to turn back because, as Henry tells us, the Phantom thinks her new foal will not be able to make the swim. They force the mare and foal into the water, but the baby begins to be "sucked down in a whirlpool." Paul jumps into the water and swims out to rescue the foal. Paul finishes the swim with the ponies, holding the baby's "head above the swirling water." As people on the shore try to figure out what is going on in the water, Maureen, accepting her passive position and celebrating her brother's heroism, "gulped great lungfuls of air" and screamed, "It's Paul!" Henry writes, "On all sides the shouts went up. 'Why, it's Paul! Paul Beebe.'"

Again (and again) Paul is heroic and Maureen is an observer. The chapter ends with Paul receiving great praise from their caregiver, their grandfather Beebe. He is understandably proud of Paul. Yet the grandfather's words leave me wondering about all the little girls who watch the story unfold, Maureen and the many girl readers as they witness his praise: "'Paul, boy,' he said, his voice unsteady, 'I swimmed the hull way with you. Yer the most wonderful and the craziest young'un in the world.'"

Running Away with Horses

Many girls like me would get lost in horse stories, reading them over and over again. For some horse-crazy girls, their whole relationship with horses was grounded in reading and imagining, rarely having contact with actual horses. For many of these horse-crazy girls, pony books and other horse stories offered a place for becoming.

Horse and girl and boy characters in horse books played the role of symbolic capital, normalizing race, class, and—particularly in the U.S. stories—gender, inside the horsey stories where they lived. And horse-crazy girls—girl characters in books and actual girl readers—accepted some of the constraints. Yet in reading and imagining and reading again, in making their own stories and as characters in stories (sometimes written by horse-crazy girls), the girls were to some extent unruly. They ran away with their fantasy horses. With their horse friends, they imagined a world where they were active and heroic girls.

Through the relationships they had with imaginary horses, girls gained strength. Jenny described how she played horses with friends:

[M]y friends and I would get together and play. Horses were often involved, and sometimes there were princess themes and there would be a prince. And we would be riding horses and the prince would just be off somewhere. We would be inventing kind of a western play game, you know, like riding horses across the plains kind of thing. . . . So it was about stories, you know, and storytelling.

Describing her fantasy horses, Jenny said, "I remember dreaming of riding a very strong horse and kind of borrowing that strength. . . . That dream, that was very vivid." Jenny clarified, "I wasn't very princessy. Like I wasn't very [into] dress up."[81] In contrast to the heteronormative demands of the world around them, girls with fantasy horses told their own stories and placed themselves in the middle of the action.

The author's horse-crazy great-great-aunt Ruth O'Malley
with her beloved horse, in Missouri, around 1920

The author and
a friend with
the author's
Shetland pony,
Dolly, in Laramie,
Wyoming, 1977

The author at eleven years old with a pony named Dinky that a farmer
down the road loaned to her for some months in 1978

Dinky in the old barn where
the author kept him, 1978

The author's horse-crazy friend Annette with her horse and the
author's horse, Snipaway, standing nearby, in the mountains near Laramie,
Wyoming, where they often rode, 1983

Annette on her horse with Snipaway standing nearby on the author's driveway, 1983

Cattle being moved in Wyoming, 1984

The author's horse Snipaway at the place she boarded him with Mike and Diane near Bozeman, Montana, 1986 (Mike and Diane's buckskin gelding, Buck, stands nearby on the edge of the photograph)

Snipaway, where he was boarded near Bozeman, Montana, 1995.

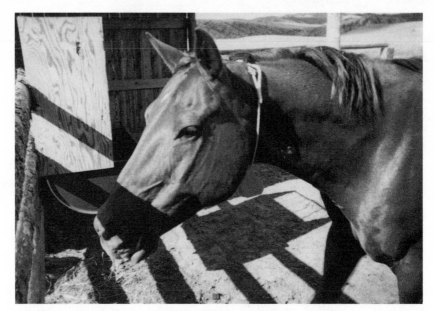

Snipaway at Margie and Hank's home, 1995

A drawing of a horse by horse-crazy Lena Halley-Segal, at age eleven, 2017

The Past That Is Still Present

Stories from My Riding Life in the Western
United States, 1970s to 1990s

In the current chapter, I move my focus from the broad to the narrow, from many girls and many horses to one girl and one horse—and to one (somewhat more) specific place, in the northern Rocky Mountains of Wyoming and Montana during the 1970s, 1980s, and early 1990s. Here, I tell a bit about the changes happening in that place, about a particular girl-horse love, and a particular horse that I loved. I argue that my relationship with my horse was noninstrumental and embodied Nikolas Rose's concept of vital politics. For me, being with my horse was life giving. He was my companion, my friend, my love.

As a child, I experienced terrifying violence and deep loneliness. I spent a lot of time lost in books, a lot of time afraid. Sometimes I wonder how I made it through my childhood. I had a courageous and loving mother, but she was on her own with three children, no money, and trying to make it through school, and I had my horse. And therein lies a second story, a story happening simultaneously to the one about a difficult childhood, and that is the story of my relationship to, and with, horses.

In my girlhood, I remember silence and silencing in many spaces where I lived. With my horse I spoke, literally spoke to him at length about myself, about my day-to-day events, about my becoming. Yet I also spoke metaphorically with my horse, I took up space, I became body with my horse, and I mattered. In the rest of my life, I rarely challenged anyone. On my horse, borrowing from him, I gained strength and courage such that I willingly rode past an angry adult who was shooting wildly at me, so that I could go somewhere that I desired. My horse carried me to places I loved, to forests and to freedom.

It might be obvious to state, but horseback riding is dangerous. Horses are big and flighty animals. They are ready to run at a moment's notice, the flap of a shirt on a clothesline, the bang of a car door being shut, the sudden rise of birds into the sky, a gust of wind blowing one's hat off and onto the rump of one's horse. Sometimes my pony, Dolly, would run away, not from fear, but from her desire to relieve herself of the small girl on her back. Between the two, her fear and her desire, she ran away with me regularly. Once or twice she wisely ran me under branches that swept me off her back and sent me flying through the air.

Horseback riding is dangerous, but as was the case with many of the women I spoke with, it rarely occurred to me to feel afraid. I was afraid in school and at home, afraid when we traveled, afraid most of my life, but with my pony and, later, with my horse, I felt safe. This in spite of the real danger to humans who ride. Former horse-crazy girls whom I spoke with described multiple injuries, from broken arms to broken legs to being thrown, hitting one's head on a rock and being knocked out. Of the many women who described their horse-related injuries, only one of the twenty-five women I interviewed, Sonya, in her early sixties, had stopped riding for a period of time due to her experience of fear. And it took being knocked out and hospitalized for several days for a horse-related injury to scare her. I myself endured multiple concussions, bumps, bruises, a broken thumb, sunburns so deep they made blisters the size of quarters up and down my arm, and perfect teeth marks indicating a nice, deep bite across my face. My feet were stepped on regularly, and as I mentioned above, from time to time I was thrown off. During grooming, I was periodically bumped over and sometimes leaned on by an over-eager horse. Yet I did not own and never used a helmet. I had but rarely used a saddle, preferring to jump up on my horse's bare back and ride off from where I caught him in the pasture. The occasional fear I did feel never stopped me from riding. I rode for hours and miles and miles, starting at age eight, by myself with my pony on the Wyoming plains and, later, by myself with my horse in the Rocky

Mountains of Montana. I found my way or, when I was unsure, relied on my small pony or my red horse to help.

And for nearly all the former horse-crazy girls that I interviewed, horseback riding and their lives with horses gave them courage and confidence in other areas of their lives. For me, while perhaps more slowly, this happened too. At any rate, I *always* felt markedly safer when I was with, on, or around my horse. And as I grew up, I found my way out of my childhood world and managed as a young adult to face my history.

In riding I pushed the limits in myself and in my life. My horse-girl relationship could not be fully contained by the strict ideological rules about being a person, being a girl in my social world. Rather than reproducing the life of a "normal" (and normalized) white girl, my riding manifested Rose's politics of vitalism, as quoted in chapter 1, namely, that which is "in favour of life, of the 'obstinate, stubborn and indomitable will to live,' of the conditions that make possible the challenge to existing modes of life and the creation of new modes of existence."[1]

This politics "in favour of life" is a concern that runs through my work. In an earlier book, I write about my interest in "something that is at the edge of my story, and perhaps at the edge of every story, that is, life's potential. Somehow, in the midst of everything, sometimes in the midst of terrible odds, life does, often, go on. In spite of everything, it certainly has for me. . . . It seems that life pushes for itself. We tend to turn toward the sun."[2] Being with horses, for me, and I believe for many girls, is a kind of turning toward the sun.

This chapter is also about that social world, a tiny taste of the gritty here and now where I lived and loved my horse. In this chapter, I consider my horse love and the limits to that love; it is so hard to know another, to know another being, horse or human, outside of oneself. And I consider the setting of my horsey love, a changing rural West, changing with or without me. I stand upon these stories, they are the context from which my now has come, and they represent themes that run throughout my book.

As long as I can remember, I have been passionate about horses. I loved horses when, at three, my grandfather sat me on the back of his old quarter horse, named Red, like so many other chestnut horses in the western United States, at the sale barn that my grandfather owned and operated in

Wyoming. I loved horses through the horseback-riding lessons that my parents finally relented and gave to me at ages six and seven outside of our little town of Laramie. I loved horses when I was eight and my father surprised me with a small dusty brown Shetland pony. And I loved horses when, at thirteen, having seen me outgrow my tiny pony, my father bought a quarter horse yearling for me. This love, my own very personal passion for horses, flows out of a larger history of horses, a history embedded in the West and specifically in Wyoming and Montana where I grew up.

I come from two small, predominantly white towns of about twenty thousand people each—at least they were that size during the 1970s and 1980s when I was a child. The first of these towns was Laramie, Wyoming, where we lived—my mother, brother and sister, and I—with my father until 1973 when I was six years old, and then without him after my mother left him and went back to school until I turned thirteen in 1980. In Laramie, at age six in the first grade, I took my first horseback-riding lessons outside of town with a little boy named Sal. I remember his mother driving us out to the riding school. I sat in the back seat of the car, daydreaming as I looked out the window. She would stop at a gas station and let us each pick out a candy bar. I chose, perhaps each time, a Marathon Bar, a candy bar I can no longer find, a long thin strip of caramel woven into a design that left periodic holes in the caramel. The whole thing was dipped in chocolate and delicious. My mother did not buy us candy bars, so picking one and eating it stays lodged in my mind, along with the horses and the arena where we rode—still today, two of my favorite things, candy and horses. I remember riding around and around the arena with Sal, each of us on our own horse. Suddenly I was large with power and life and beauty between my legs.

The lessons did not last long, not even one year, probably due to the expense. My mother had no money to spend. My father had money but did not want to spend it. He did, however, buy me a pony when I was in third grade. In the 1970s in Laramie, Wyoming, buying and keeping a pony was not very expensive compared with taking horseback-riding lessons, which were costly. Once I had the pony, my mother encouraged my father to give me more riding lessons, but he said that I could learn to ride by riding, just like he and his brothers had done. And so I did. At that time in the West and other rural areas in the United States and the United Kingdom, it was common for little girls to learn to ride simply by riding. Michael Korda writes about his horse-crazy spouse, Margaret, who grew up in the 1940s and 1950s in rural England:

> Like a lot of little girls in those days, Margaret didn't get any formal riding instruction—the pony was her teacher, basically, and she learned to ride by trial and error, which, when combined with instinct, boldness, watching other people ride, a natural sense of balance, and the well-known ability of a child to survive unharmed from falls that would break an adult's bones, was enough to point her in the right direction.[3]

From the cultural context in which I now live, it is hard for me to believe that my parents let me ride for hours alone on open Wyoming prairie with no humans around and no helmet on my head. Often the only creatures I would see were antelope, jackrabbits, and sometimes frogs. The only difficulty I faced was catching my pony.

    In the spring and early summer, one of my favorite riding destinations was a small, murky, temporary pond. It was not really a pond but an indent in the land that caught the spring rain to become, for a while, a pond. Then, after the heat of summer, by fall, it was only an indent again. But in the spring, if I brought a sack lunch, this was a good place to stop and eat. Dolly could drink out of the pond, and I could sit at the edge watching the miniature frogs that lived there. Sometimes I would catch one and hold it in my hand so that we could look at each other. I'm not exaggerating when I tell you that these frogs were miniature. They were no bigger than an adult's thumbnail. And yet they had everything one expected of a frog—little webbed fingers, small eyes on a flat face, speckles on their backs. Holding one in the middle of my palm, I would carefully examine the frog while it stared seriously back at me. You may not have spent much time with frogs, but I can tell you that they are very serious creatures.

All by myself, with Dolly, and periodically some tiny frogs, I was unafraid.

Horse-girl relationships, like any relationships, happen in social, historical, and cultural contexts. These contexts matter in that they make life more or less possible, often more for some and less for others. My two childhood towns, Laramie, Wyoming, and Bozeman, Montana, housed state universities and a mix of working- and middle-class people. Bozeman was almost completely white, while Laramie had a significant Latinx community making up perhaps 10 percent of the town's population, many who identified as Mexican American. The town was small, but there was more than enough racism among the white community to go around. My siblings and I breathed in the racism, and my mother, a deeply good person who had her hands full trying to keep us all above water, worked hard to counter that violent and violating thinking whenever we brought it home. Just existing as a white child in Laramie, I learned that "Mexicans" (most white people I knew refused to use the term "Mexican American," and many used the racist one, "wetback") were dangerous and should not be here, and that English was the original language spoken in the United States and should be the only one. In school, I should have learned the history of the land I called home and of the first people, those whose home it truly was. Instead, racism masqueraded as education and was supported and reinforced. My education taught me that as a white person, I belonged where I didn't, that my language was the original language, that my people were good and right when they clearly were not. At home, my mother faced an uphill battle challenging normalized racist ideology. To the extent I have learned to see how sick and deep and pervasive racism is in the United States, I owe that seeing to my mother. In my experience as a white person, whiteness and the racism inherent in it wraps white people up tightly. Puncturing it is no small feat.

In each town, locals used to note that the population went down to fifteen thousand in the summer when the students went home for vacation. During my childhood, working-class people could afford to, and did, live in both towns. There were few restaurants, and diners played the role of coffee shops, no espresso to be seen, tasted, or smelled anywhere. Coffee had a faint brown color and an even fainter taste of coffee beans. Old ranchers eating breakfast at a local diner at 4:00 a.m. had cup after cup. When the first Chinese restaurant opened, I ate my first semi-Chinese meal at the age of fourteen, sautéed broccoli covered in thick brown gravy.

In the late 1980s I went to college in Colorado, only returning home to where my mother lived in Montana for the summer and winter vacations. Perhaps I saw the changes more clearly having been away. Over the next decade, the 1990s, wealthy urbanites discovered Montana and began buying land for their vacation (second or third) homes. Land and housing prices went up, and the few productive jobs disappeared. Mining and logging slowed. Competition from major agribusinesses and factory farming bankrupted the already dwindling small farms and ranches. Working-class people were left with little to do except serve the affluent and the tourists who visited or lived part-time in town. These service jobs paid too poorly for workers to live in my now-expensive, small-but-growing city. Working-class, and increasingly poor, people moved to the margins of the community or further out of town onto the limited, less desirable land.

As with gentrification in other places, the changing social landscape in Montana brought profound and complicated tensions. The new affluent and largely white "Californians," as the locals called them, brought liberal and environmentally conscious politics sharply at odds with the political sentiments of the "local" white Montanans they encountered. Of course, these "locals" were only a little less recently local than the Californians, their people having arrived only perhaps 100 or 125 years earlier. The only real locals were the Native American communities living completely segregated from both the new and "old" white communities.

There were lots of Native Americans living in Wyoming and Montana throughout my childhood, and there still are. In Wyoming, the Eastern Shoshone, with more than 4,000 members, and the Northern Arapaho Tribe, with more than 9,000 members, share the Wind River Indian Reservation, 2.2 million acres in the central part of the state.[4] The Montana tribes include the Blackfeet, Chippewa Cree, Confederated Salish and Kootenai, Crow, Fort Belknap, Fort Peck, Little Shell Chippewa, and Northern Cheyenne. The Crow reservation was only a couple of hours' drive east from Bozeman. In Montana, a two-hour drive is nothing, and yet I never visited this or any reservation. On the Crow reservation lived 7,900 Crow people. They were about 75 percent of the 10,000 or more enrolled members, of whom 85 percent "speak Crow as their first language."[5] A vital, alive people—very different from me and holding a claim I could not match to the land I loved—lived near me throughout my childhood. Both inside and outside of school, I knew nothing and learned almost nothing about them, as though they did not exist. But of course white oblivion cannot really erase a people.

I do remember hearing of desperation on the reservation, hearing of drinking and car accidents, hearing of death. One woman shot herself in her little home, leaving blood and tissue all over the walls. As I remember the story, someone that my mother knew helped clean the walls so that the child living there could return. Strange to have that be the only news that made it through the wall of whiteness surrounding my town. The segregation was so complete that I can count the times I actually saw—or knew that I saw—a Native person on one hand.

I knew seven-year-old Cody and his mother who lived on the other side of the alley from my home on Rainbow Street in Laramie. His small, quiet house was filled, like mine, with the gentle, inexplicable scent of sadness, making me at six feel comfortable whenever I visited him. There was thirteen-year-old Winnie Old Coyote, who was moved from her reservation home and placed in a foster family in Bozeman for reasons no one bothered to consider. Other kids tormented her, the only known indigenous child in our racist and white junior high. I, an invisible and friendless white girl, also thirteen, should have, and knew I should have, done something but did not do anything to help Winnie. She disappeared as suddenly as she had arrived. I remember that no one seemed to notice.

White locals understood the also-white newcomers' environmentally conscious politics as responsible for the loss of local jobs, jobs that literally mined, in Butte, Montana, the land for resources such as coal and lumber. When they did not call them "Californians," the white working-class couple, Mike and Diane, who boarded my horse for me, called the newcomers "treehuggers" and complained bitterly about their liberal politics. Standing outside their house, on their cement driveway, while I groomed my horse one summer day, they told me that the treehuggers supported welfare and laziness; and the treehuggers believed in saving the environment at the cost of jobs for hardworking decent people who had lived in Montana a long time, that is, people "from Montana," who deserved to work. Diane and Mike did not of course mean the people who really were from Montana. Somehow to many local white Montanans, Native people, like the California treehuggers, had the status of foreigner. In Minnesota in the late 1980s, when indigenous people rallied against infringements on their water rights, the nightly news covered one older white man who suggested that they "go back where they came from, if they don't like America."

The coming together of the out-of-towners' environmentalist politics with the (white) locals' anti-environmentalist politics brought tensions to everyday life. Sometimes as I was bicycling around town, people would yell at me from their cars. Having and riding a bicycle turned me into a treehugger in the eyes of some. At the more violent end of the antagonistic continuum, some practiced "dooring" bicyclists. This entailed opening one's car door fast and hard to hit the bicyclists with it as one drove by them. Although my mother does not remember the details of her accident in 1992, we believe someone "doored" her one day as she finished a bike ride outside of our town. That same person probably made the anonymous telephone call to report her lying unconscious with her smashed helmet and bent bicycle on the side of the road. Luckily she had started to wear a helmet by this time. When the medical professionals came to pick her up, she did not know her name, place of work, or address, and she complained of not being able to hold up her head. The health care providers who picked her up did not make the connection between her obvious head injury, completely destroyed helmet, and inability to hold up her head. They had her stand up and ride, sitting up without support, in their vehicle. It was hours later at the hospital, as they tried to figure out who my mother was, that someone did the math and realized her neck was broken in two places.

Mike and Diane were kind and incredibly generous, charging me next to nothing, fifteen dollars per month, to keep my horse on the rented property where they lived, inviting me to enter and use their house whenever I wished, go to the bathroom, get a drink, wash my hands and whatnot, and allowing me to borrow their horse whenever I liked as well. For the fifteen dollars, they made sure my horse had fresh water, a shed that offered some shelter in a heavy snowstorm, and hay through the winter. They had a grumpy old buckskin gelding named, like so many buckskins, Buck. On the rare occasion that I brought friends or family out to ride, Diane and Mike shared Buck and let my visitor ride him. My best friend from Tanzania rode Buck once and seemed to fly several feet above the horse, who suddenly decided to leap, with a big buck, across the "crick," the western word for the small river or creek we were crossing.[6] The two horses, Snip and Buck, and sometimes one or two more, grazed in the rich green pasture during summer and were fed hay through the long Montana winter when dense, deep snow covered the land.

Their place, on stunningly beautiful land, was up above and looking down on our small town. My horse and I could stand at the edge of their pasture and watch the sun set, each time magnificent, a quiet, stunning performance of light, clouds, and land. Because I loved the place, I buried my beloved childhood cat, Thomasina, there when she died, and in her left some of me forever looking down on sunset.

Mike and Diane's home was also right at the edge of the forest, trees rising up behind their house high into the mountains. Sometimes I rode in the pastures and dirt country roads around and below their house. I watched as the land "developed" and houses filled up more and more of the open space. Other times, I rode up from their home into the mountains and forest. An old cabin stood lost among the trees and winter snow. The doors and windows shielding the one room had long ago given up the ghost, falling into the cluttered rubble that once was someone's life.

Riding past the cabin and its scattered contents tempted me to explore. One day I jumped down from my horse and climbed up to the open doorway. Strangely, in my memory the house is elevated, built up upon a hollow wooden platform, perhaps to keep it from being completely buried in Montana winter snow. Standing in the doorway, I peered in at someone's demise. Something, perhaps the rusty nails stretching out from broken wood like eager worms, perhaps the sadness of life's inevitable coming undone, kept me from entering.

Riding my horse gave me a courage I did not ordinarily have in life and, in so doing, engendered vitalism. Growing up, I remained silent and nearly invisible in most social situations. I remember finding safety by reading in a bathroom stall at school. I remember sitting quietly, unseen, in my desk, in my row, among rows of desks, among rows of children. I remember quiet. With my horse, he and I together, I became someone, someone who spoke, at least to him, someone who took up space, at least a little bit. British pony book author Patricia Leitch describes this becoming, becoming more, becoming horse, in her novel *The Magic Pony* (1982) with her hero, Jinny, and Jinny's horse, Shantih, as they ride. "Over the moors they galloped. Drystone walls rose up before them and fell away behind them as Shantih soared over them and galloped on. There was no tomorrow, only this now of space and light. Joy in Shantih, and in this flying freedom sang through Jinny's whole being. She rode entranced, the Arab mare part of her own being. On and on they went."[7]

Before I moved my horse to stay at Diane and Mike's in the summer of 1986, I kept Snipaway at the place he had been bred and born. It was a small horse-breeding operation belonging to a wealthy alcoholic couple, the Whites, whose already-alcoholic daughter went to my junior high. While boarding my horse at the Whites', I periodically encountered an angry old local, living nearby, who challenged me to make my own demands on life. She was the real thing, a relic from Buffalo Bill's Wild West past. And in stark contrast to my fearful acquiescence in most situations in my life, with my horse, from time to time, I would even defy that angry old woman.

The old woman did what cattle ranchers and sheep herders, like some of the men in my familial past, had done—she contested the fences. In the first decade of the twentieth century, railroads came to Montana and other places in the West. Like most humans in business, the railroad barons were in it to make money. The common good was not their goal. To make money, railroads needed humans with money to pay for their services. To this end, they promoted the western places through which the railroads traveled. They encouraged humans to move west and set up homes on the relatively empty land. Native Americans lived in the West on the open prairies, as did the cattle and sheep with their accompanying ranchers and herders. Those humans were never plentiful enough or enough-in-need of trains to fit the bill (literally); the railroad barons started selling the idea of living in the West to white people (or soon-to-be-white people like the Irish) from the eastern United States and parts of Europe.

The railroad interests worked to get a bill called the Enlarged Homestead Act through Congress. With it, the railroads hoped to entice more people to live out west near the railroads. The Enlarged Homestead Act passed in 1909 and gave homesteaders living on semiarid land a homestead that was double the size of other government homesteads, "from a quarter section to a half section; from a hundred and sixty acres to three hundred and twenty." About this act, journalist Jonathan Raban writes:

> One did not have to be an American citizen to stake a claim—though it was necessary to become one within five years, when the homestead was "proved up." The proving-up was a formality that entailed the payment of a small fee and an inspection of the property to verify that it had been kept under cultivation. That done, the full title to the land was granted to the homesteader.
>
> Three hundred and twenty acres. In such a space one could imagine a dozen big fields, filled with rippling crops of wheat, oats, alfalfa, barley. . . . It wouldn't be a farm, it would be an estate. It was an astounding free offer by any reckoning.[8]

The ranchers and sheep herders, people like my father's father and grand-father, were against the Enlarged Homestead Act. Like the railroads, they too lobbied but lost. Homesteaders came and homesteaders fenced. They fenced and they fenced and they fenced. Raban writes, "The fences are still a wonder. You can sight along a surviving line of posts, and not a single one is out of true, though the ground on which they're set dips, rolls, and breaks.... People were proud of their fences." Raban explains, "The fences were not merely functional. They were a statement of the belief that this unruly land could be subdued and civilized" (69).

The Old Woman with a Mountain and a Gun

‿◦ Growing up in the rural western United States, I was sur-rounded by plains, plains flowing to meet mountains, mountains rising to forests, forests stretching to the sky. Increasingly, I also grew up surrounded by fences, fences that worked to grab up space and, greedily, hold it tight. They put a spiky metal arm around the forests and dictated which trees I could enjoy. The fences and I shared both a hunger for forest and a history of such hunger. Like the fences, my own white-girl presence on that Montana land flowed from our common colonial history.[9] And, unlike a certain old woman, I usually knew my place; it rarely occurred to me to either protest, or celebrate, the fences.

The forest was different. My love for it nudged me into wanting, into pushing limits, so as to be surrounded by shade, surrounded by cool and sweet pine scent, surrounded by silence. I still do love the forest. I especially loved riding my beautiful red horse away, away into forest. My favorite forest rested high above my little mountain town, near where I first kept my horse, the place where he was born and bred. Once the old woman almost killed me there.

That day, as usual, I bicycled the six miles to where my horse grazed in a large gently green pasture snuggled close to Montana mountain. In the 1980s, before my mother's broken neck—when things had started to change and she had a helmet on that saved her life—no one I knew wore helmets, not for bicycling or horseback riding, skating or skateboarding, skiing or ice skating, really not for anything. So helmetless, I bicycled my very familiar route on country roads, six miles to my horse, six miles back to town, every day during the summer, and on weekend days through the fall until snow came. I can still see the road's edge between asphalt and rocky dirt. Out of the corner of my right eye, biking from home, I could see cornfields; from the other eye I could see a row of trees across the road and the little houses hidden behind them. One year when the grasshoppers were especially bad, they made a thin haze over the corn and around me on the road, slamming their little bodies into mine, crunching under my tires, and smacking into my mouth and hair.

As I biked, I tried to stay as close to the dirt as I could without slipping onto it. Cars rushed past; possibly contrary to popular knowledge, cars drive fast in rural areas. People move slowly, but cars move quickly, speeding down small roads that the drivers know too well for caution. Cars and wind and bugs whipped by me on my bike, and the wind pulled at my oddly fine-yet-thick brown hair, tangling it slightly, and once in a while catching a bug in the tangle. I was neither scared of the cars nearly touching me on the narrow, stingy line of asphalt called a highway nor conscious of my hair. Headed to my horse, I ceased to care about the demands of girlness.

Reaching the ranch and swapping my bike for a bucket of oats, I walked quickly out to his pasture and called my horse's name. Seeing me, seeing the bucket, he hurried over and pushed my hands out of the way so as to plunge his large head into the bucket, into oats. Happily munching, he pulled his head out of the bucket and looked at me, giving me a gentle push with his muzzle and dripping a mushy mixture of saliva and oats on my legs, shoes, and the ground. I kissed his soft nose and came away with a few oats on mine.

Usually I brushed my horse after we rode, sometimes before too. That day, I quickly pulled my bridle with its gentle D ring snaffle bit over my horse's head and into his mouth. I snuck the bit in by holding his chin and sticking my fingers in the toothless spot that horses have, near the back of their lips, so that he opened his mouth. Our preparations ended there. Putting both hands on the curve of his back, I jumped up and swung one leg over, settling comfortably in for a ride. I almost never bothered to put a saddle on. We loped to the gate, where

I jumped down and opened it up for him to follow me through, closing it carefully behind me before using the fence to climb back onto my horse's smooth red back. This fence represented the boundary around my horse's pasture. But it was merely the first fence we would meet that day.

The fencing process is not over; new fences still march across both prairie and mountain. Some places are rich with them, other places less so. In the 1970s, when we still lived in eastern Wyoming, I could ride all day on the plains and rarely be deterred by a fence. In the southern Montana Rocky Mountains, in the early 1980s, it was already different. I could not ride very far without running into fences, some with gates I could open, some not.

Having left behind our first fence, we walked, clop ca clop, clop ca clop, clop ca clop, down the dirt road headed toward the mountains. Sometimes before riding I had a farrier come to put shoes on my horse, but often, because we would only be riding on soft dirt roads and trails, he went barefoot. That day he was barefoot, and this meant I needed to ride slowly on the hard-packed and somewhat rocky parts of the road. I decided to ride up the dirt road into the forested mountains above the place where my horse lived. That forest belonged to the forest service, so anyone could use it, at least for benign activities like hiking or horseback riding. In spite of my passion for forests, and although this forest was especially beautiful, nearby, and in the public domain, I rarely chose to ride there.

It is odd that I avoided a place so beautiful and so fitting for my ongoing longing to be surrounded by trees. I still feel this way, still breathe easier when I find myself held tightly by their firm bodies, canopied by green as they reach up and up to the sun. Nonetheless, I rarely rode this way because of the old woman with the gun. Indeed, what is even odder than my avoiding this forest place is that I ever went there at all, given my well-practiced fearfulness in most parts of my life. The periodic courage I credit to my horse.

That old woman lived in her old and rickety little house tucked right next to the forest service land. Like many problems, the problem she and I had lay in a difference of opinions. I believed that particular forest belonged to the forest service. The forest service believed that it belonged to the forest service. But the old woman did not. According to the old woman, this was *her* forest. It always had been. And contrary to all evidence—the truth is that we are here for such a short, such a quick little time—the old woman seemed to believe this forest would *always* be her forest.[10]

But on that day my horse and I approached the turnoff to the smaller dirt road, the forest service road that led up and up into deep, green pine. My heart shifted to high speed and my legs gripped the body of my horse tightly. In response, his ears perked up and forward. *Steady*, I said, ostensibly to my horse, but really to myself. We moved softly, slowly, slowly up the road. Soon I could see her little house enclosed by trees, off a bit from the road on its left side. At any moment she could emerge, and then we would have to run for it, run fast into the forest. It was risky.

Twice I thought I heard her coming, and twice I was wrong. Then, suddenly, there she was running, running fast herself, quicker than one might imagine an old woman being able to run. She was yelling and waving her rifle, held by both hands, in front of her. *Now!* I shouted to my horse, leaning forward and giving him full rein over the bit while nudging him with my heels. He leapt ahead, and we flew past her as she stopped and aimed her rifle. I heard the crack, and another crack of the gun as she fired and my horse ran faster. She did not, she never, hit us. Perhaps her vision had gone the way of her mind. Or perhaps she never intended to hit us, only to scare us from riding on what she knew to be her land. In this she was successful. I almost never rode my horse up to the forest service land beyond the pasture where she lived. And when I did, the price I paid to be in that enchanted place was my anxiety. I knew she would be waiting, ready, when we came riding down the road again.

Pinochuck, My Horse, and the Many Ways We Do Not Know Each Other

Mike and Diane ran a gasoline station at the edge of town, and they attended an evangelical Christian church near the station. Sundays they spent at church, and the rest of the week they worked long hours at the station. So when I went out by bicycle or borrowed my mother's car, the house, the hill, and the pasture were usually empty, except of course for Snipaway, Buck, and me. Like most people in Montana back then, like my mother and everyone I knew, Diane and Mike kept their house unlocked. Usually alone, I rarely borrowed Buck. Not wanting to intrude, I rarely entered their house, except to use the bathroom from time to time. Their house looked like my bedroom, the domain of a highly compulsive person, and given their conservative beliefs, that compulsive-cleaning-up person was probably Diane. Like me, she kept every pencil in its place, the sharp points all going the same direction. The insides of that house felt like a museum of Americana, a place where no one lived or breathed or dared touch anything.

Once, chatting with Mike and Diane as I groomed my horse on their driveway, I told them that my mother was on her way to El Salvador for a year. A psychologist, she planned to work with families who had lost someone to the death squads of the brutal and U.S.-supported government. Excited, Diane told me that someone from their church was just leaving too, to go to Chile and help Pinochet— she called him Pinochuck—fight the communists. Diane wondered if my mother and their friend might meet up.

Although they kept my horse for over a decade and I liked them immensely, somehow we never did manage to know each other, Diane and Mike and me.

Mike and Diane were good people, albeit perhaps too relaxed about the upkeep of their pasture. And I, unfortunately, did not do what I should have done and checked the pasture carefully, that is, checked it before letting my horse roam freely in it. One summer morning, I arrived on my bicycle at Diane and Mike's home to find my horse tied by the house, the veterinarian looking at him, and both Mike and Diane standing nearby, looking worried. Snipaway had caught his leg in some old and hidden barbed wire, part of some past fence, in the far corner of the pasture. Before being found and disengaged from the wire, he'd torn his leg up badly. It will probably never heal, the vet told me. He recommended that I put my horse down.

The leg never did fully heal. My red horse was only ten years old when he encountered that wire. And he limped, on again, off again, through the next fifteen years.

I do not fully understand what it means to know someone, to know a person, to know a horse, to know another. In some way, I did not, could not, really know Snipaway. I only traced the edges of myself in the exchanges I had with him. When I wonder what my horse felt, what he experienced, for example, that day caught in the wire, I feel my stomach clench. I feel my longing for his well-being. I feel myself.

I have always had an odd tendency to want to experience the pain of a beloved, upon learning of it. Because the other is, always, unknown, my knowing the other's experience would become a place of connection. Yet even more than that, it is as if, somehow, if I can feel Snip's experience, experience his pain, perhaps I can soak up that pain, call it from him into me and relieve him of it, even today, years past the pain, years past his life, and death, years and years past. Only a silly wish, a desire to be with, to be of the other, I hope to relieve us both of our suffering, at least insofar as it is born of separation.

My horse must have been scared, and from the look of the wound I do know that he fought hard to free himself of the trap the wire made. The thought of my beloved, gentle horse, so afraid, so hurt, carries itself through me in waves of nausea, and I experience the edge of myself again, the limit of my ability to experience the being of another. I am reminded, again and again, of how little, how very little, I know.

Eventually Diane and Mike had to move, leaving their beautiful view of the valley where our town lay quietly resting against mountains, leaving that view to wealthier people, perhaps tree-hugging Californians. When that happened in the mid-1990s, I had to find a new place to board my horse. Mike and Diane did not know where they would end up. They just knew that they could not afford our little town anymore. So we said goodbye, by telephone, as I lived in New York City while I worked on my doctorate in sociology. And social class working as it does, and I being middle class and complicit, I never saw Diane, I never saw Mike again, they who had been so good to me, so generous, so kind.

On Losing Things: A Contemporary Horse Thief

🪱 When Mike and Diane were forced to move, I had to find another place for my horse by long distance. I could not afford to fly to Montana, so I put an advertisement in the local paper looking for a caretaker and rider for my beautiful chestnut quarter horse–appaloosa mix. (To register as a quarter horse, a horse has to be "pure" quarter horse and able to prove his or her bloodlines. Snipaway could have been registered as an appaloosa if he had "colored" with appaloosa spots across his red rump. But his spots never came. Without them, he remained an unregistered, solid-red-rumped mutt.) I received numerous calls. Most were not interested once they learned that Snip limped after a ride and could not be used for jumping or hard cross-country riding due to his injury. Finally a young white man named Dave, originally from Minnesota, responded to my notice. He was interested in caring for and riding, in a leisurely fashion due to the limp, my sweet red horse. He now lived in Montana near my little town and worked as a ranch hand. He was allowed to keep a horse at the ranch where he worked.

Perhaps it was a different time. Or, more likely, it was simply my ridiculous naïveté. I do not remember getting references, speaking with anyone who might recommend Dave, laying my hands on Dave's résumé or on a letter from someone he knew. Nothing. I just spoke by telephone with this complete stranger, decided I trusted him with my beloved horse, and arranged for him to pick up Snip from Diane and Mike's old home.

A couple of months later when I was able to get to Montana, I visited Snip in his new home. He seemed happy to see me, generally healthy and well, and as beautiful as ever. I guess I have already mentioned that Snip was beautiful, the kind of horse one turns to watch as he moves, truly beautiful. Dave was a chatterbox, and he proceeded to chatter his way through the time I spent with my horse. It turned out spending time with Snip meant spending time with Dave. Yet this arrangement also meant that I did not have to do what seemed unbearable: give up my horse. So I hung out with Snip and hung out with Dave on that trip home.

By my next visit home to Montana, things had changed. In particular, both Dave and Snip had disappeared. They probably disappeared a bit before my visit. In fact, I had not heard from Dave for a month or two. But at the time, that did not seem especially unusual. As long as things were fine, there was no reason for Dave to be in touch with me or me with him. I had assumed things were fine.

When my mother picked me up from the little local airport, we drove directly out to see my horse. When we arrived at the ranch where Dave worked, we could find neither horse nor Dave. I panicked. Dave could disappear, just not with my horse. The people at the ranch said that Dave had left. They were not sure where he went, but, it being winter, work slowed. Dave had taken "his horse," they said, and moved on. So my mother and I started out on a quintessential wild-goose chase from ranch to little tucked-away house to farm to little house to tiny town. The people at Dave's ranch told us that Dave had some friends living in a small house, tucked away, up the road a couple of miles. We headed to that small house, my mother driving, and me crying.

The small-house people were not home. No one answered but a barking dog. We decided to go to another house, a farm, up the road again, to see if they could tell us the whereabouts of the small-house people. They were not home either. We sat in the car trying to decide what to do. We decided to try the small house one more time.

Miraculously on the second try, the friends in the small house were home. Not-so-miraculously, they had no idea where Dave went. Do you know where Dave is? we asked. Nope, the man told us, but if you find him, tell him to be in touch because he owes us money.

The small-house people thought Dave was friends with Margie and Hank who worked in a wood-carving business in a nearby, tiny town. We climbed back in the car, my anxiety swirling around me and through me, making me dizzy and faint. I am a crier, so I started crying again. We drove to the tiny town and asked a man working on his car where the wood-carving business was located. Unsure, he directed us around a series of rights and lefts and another right. And we drove round and round that little town until we found the business. It turned out Hank did not work there or anywhere, but Margie did. Dave, like

Hank, preferred to abstain from work when possible. This was why he also owed Margie money. She said that Dave owed her and Hank money. Later, knowing a bit more about Margie and Hank, I thought that was a generous way for her to put it, given that it was she who earned the money; Hank merely spent it, and as it turned out, Hank merely spent it on Hank.

Hank smoked a lot of marijuana, and, I learned, Dave did too. It is not the most expensive habit in the world, but like most habits, it does come with a cost or two, one of those being financial. Not wanting to work, but wanting to smoke and also live indoors with food and water and heat, presents a challenge for those of us in the working and middle class. Dave had solved this problem temporarily by selling my horse to Hank and Margie. They were buying Snipaway from Dave. Money was one problem for Dave, me showing up was another. Margie was surprised to learn that Snipaway did not belong to Dave. Luckily, they had not started the payments. Unluckily, Dave owed them money (too), and now it seemed a reduced price for Snipaway was not going to work as a solution to his debt.

Could we buy him from you? asked Margie. Margie explained they wanted a horse for their daughter, Amber. I had no intention of selling Snipaway. And I was desperate to go and see him. So Margie told me how to get to their home, where Snip was waiting, and we worked out the same deal that I had with Dave, minus the stealing. They would keep and care for Snipaway in exchange for being able to ride and use him. And that was how Snip came to be at his final home.

I did try to press charges against Dave with the local police. It used to be that stealing a horse was considered a major crime in Montana. According to the old western movies I saw as a child on Saturday afternoons at the local movie theater with its magical single screen, men were hung, and not in the pornographic sense, for stealing horses; women didn't do much of anything in the westerns except pine for men, both hung and unhung, again, as far as I know, not in the pornographic sense. I did not want Dave hung, but I was pretty unhappy with him for stealing my horse. At the police station, I spoke with an older white man in his police uniform sitting at the other side of a counter, perhaps waiting for people like me to come in and report crimes. He did not appear to be doing anything—neither accepting crime reports nor filing police paperwork, answering the telephone, or even reading the newspaper. I told the man my story in all its detail. The man waited. When I finished, he waited some more. After a long pause he spoke slowly, like people in Montana do. Taking a breath in preparation, he said, You got your horse back, didn't you? Where's the crime?

Unless his creditors presented a threat, Dave was safe from hanging for the time being. Times had changed.

Snip's Death

Knowing a bit about slaughterhouses, including that laws exist forbidding people to take photographs of them or even around them, I know they shelter ugly deaths. These deaths exhibit the lifelessness of even life itself—at the hands of a capitalist economy—not life but things becoming other things, profits ebbing and flowing like blood. Dolly died that way. My horse died differently. Perhaps he suffered, perhaps not. Yet to some extent his death happened on his own terms. He chose the place and in some way chose the time.

The rest of Snip's life right through to his death and burial at age twenty-five in 2004 happened at Margie's home. He was in a pasture near her home, a trailer sitting on what might be the most beautiful land in the world. The golden curves of grass and land and sky moved like water toward a horizon filled with light blue mountains, somehow gentle when seen from such a distance, as though they were the painted-on edges decorating a new baby's room, a baby born to the gods.

Because many things are slow in Montana, the news of Snipaway's seemingly gentle death took months to reach me. When it did, I was at work in my office at the private college where I taught, with a guest speaker about to give a lecture to my class on the family. I remember looking out my office window and thinking of this one, of my family, now gone.

Snip had laid down and died one night, Margie's email said. They found him in the morning. They used a backhoe to dig a large hole right out there in his pasture and buried him in it. From grass he came and to grass he did return.

5

Ways of Thinking about Normal in the United States

Horse-Crazy (White) Girls in the Late Twentieth Century

> In a phenomenon too prevalent to be mere chance, little girls all over the Western world wake one day to find themselves completely taken over by the love of all things equine.—Melissa Holbrook Pierson,
> *Dark Horses and Black Beauties* (cover copy)

In my interviews with women who were once horse-crazy girls, I asked them why U.S. girls love horses, dream of, pretend to be, talk and obsess about, draw, and, if possible, care for and ride horses and more horses. They responded that it was both *because of* this love, that is, because of their relationships with horses, and because in these loving relationships they gained a kind of freedom and power by becoming something more, and by coming to belong. With horses, girls enact themselves as loving beings; they become themselves in ways that at times reinforce but in important ways challenge "normal" roles for girls in the world. In this chapter I describe the women (the former horse-crazy girls I spoke with), explore their horsey bonds, and investigate the ways that girl-horse relationships offer a place to belong and a challenge to the demands of being a "normal" girl. Girl-horse relationships undermine the normalization and heteronormativity girls face; I will define and explore this phenomenon via the work of Michel Foucault.

Girls in the United States today face a number of pressures or normative demands as to what it means to be girl, to be acceptable, to be safe, to manage their lives. These pressures, which are not always logically consistent with one another, include that they be beautiful objects; that they be caring, caregiving, loving beings; that they be able to manage in the world as well as provide care in the home. Growing up female means finding one's way through this social order and making a life, for better or worse, a more or less livable life.

Horse-crazy girls, to some extent, refuse to be beautiful body-objects. They make space for, value, and enact girl experiences that weave together caring for other beings with acting in the world. And as they find a power and safety with horses, they exhibit courage and strength in their day-to-day horsey lives.

The Former Horse-Crazy Girls

As discussed in chapter 1, Foucault's concept of normalization refers to the process through which "people come to demand of themselves, as the larger society demands of them, that they reproduce 'normal' standards of action."[1] Social power materializes and is reproduced through this process. Foucault claims that "normal" means different things to different groups of people, that diverse societies have different ideas of what normal is, and that within a given society, what is normal changes over time. I interpret Foucault to mean that those who are powerful play a bigger role in shaping how their society understands what is "normal" and that the powerful benefit from these ideas of the "normal." Social power in this case results from the forces by which identity is formed, and it produces the "normalized" self.[2]

How should a girl live? In this chapter, I describe "models" or ideological formations of "proper," "normal" behavior. For the purpose of my argument, a model is a comprehensive framework for how to live. Many model answers, for correct living, are given in mainstream U.S. society, and the models are rigid and exclude other ways of being. Countless girls experience exclusion from these models: girls of color, queer girls, poor girls, girls with disability. Nonetheless, I argue that there are two dominant models of life for girls today, a mainstream conservative model based on care, and a mainstream liberal feminist model based on self-assertion. I contrast the biological essentialism of conservatives such as George Gilder—who grounds the definition of what it means to be a woman in the idea of care (he asserts that women are hard-wired to be caregivers)—with the biological essentialism of liberal feminists such as Betty Friedan, who asserts that women and men are fundamentally the same and that women are hard-wired to be fulfilled in life by careers equal to those of, and much like the experience of, men. Both are unvital, as both are static models for life. In contrast, horse-crazy girls represent what Nikolas Rose calls a vital politics. Drawing from Rose, I claim that these girls' lives are unmediated by a rigid model, since there are few such models for horsey girls.[3] While elements of horsey girl culture such as pony books might be seen as models, I claim pony books, and horsey girl culture more generally, are not models as they are neither all-encompassing nor imposed upon girls. Instead, while they normalize, they are also experiments in living and, as in the case of the pony book genre, largely written by horse-crazy and former horse-crazy girls.[4]

In combining care and self-assertion, horse-crazy girls exemplify a different mode of living, one that is, like love itself, its own end. I call this mode of life *vital care*.

Love and Freedom

In my childhood in the 1970s and 1980s, conservatives like Gilder called for girls and women to "return" to the domestic sphere, and liberal feminists like Friedan called for girls and women to assert themselves in the public sphere and leave behind the care-work of the home. Both groups focused on white girls and women and excluded other groups. Still today, strangely out of sync with a world where families need two full-time adults in the wage workforce, conservatives like Ryan T. Anderson continue to draw from Gilder and argue for women's return to the domestic sphere.

Liberal feminists push back against conservative visions of girlhood and encourage girls and women to take an equal place in the public world of work. Yet the liberal feminist movement has tended to downplay the importance of domestic and care labor, although its proponents have been correct in their demand that women have freedom and choice to leave the domestic world.

I claim that horsey girls rebuff the ongoing binary framing of gender by both mainstream liberals and conservatives. Horse-crazy girls exemplify a mode of life that is not binary, that resists these dualities—for the liberal feminists, girls having self-assurance and *not* focusing on care-work and on caring; and for the conservatives, girls *not* self-asserting and instead focusing on caring.[5]

Michael Korda inadvertently describes the both/and appeal of horses for horse-crazy girls and the vitalism in their ways of being. On one hand, he argues for the power and freedom offered by horses and ponies when he says that for children, a pony involves "some of the same desires that center on learning to drive and owning a car today for teenage Americans—freedom to come and go as you please, responsibility . . . a sense of power and control." On the other hand, about love and care, Korda explains that horses and ponies are "warm, furry," and they accept "treats" and respond to "love, affection, and attention."[6] Horses offer girls loving relationships and power. About this range of ways of being involving power and care, gender studies scholar Birgitta Plymoth writes, "Women in equestrian sports are active in a full spectrum of roles ranging from that of the groom, doing the mucking out, to training and competing at elite level. In competition, they frequently face male competitors. Boys and men are to a considerably lesser extent engaged in the daily tasks of caring for the horses in riding schools and elsewhere."[7]

Foucault is useful in understanding horsey girls because he describes processes by which girl identity is formed, and formed in ways that are more or less constraining, that offer some freedom. By freedom I mean that, as the women I spoke with described, their girlhood selves had a more fluid, and therefore more vital, self-identity. Horse-crazy girls had more freedom to become themselves through the unfolding of their own activities, which means their lives belong more to themselves, as something valued for itself. Conversely, they were less frozen in stereotypical "girl" roles or models that deaden activities, that make ways of being valuable only for some instrumental value to come. Normative culture, for example, pushes girls to work toward and obsess about thinness, beauty, and sexual appeal. Dieting is not an enjoyable activity, worthwhile in itself; one diets for an instrumental end, to be thin, to be, in the terms of mainstream culture, beautiful.

The relationships of girls to horses matter because they enlarge the girls' world rather than shrinking it to fit a model. In an odd way, girl-horse love does replicate social demands on girls that they tame wild beasts (men and horses), as Gilder and Anderson argue it is their instinct to do (see more on this below). Yet in important ways girl-horse love does *not* replicate these demands; in contrast to Gilder's passive, ideal women, horsey girls do not merely tame; they master horses as well as themselves and thus engage in a vital politics of life. Horsey girls challenge other conservative binary frames as well, such as the linking of girls to instincts and boys to rationality, girls to caring and boys to competing, girls to private spaces and boys to public.

I suggest "vital care" as a term that describes the ways in which the separation and potential antagonism of care and self-assertion is abolished. In the same way that creative labor brings together the potentially discordant ideas of the noninstrumentality of creative activity with the instrumentality of work and labor, vital care brings together the confidence and action of self-assertion with the action of care—but not in the way that care is often understood as subordinating the interests of the self to the interests of someone else. In vital care, care and self-assertion are not distinct but are simultaneous—they are inseparable parts of the same experience, a relationship with a horse. There is no distinction between self-assertion and care in a horsey girl's mental framework, there is only a relationship. And there is no public or private space but only the created world of the companionship.

Horse-crazy girls shake loose power and find their own ways of being. Girls with horses find a kind of freedom from the normative demands of mainstream girlness—challenging both binary conservative ideals of women's taming of men and caregiving, and binary liberal feminist ideals of women leaving caregiving and finding "success" in the (previously male) public world of wage/work. The freedom these girls find—for a moment in their lives—is more fluid and shifting, more present-oriented, and less instrumental than the alternatives offered by conservative or mainstream liberal feminist ideology. This freedom holds open possibility like life itself.

Nonetheless, there are many limits to the challenge horsey girls present. Girls with horses complicate this gendered binary frame at the same time as their whiteness gives them a power and privilege that many white people take for granted. The predominantly white girls in my study become themselves in the midst of a racist society where they work to live up to mainstream white ideals. These girls, like other white people, largely accept white privilege. As white girls, they develop within the frame of the hegemonic femininity of white womanhood. Girls of color exist and become automatically always-outside the normalized femininity demanded of white girlhood.

The white/privileged horse-crazy girls I interviewed expect and are expected to become normalized in whiteness. Race and gender interact in white girls' becoming. Like conservatives' ideal women (who are always white) and liberal feminist women (who have a history of focusing on white women's concerns), white girls who are horse crazy bring their whiteness along for the ride. Yet they also—like girls of color, like all girls—face another kind of normalized violence, the literal violence of sexual assault and the larger violence of normalized girl subjection. And some horse-crazy girls, girls with disability and queer girls, face other kinds of always-outside status, other forms of marginalization. They face these additional forms of marginalization in the midst of normalization, in the midst of their becoming.

Three Generations of Horsey Girls

Twenty-five women who were horse crazy as girls shared their experiences with me in interview conversations. Four of these women also had horse-crazy daughters about whom they told me. In this section, I describe these women in terms of their age and generation, their social class, and the degree of their ongoing commitment to horses. The women range in age from twenty-three to ninety-nine. Most, but not all, remain passionate about horses as adults. Many continue to ride or find other ways to be around horses, like the three women who volunteered in horse rescue and horse therapy organizations.[8] Not every woman had owned a horse, but all had been in some kind of contact with horses during girlhood. I do think that the experiences, dreams, and fantasies of horse-crazy girls who have no access to horses have a lot in common with those who come in contact with the real animals. Yet all the former horse-crazy girls I spoke with did have *some* access to actual horses.

Horses do not only offer something deeply meaningful to *girls*. The desire for close relationships and alternatives to heteronormativity follows these girls into adulthood. Certainly for most of the women I interviewed, being horse crazy did not stop with adulthood. Most of my participants, like Hana, in her thirties, continue to be passionate about horses in their very busy adult lives. When I asked Hana how long she was in love with horses, Hana responded in the present tense. She is still in love with horses. She said, "I really can't remember a time when I wasn't."

This seems to be a social trend. Books like *The Smart Woman's Guide to Midlife Horses: Find Meaning, Magic and Mastery in the Second Half of Life* (2011), by Melinda Folse, address middle-aged women who find their way back to their childhood passion of horses.[9] Women seem to make up most of the volunteers at many horse rescue organizations. One woman I spoke with claimed that 85 percent of the one hundred or so volunteers at the New Mexican horse rescue organization where she worked are women aged sixty and above.

A woman named Gwen told me about the volunteer work she did helping children with disability get horse therapy. Gwen works in the one stable left in Manhattan where the Central Park carriage horses live. On Saturdays some of the horses are used for equine therapy. Gwen, like Kathleen and others, cares less about riding than she does simply being around horses. And the horses adore her. Everyone at the stable teases Gwen because the horses love her so much.[10]

Ten of the former horse-crazy girls I spoke with still ride horses. Still describing riding in her adult life with passion, Fiona said, "I absolutely love horseback riding. It is the best feeling in the world."[11] Four more who do not currently ride spend significant time with horses; three of these volunteer regularly with horse rescue and horse therapy organizations. The fourth, Kathleen, owns three horses that she cares for, and loves, but does not ride.

Of the remaining eleven women who no longer ride, four plan to go back to riding someday. Hana would love to ride but financially cannot afford to do it and, as a full-time mother of a young child, does not have the time to volunteer her labor at a barn. About horseback riding, Hana said, "I cannot express how much I miss it."[12] Another woman had to stop riding because of developments in her disability that made horseback riding unsafe. Only five of the women I interviewed neither ride nor spend time with horses, having moved on from their horse passion.

In broad terms, the women I spoke with come from three generations. The oldest group are around my mother's age, eleven women in their late fifties, sixties, and seventies: Saralyn, Sonya, Gwen, Toni, Mila, Grace, Bella, Carol, Rosemary, Ruth, and one woman in her late nineties, Opal. The middle group includes nine women in my generation, in their late thirties, forties, and early fifties: Carrie, Penelope, May, Hana, Kathleen, Jenny, Lola, Paula, and Ella. Finally, I interviewed five women in their twenties and early thirties: Susan, Fiona, Donna, Helen, and Heather.[13] Horses mean slightly different things to each of these three generations of horse-crazy girls. With each new wave of feminism, the way gendering happened and the opportunities in work, sports, and other areas that were available to girls and women changed. Simultaneously, the relationships the girls had with their horses changed too.

Several of the women in my mother's generation noted that, as children, they had few opportunities to engage in sports. About this Katherine Dashper writes, "Historically, most women were excluded from sport and active physical recreation on the spurious grounds that it was unladylike and might damage their reproductive abilities and capacities to be good wives and mothers."[14] For some women in my mother's generation, horseback riding was the *only* athletic option. Indeed, equestrian sports have been an option for girls and women since the mid-twentieth century. Plymoth writes,

> Equestrian sports are fairly unique in that equality prevails in a formal sense. The Olympic Games opened up dressage classes for women in 1952; show jumping in 1956 and eventing in 1964. Accordingly, women and men could compete against each other at all levels. . . . Biological and physical factors, cited in the majority of other sports as a reason for placing men and women in separate classes, do not appear in equestrian sports discourse.[15]

All the women in my mother's generation whom I interviewed rode for pleasure. None of them competed, but horseback riding was an athletic activity that was open to these women.

One woman in her sixties, Bella, described her childhood desire to be a cowboy. She emphasized the *boy* part. Boys were heroic and had all the excitement, she explained. This former horse-crazy girl consumed a lot of popular media, reading stories about "brave cowboys" and going to the movies to see them and their adventures. One sixty-one-year-old woman, Toni, expressed her association of being horsey with masculinity. Toni told me that she was surprised at the "gentleness" in my voice when we spoke on the phone. Knowing that I am a woman interested in horses, she assumed that I would be "more aggressive and masculine."[16] Several of the women in this group called themselves "tomboys" as children. Along with their extremely limited access to sports, these women also had more limited choices in the adult working world once they became adults. This group of women was more likely to do traditionally gendered work. They did sex work and social work, were full-time housewives and office workers, and, less traditionally, became academics. Interestingly, the three women in this group who became academics all came from working-class backgrounds. They were not born into highly educated or affluent families. The women in this age group wondered if they would have been quite so horse crazy if they had been able to engage in other sports and had had more work opportunities available to them.

With Title IX, signed into law in 1972, when my mother was thirty and I was five, it became illegal to discriminate on the basis of sex in any program receiving federal funding. Athletic opportunities began to open up for the girls of my generation. Unlike the older generation of women, I had the chance to take part in organized sports by the time I entered high school in 1981. In Bozeman, Montana, my school offered girls' teams in basketball, volleyball, and short- and long-distance running. I ran cross-country in my junior and senior year. We also had more ways of being girls, more fluidity in the ways gender was understood and performed.

Yet our opportunities in sports and work were still constrained. In my little town, high rates of violence against women and profound homophobia limited everyone's lives. I knew no one who identified as gay, lesbian, bisexual, transgender, or queer (LGBTQ). I had never heard of a women's or rape crisis or queer center. And as a girl, I was restricted in what were considered acceptable areas of work. For example, like me, two of my participants (one in my generation and one in the older generation) had dreamed of being large-animal veterinarians when they grew up. In high school, I visited all the local large-animal veterinarians in town and offered to be a volunteer intern. Each one turned me down because I was a girl. All three of us, the two participants in my study and I, were told repeatedly that girls could not be large-animal veterinarians; and all of us eventually gave up on that dream. The veterinarians I spoke with as a child emphasized that girls would never be strong enough to handle and practice medicine with large animals.

The youngest women in my group, those in their twenties and thirties, had the most opportunities in sports and work, and the most freedom in sexual and gender expression. Yet their world, too, has not been limit-free. Queer people's lives are significantly less limited than when I grew up; yet LGBTQ people continue to face profound discrimination, experience regular and brutal violence, and have limited work opportunities, particularly in states where it has been legal to fire someone based on his/her/their gender or sexual identity.[17] As mentioned above, violence against women continues to be a major public health issue, and women are significantly more likely to live in poverty than men. Women continue to work a second shift, doing the lion's share of their family's unpaid domestic labor even as they also work outside the home for a wage.[18] And yet horses offered all three generations experiences of freedom, power, love, and connection.

I focused my study on girls who primarily rode for pleasure. Twenty-three of the twenty-five women I interviewed grew up working or middle class and rode mainly as pleasure riders. Two women were affluent as children. The girlhood horse experiences of the two wealthy women were different from those of the working- and middle-class women in that the affluent women did not do a lot of the physical care of their horses. They kept their horses at stables, and the stable staff did the work of mucking out stalls and feeding and watering the horses. In contrast, most of the women I interviewed actively looked for opportunities to take care of horses, horses that were usually not their own because their families could not afford to purchase, or pay board for, a horse. Caring for horses became a way to be around them. Sometimes girls even earned horseback-riding lessons as a form of payment for their caring labor.

Recognizing how expensive and thus inaccessible horses often are to low-income children, and knowing the power of the relationship children can have with horses, one former horse-crazy girl I interviewed, Paula, started and ran a not-for-profit program working to make horses accessible to low-income children.[19] One of the features of the program is that the children do the work of caring for the horses in exchange for horseback-riding lessons. Similarly, two women who participated in my study, one middle class, one working class, spent significant childhood time as "stable girls"[20] or, as they put it, "barn rats." Hana described going to her local urban stable every day after school, hanging around and helping with the horses, and hanging out with other stable girls.[21]

Sonya "grew up working class in a very large family," and her family could not help her financially with riding. As a teenager, when she was "old enough to earn money" herself, Sonya was able to begin horseback riding. "I worked at a lunch counter in Boston," she said. "I grew up in the Boston area. This was the sixties and so many towns had stables, it wasn't unusual for people to ride for an hour or two. I worked in Boston and saved enough money to get me in and out of Boston by train. And the rest went to riding horses, so that I could rent them for a day."[22]

Binary Girls

Conservative Visions and Girls Taming Horses

The conservative ideological formulation that women and girls are biologically better at care-work helps create a gendered subjectivity compelling women to do this work. Indeed, that subjectivity supports an underlying political economy in which women do the majority of the care-work in the United States, and do it largely without pay. In part due to this belief that women and girls are natural caregivers, conservatives have stood against marriage equality. For example, making reference to biology, Anderson argues against the legal right for all queer people to marry by claiming, "Marriage exists to bring a man and a woman together as husband and wife to be father and mother to any children the union produces. It is based on the anthropological truth that men and women are different and complementary, the biological fact that reproduction depends on a man and a woman, and the social reality that children need both a mother and a father."[23]

This contemporary conservative framework often envisions women as gentle beings who passively tame the wild beast inside of men. As untamed wild beasts, "men are more sexually permissive."[24] Anderson and other conservatives believe that marriage to a woman will keep men tamed, monogamous, and committed to financially supporting their wife and children. For and by a woman, and only for and by a woman, a man will be "civilized." (And being civilized means that he will become monogamous and work to support his family financially.) As popular conservative radio host Dennis Prager argued in 2011, "For all of higher civilization's recorded history, becoming a man was defined overwhelmingly as taking responsibility for a family."[25]

Conservatives today such as Anderson and Prager draw from the work of Gilder, a popular writer and onetime member of Ronald Reagan's administration. In his influential book *Men and Marriage*, which came out in 1973 under the title *Sexual Suicide* and was republished under its current title in 1986, Gilder opens with a Beauty and the Beast story in which a beautiful princess (standing in for all women) succeeds in taming—passively, just by being a beautiful, gentle woman—an out-of-control beast (men). With the wild beast tamed, civilization, such as it is in Gilder's fairy-tale world, can grow and thrive. When women neglect their job of caring for, taming, and civilizing men by leaving the domestic realm and joining men in the public world of work, men once again revert to their precivilized natural and wild beastly state. Gilder writes, "Modern society relies on predictable, regular, long-term human activities corresponding to the sexual faculties of women. The male pattern is the enemy of social stability. This is the ultimate source of female sexual control and the crucial reason for it. Women domesticate and civilize male nature. They can jeopardize male discipline and identity, and civilization as well, merely by giving up this role."[26] For Gilder, a man is tamed by his focus on providing for his submissive woman and children. He turns his naturally competitive ways into competing in the workforce to earn the wages with which he supports his vulnerable family. Prager refers to another book by Gilder in claiming:

> Men need a role, or they become, as the title of George Gilder's classic book on single men describes them: *Naked Nomads*. In little more than a generation feminism has obliterated roles. If you wonder why so many men choose not to get married, the answer lies in large part in the contemporary devaluation of the husband and of the father—of men as men, in other words. Most men want to be honored in some way—as a husband, a father, a provider, as an accomplished something; they don't want merely to be "equal partners" with a wife.[27]

For Gilder, when women leave their biologically bound role of caring for their home, children, and man, two catastrophic things happen. One, men's role in the family is destabilized and men wander from their families at loose ends. "A man without a woman has a deep inner sense of dispensability, perhaps evolved during the millennia of service in the front lines of tribal defense. He is sexually optional. Several dominant males could impregnate all of the women and perpetuate the tribe."[28] Two, the other catastrophe involves the ending of men's moral socialization by women. Untamed, Gilder warns, this same man is likely to run amok raping, looting, and plundering

(61). He claims, "Biology, anthropology, and history all tell the same essential story. Every society, each generation, faces an invasion by barbarians. They storm into the streets and schools, businesses and households of the land, and, unless they are brought to heel, they rape and pillage, debauch and despoil the settlements of society. . . . These barbarians are young men and boys, in their teens and twenties" (39). In the modern world, the nuclear family tames these young men. "A young man enters the decisive phase of his life," Gilder writes,

> when he resolves on marriage and career. . . . At this point, economic incentives and bureaucratic rules alone are impotent to make him a useful citizen. He becomes law-abiding and productive, in essence, because he discovers it is the only way he can get sex from the women he wants, or marriage from the one he loves. It is the sexual constitution, not the legal one, that is decisive in subduing the aggressions of young men.

In large part, Gilder sees his book as a challenge to the second-wave liberal feminist movement of the 1970s, a movement that he believes is set to destroy civilization because it moves women out of their natural (domestic) sphere where they gently care for men and children, and into the public working world of men. More recently, Prager echoes Gilder, arguing that one of the saddest feminist legacies "is that so many women—and men—have bought the notion that women should work outside the home."[29] Conservatives like Prager, Anderson, and Gilder believe in the natural roles of women and men in the world. In this thinking, we must do what our biology shaped us to do.[30] Here, conservatives resonate with much of the past and present-day popular literature on girls, women, and horses. Both the literature and conservatives like Gilder claim that it is instinctual for women to be who they are and do what they are destined to do—that is, gently care for others.

In the late twentieth and early twenty-first centuries, popular horsey literature echoes Gilder, and other conservatives writing today, and focuses on the idea that it is instinctual for women to connect with horses. The women I interviewed from all three generational groups also regularly raised this idea about women's instincts and their instinct-based special connection to horses. The idea reflects the broader culture's normative and binary understanding of women as intuitive, emotional, and of the body (in contrast to men being rational and of the mind). Revealing this belief in terms of horse-crazy girls,

Josephine Pullein-Thompson writes that for some, "the actual riding was not that important, it was loving and looking after the ponies that mattered and presumably satisfied their budding maternal instincts."[31]

Because women are associated with the body, emotion, and instincts, women are understood to be more animalistic and thus able to connect better with other (nonhuman) animals than men.[32] In this conservative framework, and drawing from the dualistic mind-body split central to Western thought and culture, men are the rational ones who, in spite of their strong sexual desires, while competing to provide for their fragile women and children at home, build civilization as they compete with other men. As I discuss above (and in *Boundaries of Touch*), these same womanly instincts also justify women still today doing the lion's share of contemporary domestic labor, particularly that involving children and childcare.[33]

In an essay by horse trainer and popular writer Mary Midkiff on women and horses, published in 2000, she affirms Gilder's conservative vision. Midkiff writes, "Women are gatherers, nurtures [*sic*], and teachers while men are proficient at spatial tasks, hunting, and defense. Throughout history, women have spent most of our time teaching and caring for the young. We have an innate ability to read emotions learned first by reading babies' cues without language. It all adds up to woman's 'intuition.'" Much like Gilder, Midkiff argues, "Women want to tame, save, and nurture the beast." Yet in this case, the "beast" Midkiff has in mind is a horse. "Think about it," she argues.

> What kind of person would work best with horses' behavioral characteristics? Chances are, you've begun to think in terms of the gentle touch, a soft but firm voice, an intuitive sense for the factors triggering a behavior, a calming effect, sensitivity instead of force, finesse over power, cooperation over dominance, and a constant search for more meaningful communication. This description certainly fits the human female.[34]

Interestingly, in most examples of the pony book genre from the United Kingdom, horsey girls do tame horsey beasts. And in the books from the United States, before the storybooks told of girls, before girls had a chance to exist as characters in horse books, the stories were about boys who tamed horsey beasts. In Walter Farley's *The Black Stallion*, his central human character, Alex Ramsey, adeptly fulfills Gilder's vision for women in spite of his being a boy, and in spite of the beast being a horse. Yet in contradiction to the conservative story advanced by Gilder, and as I discuss in chapter 3, the horsey girl in British pony books tames her horse not only because she is female and therefore has a "natural" gentle and pure way, but also because of her particular character. She is thoughtful and kind, smart, industrious, and brave.[35] She is not an overly social girl, although she has friends. She is not concerned with what the story deems to be superficial matters like her appearance. She is connected to her family. She loves to be alone with her horse and perhaps is most comfortable, most herself, most confident, when with her horse.[36]

As with depictions of horsey girls in pony books, Plymoth finds, in her study of the media coverage of Swedish equestrian sports and the girls who participated in them, challenges to traditional ideals of girlhood. In those media depictions, the horse-crazy girl is "described as competent, energetic and brave; [and] that she has learnt how to manage, and has acquired leadership abilities, characteristics that can be described as traditional male qualities." Yet Plymoth also observes more conservative horsey-girl femininity "described as 'different' and separate from that of sportsmen." She writes that in these more traditional depictions, "The female equestrian is described in images of motherhood and glamour reflecting a more traditional gender norm. The image of the caring 'horse girl' being promoted also within the equestrian sports helps perpetuate traditional ideals."[37]

Like Plymoth, Dashper finds, in her study of gender in equestrian sports in the United Kingdom, both challenges to and the perpetuation of traditional gender ideals. Dashper explains, "Women in equestrian sport walk a narrow line between acceptable toughness that is needed to succeed in sport and acceptable femininity, which is still commonly understood to be more submissive and demure."[38]

Foucault helps us see gender as historical when he explains the process of normalization (discussed in chapter 1). Challenging conservative thought, Foucault shows how gendered self-understandings emerge out of changing social practices, rather than being a manifestation of "natural" or biological facts about people. In contemporary conservative thinking wherein girls are "naturally" caregivers, and wherein being a girl always means having a vagina, those of us with vaginas are understood to be better at giving care because, in this way of thinking, we are born that way. And as discussed above, when it comes to horses and girls, people often believe that girls are good with horses because girls are good at caretaking (in this case, the caretaking of horses). Thus, the experiences of horsey girls can reproduce and reinforce normalized "naturalistic" interpretations of being female. Yet even if the girls' horsey experiences reinforce some social ideas about being a "normal"—caregiving—girl, I believe the horsey girls I spoke with chiefly challenge basic gender norms.

From horsey girls we can learn to value care itself and to value being-with-another for no end outside of the intrinsic worth of being-together. The contemporary conservative man is most comfortable competing, fighting to support his wife and family (good) or fighting to fulfill his sexual urges (bad), but still most comfortable in the midst of battle with other men. For conservatives, women merely give him a reason to battle. For horsey girls in the stories and as described by the interview participants in my study, the *relationship with* horses fulfills them. For some, certainly for me, the relationship allows for, brings forth, their being, being-with-another.

Second-Wave (White) Feminist Ideals and Horse-Crazy Girls in the World

Gilder wrote his famous book in part as a response to the second-wave feminist movement of the 1970s. To Gilder's dismay, second-wave feminism has helped make many things possible for U.S. girls and women. Yet the feminist movement, like any social movement, has had limits. It has reproduced, in some ways, the oppression it addressed. In this section I address one important branch of the second wave, still important today, that is, liberal feminism. Neither of the two most important branches of second-wave feminism, liberal feminism nor radical feminism, addressed domestic, caregiving labor except to focus on freeing women from such work. In her brilliant study of feminism and its co-option by global elites, Hester Eisenstein defines liberal feminists as "those who believe that women's liberation can be accomplished through the current system, with sufficient reforms to allow women access to all areas of economic and public life." Eisenstein explains, "Basically, liberal feminism accepts the modern capitalist system."[39]

The potential liberation for girls in both the fictional world of the pony genre and the real world of horses offers a point of contrast to that of liberal feminism. Perhaps it appears odd to compare feminist thought to horsey girls' worlds. Yet both have in part challenged gender norms, albeit consciously in one case and perhaps unconsciously in the other. There are some interesting links to be made between the visions of U.S. feminists and the worlds of horse-crazy girls. In particular, second-wave liberal feminism worked to open space in the traditionally male wage workforce for women. Liberal feminists argued that men and women are essentially the same, wanting the same things from life, having the same basic physical and emotional experiences. They argued that because women and men want and need the same things, women also want and need to work at creative and engaging jobs in the wage workforce, and women should be allowed, indeed encouraged, to do so, and to do so for the same wages earned by men. Liberal feminists idealized the public world of wage work and worked to free women from the domestic labor of care so that, in this way of thinking, women could do "real" work, work that mattered, work that fulfilled the human need for self-actualization.[40] In her famous study that helped spark the second-wave feminist movement in the United States, *The Feminine Mystique* (1963), Betty Friedan argues, "We can no longer ignore that voice within women that says: 'I want something more than my husband and my children and my house'" (27). That "something more," argues Friedan, is a career.

Friedan explains, "Women, as well as men, can only find their identity in work that uses their full capacities. A woman cannot find her identity through others—her husband, her children. She cannot find it in the dull routine of housework." Only through "education and the right to participate in the more advanced work of society" would women have the opportunity to "find their identity" and to live their lives fully (324).

Friedan and other liberal feminists, such as Gloria Steinem, founding editor of *Ms.* magazine, and Bella Abzug, former congresswoman, tended to focus on getting women into the wage workforce without also thinking about the domestic sphere women might leave behind. They pushed for programs like the popular "Take Your Daughter to Work" day to teach girls that they do belong in the public working world. Unfortunately, the liberal feminists did not push for a "Teach Your Son to Do Domestic Labor" day. Indeed, liberal feminists in the 1970s and 1980s, like the larger normative culture, prioritized and idealized the public working world and too often ignored the private one. After white middle-class women increasingly entered the wage workforce, a gap emerged in the domestic labor of care. That gap was often filled by working-class and working-poor women, white and of color. As feminist theorist bell hooks eloquently explains, Friedan addresses the situation of white middle-class women, not all women. About Friedan, hooks writes,

> She did not discuss who would be called in to take care of the children and maintain the home if more women like herself were freed from their house labor and given equal access with white men to the professions. She did not speak of the needs of women without men, without children, without homes. She ignored the existence of all non-white women and poor white women. She did not tell readers whether it was more fulfilling to be a maid, a babysitter, a factory worker, a clerk, or a prostitute than to be a leisure-class housewife.[41]

The new domestic laborers in middle-class homes were themselves often underpaid, without health care, and undertrained. They stepped into the middle-class home, out of necessity, at the expense of their own homes and children.

Many other times instead of hiring someone else, as described by Arlie Hochschild with Anne Machung, women stretched their labor into two shifts and did *both*, the wage labor outside and the "second shift" of domestic labor inside the home.[42] Some women did attain the goal set forth by second-wave liberal feminist thought. Yet too often it was at the expense of other less powerful, more marginalized women, or at the expense of "trying to have it all" and having to *do* it all.

This happened instead of liberal feminists agitating for state support for families, instead of men playing a bigger role in the domestic sphere, and instead of the public work world becoming more family friendly. Liberal feminists did not value domestic labor. It was something from which women should be liberated.[43] This view has largely remained up to the current moment.

Vital Care: Linking Assertion and Concern for (the) Other(s)

For Gilder and liberal feminists, the interplay of care and self-assertion constitutes a zero-sum game. When one is gained, the other is lost. In vital care, horsey girls transcend that duality, where care and action are not separate and where they assert themselves in their care.

Courageous Girls and Horse Power

Liberal feminists demand that girls and women gain worldly power, and horsey girls do. In riding horses and in their dreams of riding horses, girls become stronger, faster, more powerful physically. As horseback riding has become the domain of girls and women, it has offered them, Dashper writes, "many opportunities to demonstrate their physical capabilities, skills and prowess in what was once a strongly male-dominated milieu."[44] Indeed, scholars such as Laura Sanchez, who study risky play, argue that horseback riding is the riskiest sport of all. Sanchez writes, "Equestrian sports and horseback riding are quintessentially high-risk activities with the highest epidemiological rates of traumatic injury and mortality, of all sports."[45] Horseback riding being something that girls dominate, in its very riskiness, it offers a profound challenge to stereotypes about girlhood.

Horseback riders often exhibit courage.[46] It takes courage to ride an animal regularly weighing over one thousand pounds, and courage to move among and care for these large, flighty creatures. In an article on gender and stable culture, Gabriella Thorell and Susanna Hedenborg explored riders' taken-for-granted courage and "the importance of 'not chickening out.'" One student they interviewed, Charlotte, said, "We fell off, probably eight to ten times a week because we rode young horses. We rode outdoors, and the horses weren't exercised over the weekends [and therefore had some excess energy on Mondays]. But we were never really injured. Naturally it hurt sometimes, but we laughed it off. . . . [F]alling off was just something you did."[47]

The stories of courage women told me were most vivid when they described getting back on their horse after an injury or accident. It is a commonsense idea in horsey worlds that one must get back on one's horse after falling off (as, in the prologue, my father insisted when my sister fell off and broke her arm). If you do not get back on, the worry is that you never will. Your fear will get the last word and keep you from riding again. Horseback riders usually live by the rule and insist on getting back on a horse even immediately after a serious injury.[48]

Sonya, discussed briefly above, described multiple and serious injuries. She came the closest of all the women I spoke with to giving up riding after having been gravely injured in an accident. In one incident Sonya described, she was riding her mare, Sage, near her home, and the horse was "just being a brat"; Sonya wanted to continue riding and the mare wanted to go home. "We cut a tiny trail around our land," Sonya said.

> I had been riding on that and we were coming out of the trail and across our driveway. I was prepared to go one way, back to the trail, and she wanted to go down the driveway. And she just took off down the driveway toward the barn. I went flying. My leg twisted, and it was just ewww. . . . It was really bad, a spiral break. Luckily, I did not get caught in the stirrup.

> Sage panicked as much as I did. She ended up running around and over to the other side of the pasture. And then she went to stand at the gate from where we usually bring them back in. She just stood there waiting for somebody to come and bring her in. She was scared. I was a wreck. It's not like a huge property, only five acres. But I was far enough from the house and nobody could hear me. So you know I'm dragging myself back with this broken leg. It was ridiculous. The break was a spiral fracture. And I now have a bunch of metal in my leg.

In spite of the severity of her break, when Sonya got home from the hospital, she headed out to the horse. "When I got home," Sonya said, "I mean the minute I got home, I got up on the back of the truck." Sonya told her spouse, Maya, to get the horse. "I need to do this," she said, and added, referring to the mare, "she needs it as much as I do." Sonya was "scared to death." She asked Maya to hold the horse for her, and from the truck bed, Sonya was high enough to swing her broken leg over the mare's back. She said, "You know, I was getting on the wrong side but that was okay." Sonya mounted Sage from the wrong side, on the horse's right rather than left,[49] and Sonya said, "She didn't care. I just swung my leg around and that worked fine." Maya walked Sonya on the mare around the paddock "like you walk a little kid." "I was terrified," she said, and "holding on to the horn." Yet she explained, "You know, you get back on the horse."

More recently, Sonya sustained an injury after which she did not get right back on. She had been bedding the horses down at night. "We probably baby them more than we should," she said. "We put them to bed at night. And when it was my turn to put them in, I would go out and ride around the paddock bareback." On the night the accident happened, Sonya had caught the horses in their pasture and was riding one back to the barn bareback and without a helmet. She said, "Bareback was okay, but without a helmet was just stupid." Sonya does not know why the horse took off, but she did. "My only guess is that she heard something I didn't when I was riding her, and it scared her and she took off like a bat out of hell." The horse was "running scared," and Sonya fell and was knocked unconscious.

Remarkably, when Sonya came to, she "finished putting them to bed" as though nothing had happened. In her disorientation, Sonya neglected to fully close Sage's stall. "Sage is very clever and will let herself out of her stall," she said. "She'll open up the bar just cause she's smart. And so we put a clip on it. She can't manage the clip." Sonya described the night of the accident:

> And so I had finished putting them to bed, given them hay and water, cleaned the stalls and did everything. The only thing I didn't do was that clip. . . . I went in the house and said to my daughter Bonnie, 'I fell. I got a bump on my head. You want to check it?' She said, 'Yeah, it looks pretty bad. You should probably put some ice on it.' Now this is Bonnie telling me this story. I don't remember any of this. Twenty minutes later I said, 'Bonnie, I have a bump on my head. Would you look at it and see what you think?' And she said, 'Oh, shit.' And I became more and more confused. . . . Bonnie was convinced I was dead. You know, she's a nurse, [so] she knows this is really bad.

Fortunately, after several days in the hospital, Sonya did recover. Yet when she came home, she was scared to ride. "By the time I got home, I thought, 'Oh, my God, I don't know about this.' . . . It scared me. It scared me." Notably, and in spite of the severity of her injury and her fear, Sonya has slowly started to ride again, including going for pleasure rides in the woods near her home.[50]

In contrast to the fear many people feel interacting with such a large animal, horse-crazy girls often feel more, not less, safe with horses. Describing her girlhood passion for horseback riding, Sonya explained, "I liked the independence. I liked being in the woods and feeling safe." About this sense of safety, another interviewee, Jenny, mused:

> It's interesting; why not dogs or cats? Why not dogs or cats allowing for a kind of safe space or something? Dogs and cats can give and allow for great affection, the need for care, love, and all those things. The horse is big and it's powerful and it has all of those things, you know? So to me, this says something about being aware that in the world there are entities much bigger than you are and more powerful than you and not benevolent, i.e., men. And that gets transposed

onto this really large, powerful . . . figure of the horse, you know, that's safe and benevolent.[51]

Many of the women I spoke with shared the experience of feeling safe with horses. And with this experience of feeling safe came a sense of greater independence and freedom. As Helen described her experience (also quoted in chapter 1), "I feel very independent, like I am free."[52]

In the Pullein-Thompson sisters' pony stories, ponies and horses clearly offer not only independence to "worthy" girls—young female characters deemed worthy due to their passion for horses, honesty, and willingness to get dirty and work hard—but also a chance at empowerment. Both the fictional and real horse-crazy girls who might—or might feel pressure to—obsess about boys and their appearance, obsess instead about horses and skill at horseback riding. In this they move from striving to be the beautiful objects of someone else's desire—the form of worthiness demanded of girls by the dominant culture—to becoming subjects as skilled horse caregivers and athletes. In becoming accomplished riders, they step into a skilled-at-sports focus usually reserved for boys.[53] Haymonds writes that in riding, a girl learns "to assert herself as the equal of males."

Haymonds clarifies about girls as riders and as pony book readers. "Astride a horse, a girl becomes powerful and gains self-esteem in the process. However strong and difficult the horse is to ride, the girl is the dominant partner in the relationship, mastering him by love and patience." Haymonds describes a typical pony book girl's relationship to her pony in the story:

> She has chosen the horse, she has bought him, or rescued him. When the girl in the pony story sets her eyes on the pony for the first time, her reaction is immediate and possessive, "the pony must be mine." Even the titles of pony stories echo this new assertiveness—*I Wanted a Pony, I Had Two Ponies, A Pony of Our Own, Janet Must Ride*. At last, it is the girl who is saying what she wants, not what society wants for her.[54]

Horses in literature, as in life, allow women a kind of power they would not otherwise have. Cunningham writes, "[T]he horse has, from the nineteenth century at least, occupied a unique and significant place in the empowerment of women. This can be both literal—what a woman could do on a horse which could not be achieved by any other means—and symbolic—what the idea or image of the horse can represent for women or (more usually in the modern period) girls."[55] Jenny, quoted above, explained this gain in power in the context of the relative powerlessness of girls. She noted that we do not have the social phenomenon of "dog-crazy girls"; other animals do offer girls love and connection but not the power offered by the horse. Girls gain power through their relationships with horses.

There is power and safety in the community that many girls build with other horsey girls and women in the rare female-dominated public spaces at stables. In one of the few studies of girls' communities at riding stables, Karoliina Ojanen, writing about Finland, shows that the girls in her study mirror the U.S. girls' challenge to binary culture. Ojanen examines the care-giving role of stable girls. She notes, "The stable is an important place to meet with friends and spend time with other girls." As a girl in Ojanen's study put it, in this community of horsey girls, "You get to know people, you know. . . . You become someone."[56]

There is also power in being connected to an animal who is itself so physically powerful. I spoke with the seminal feminist and vegetarian writer and activist Carol J. Adams, who gave me permission to use her real name. She was a horse-crazy girl whose family owned several horses. Indeed, Carol's relationship with her pony and her pony's sudden death led her to write her famous book on feminism and the shared oppression of women and other animals, *The Sexual Politics of Meat: A Feminist-Vegetarian Critical Theory* (1990).[57] Carol grew up riding and riding and riding with her sisters and her community of close friends. They seemed fearless. They would race their horses, swap horses while the horses were running, and have the horses run under trees so that the rider could grab a branch and swing off and then back on her horse. Carol explained to me that there was something extraordinary about the power gained from riding, from the connection with the horses, the motion and the ability to move so fast and so freely.[58] Similarly, Korda quotes his horse-crazy spouse, Margaret, on her girlhood: "You don't know what it's like for a little girl to sit on a horse's back in a dress, with your bare legs pressed hard against all that warmth and power."[59]

There is power in fulfilling one goal of good horseback riding, which is being one with the horse. Girls can *literally* move faster, jump higher, and do more on the backs of these powerful animals; they borrow from the horse's power. About girl riders, psychologist Delphi M. Toth writes, "Her ability to exert control over this powerful creature gives the adolescent girl confidence and a sense of accomplishment that generalizes to other parts of her life."[60] Children's author Patricia Leitch, in her pony book *Jacky Jumps to the Top*, which came out in a revised version in 1973, illustrates this power, and the freedom it brings, through her character Jacky, as the girl rides the horse she loves: "And in those moments nothing existed for Jacky but the willing pony beneath her, the surge and power of the gallop and the freedom of the open land and sky. They had escaped from time. No yesterday. No tomorrow. Only now. The drumming freedom of the now."[61]

Caring for Horses

Horsey girls both find freedom with horses, *and* they perform extensive care-work. In this, they continue to value the traditionally girl work of caring. As they care for horses, the girls spend many hours grooming and feeding horses, cleaning their stalls, and braiding their manes and tails.

Indeed, grooming and caring for horses was central to the experiences of the horsey girls I interviewed. Horses require a lot of care. If one enjoys caring for horses or wants a horse but cannot afford to hire the necessary care, one must take on a significant amount of daily work. Of course, to some extent this is true with all animals. Having animals entails care-work. Even a pet goldfish must be fed and have its water periodically changed. Dogs, cats, rabbits, and birds often require daily care. Yet, in contrast, Korda points out, horses entail a major life change that is bigger and "more demanding." He writes, "They can't easily be put in a carrying case and taken to the city, or down to the vet's to be boarded for a few days while their owners fly away to Jamaica to catch a little sun." Horses, Korda explains, "need constant care, supervision, a firm schedule, and in bad weather, careful treatment, well thought out in advance."

> If it's going to pour rain, or turn freezing cold, or if a snowstorm is on the way, thought has to be given about what to do with the horses, and preparations made in advance. The middle of a winter night during a bad storm, with snow and ice on the ground, is not the time to be going out into their fields in boots and pajamas to get their halters on and bring them into the barn, or putting salt on the paths so they don't slip.... You have to make sure that they've got fresh water, and that it won't freeze solid on them in the winter and they can't kick it over accidentally in the summer, and that they've plenty of good hay where it can't get

wet or muddy, if possible, and that there's nothing in their field or paddock they can hurt themselves on.[62]

The difference in the amount of time my nonaffluent and affluent interviewees spent caring for horses was striking, and with it came other differences. The relationships that the less affluent girls had with their horses were not likely to involve competition. The world of showing and jumping horses is expensive. It is, probably, partly as a result of their financial limitations that competing (and winning) was less important to these girls. For example, Hana told me about showing, "My family didn't have a lot of money and it's very expensive." The middle- and working-class girls described the pleasure of riding for riding's sake and the pleasure of caring for horses. Hana explained about competition that she "didn't really love it." She added, "I'm not very competitive by nature." The fulfillment they experienced in the relationships they had with horses was less connected to competition and less about instrumental goals. For noninstrumental reasons, many girls spent any available time and money toward the goal of being with horses. "I just wanted to be around them," Hana said.[63] Sonya explained, "I spent, for several years, most of my free time and all of my free money on riding horses." Sonya did not compete. She rode simply for the pleasure of riding and being around these animals whom she loved. Sonya said to me, "I liked the horses." And then she added, about her present-day life, "You know, I just like the horses."[64]

One former horse-crazy girl, now horse-crazy woman, Kathleen, exemplified this commitment to care. Kathleen now owns three horses, an old injured lesson horse that she purchased from a riding school in a major U.S. city when the school shut down; a pony named Merrylegs after the pony in *Black Beauty*, which her friends' children ride but is too small for her to ride; and a fat miniature horse who can pull a little cart but is too small to be ridden even by children.

Kathleen keeps her three horses at a stable where she pays for their care. Even so, Kathleen visits and cares for them herself each day. Kathleen's relationships with her horses revolve around this care. She rides none of them, one being lame and the others being too small for her to ride. She loves her horses profoundly. Indeed, she bought the lame gelding for $30,000 in spite of the fact that the veterinarian told her not to buy him.[65] The vet argued that given his injury, $1,000 would have been too much. Kathleen said she paid that much because that is what the riding school owner asked for him, and Kathleen worried that if she did not purchase him, the gelding would end up at a slaughterhouse. Kathleen started to cry when she told me of her hope that the old horse would live peacefully loved and cared for by her, for as many years as he had had to live mistreated at the stable.[66]

In her study of stable girls, Ojanen argues that, like Kathleen, these girls do the work they do at stables out of their love of horses, their desire to be near them. And like unpaid and gendered domestic labor, a supposed "labor of love," stable girls earn no money. Ojanen writes,

> A stable girl refers to a girl who visits the stable many times a week and takes care of horses without receiving any monetary reward; stable girls have an established standing in the community. Although these girls go to the stable many times a week, they usually ride only once a week. Horseback riding is only one aspect of being a stable girl—in fact, being a stable girl has more to do with tending the horses and spending time with friends.[67]

In Finland, as in the United States, horse-crazy girls abound. Since the 1970s, horseback riding has been a common leisure activity, particularly for girls. Ojanen notes, "About 60,000 people under the age of nineteen have riding as a hobby, and 98 per cent of them are girls" (139). Indeed, Ojanen explains that horseback riding is widespread in other Scandinavian countries as well as in central Europe. Stable girls often start out taking once-per-week lessons at a particular stable, some when they are as young as six or seven. Most stable girls do not own a horse; instead, as they visit the stable regularly for their lessons, they develop a relationship with a horse, often one owned by the stable. These caregiving girl-horse relationships usually take about a year to develop, such that the girls go from being weekly horseback-riding students to *also* taking regular care of a horse and visiting the stable more often.

Ojanen found that girls do not normally pick the horse with whom to develop a relationship. Rather, the relationship develops based on the horse's need for care. Ojanen writes that the girls "are eager to tend any horse without a regular caretaker. These horses are owned by the stable and used in the riding lessons. As time passes, however, girls may also start taking care of horses that are in private use" (139). The stables hire very few people for pay. So those they do hire can use the stable girls' volunteer labor in giving each horse an abundance of love and attention. Whereas, in many cases, the stable and horses would manage without the stable girls' help, they can certainly make good use of the girls' unpaid work. However, for some stables, only with the volunteer labor of girls and women are the stables financially able to function.

Girl-horse love, like all love, entails relationships that emerge in a larger network of social meanings. Horsey girls both transform and are transformed by these meanings. Girls who love horses both yield to and challenge the dictates of normative conservative thought about their "naturalness." And these girls take up the promise of liberal feminism to open the world for girls and women. Yet horsey girls do not leave care behind; instead, they bring the work of care into their life-altering relationships with horses. Their horse relationships are largely noninstrumental and for the present-oriented experience of love.

Conclusions: Problems of Care and Self-Assertion

Here I must note that, according to Foucault, these challenges to normative gender, too, must be problematized. Gender, for example, is never *not* a problem; it is always fraught with dangerous potentials. Yet I propose that horsey girls, in their challenge to gender norms, open up their world for their becoming in a way that moves toward the possibility of freedom. For Foucault, this means that we must always question the self that we are, that we will never understand ourselves or our world as, finally, finished with the process of becoming. There is a freedom in this questioning, a freedom in being always unfinished.

We know that there is a problem in the United States today that resides between the needs of those requiring care and the needs of the caregiver for self-assertion. Is there a way to think of a linkage between them? The importance of this problem can be seen, for example, in the popular mainstream debate prompted in 2012 by Anne-Marie Slaughter's highly referenced article in the *Atlantic* on gender, care, and "Why Women Still Can't Have It All."[68] Slaughter focuses correctly on the structural issues that make "having it all"—having a highly successful and demanding career *and* having, raising, and spending lots of time raising children—impossible. In a capitalist society such as ours where profit matters more than anything else, more than life itself, very few women get to "have it all."

In sharp contrast to people's instrumental reasons for doing things in the larger adult-run capitalist world, horse-crazy girls predominantly ride and spend time with horses for the love of it. I argue that in terms of both care-work and agency, girl-horse love and Haraway's work on companion species (discussed in chapters 1 and 6) help to both describe and explain the complicated nature of girl-horse relationships. Here I argue that care does not have to be in a dichotomous relationship with empowerment. Both empowerment and care can, and in the case of horse-crazy girls, do happen together.[69]

In spite of the second-wave liberal feminist focus on working outside the home, and in spite of an ongoing demand by U.S. conservatives for women to value staying home with children above all else, most women since the second wave have *needed* to work for a wage *and* do the domestic labor involved in having children in order to, in Slaughter's words, "have it all." Thus in response to the home/work binary, many women, particularly affluent and predominantly white women, have attempted to do both, caring for a family and working at a career, by hiring other (less affluent) women to help with the domestic labor. Working-class and working-poor women, often women of color, have filled in the gaps in the lives of women like Slaughter, that is, more affluent women's lives. Nonetheless, in her article, Slaughter—who has two children—argues that even affluent women cannot "have it all." She asserts that caring for a family and working at a demanding career cannot happen in our current social framework. "All my life," including for years after having her two sons, Slaughter writes,

> I'd been the woman smiling the faintly superior smile while another woman told me she had decided to take some time out or pursue a less competitive career track so that she could spend more time with her family. I'd been the woman congratulating herself on her unswerving commitment to the feminist cause, chatting smugly with her dwindling number of college or law-school friends who had reached and maintained their place on the highest rungs of their profession. I'd been the one telling young women at my lectures that you *can* have it all and do it all, regardless of what field you are in.[70]

Now, based on her own experience of trying to do and have "it all," Slaughter has changed her mind. In her 2012 article, Slaughter explained that even for affluent women like herself, having it all is not possible, "not with the way America's economy and society are currently structured" (86–87).

Furthermore, Slaughter rightly argues, to believe women can have a successful career and raise a family, "have it all," is to believe that the women who do not have it all are failing in one way or another. This belief echoes the highly problematic broader normative U.S. thinking that if one tries hard enough, one can do and be anything. Slaughter delineates the ways this try-hard-enough ideology blames women. And she argues against the idea that if a woman does a number of things correctly, *then* she can have it all. According to this deeply problematic, individualist way of thinking, to succeed, the individual woman must be committed enough. She must "reach for the stars." She must choose the correct life partner. Slaughter herself writes, "I could never have had the career I have had without my husband." Slaughter's husband, Andrew Moravcsik, has spent more time with their two sons than she has. Along with finding another Moravcsik, the successful woman must sequence her career and childbearing correctly. Usually this means waiting to have children until a time when she might no longer be biologically able to do so. If the woman fails at any of these important choices, then *she herself* is the reason for her not being able to have it all (90–93).

Of course, Slaughter speaks to and about elites, "highly educated, well-off women who are privileged enough to have choices in the first place." Most women, as she herself writes, "face much more difficult circumstances. Some are single mothers; many struggle to find any job." Some women support partners who cannot find work. "Many cope with a work life in which good day care is either unavailable or very expensive." Slaughter acknowledges that many women "are not worrying about having it all, but rather about holding on to what they do have." Yet in the United States, Slaughter explains, "women are less happy today than their predecessors were in 1972, both in absolute terms and relative to men" (89).

The political-economic element of Slaughter's problem is connected to the ethical. Despite widespread appeals to the centrality of family and children, care-work is devalued as "women's work" and so not paid sufficiently or at all. First, to have it all, we as a society must value care and the work of caring. Once caregivers stand on the firm ground of a society that financially supports their labor, then we can move our attention to vital care. In vital care, I show how self-assertion and care can come together in the same universe of experience, through the care relationship. Self-assertion is not lost in the experience of care. This revaluation of care as a form of self-assertion, or care as embodied in an experience of self-assertion, might reframe the debate. Beyond the political-economic issues, Slaughter's problem of "having it all" lies in how care and self-assertion cannot be reconciled when they stand opposed. While horsey girls experience something unique in their riding and their love, this experience at least offers an example of how this opposition might be overcome.

6

Horsey Girls

Heteronormativity and Otherness

In chapter 5, I argued that horse-crazy girls shake loose the confining models of either being a caregiver or engaging in self-assertion. I showed how an alternative mode of agency, that of vital care, is freer in the sense of being less restricted by these normative models. Girls become themselves in that their development is somewhat freed from the larger mainstream society's demands of who they ought to be. Vital care constitutes a unique union of caring and putting forth the self.

In this chapter, I explore the horsey girl challenge to heteronormativity. I am interested in heteronormativity as the cultural imperative for girls and boys to come together in romantic and unequal relationships, a requirement that comes with normative understandings of gender and sexuality, and a normative model for how girls should live. A social world like the mainstream United States "that assumes and promotes heterosexuality is a heteronormative world." Amy Eshleman and I write about this, "The normality of heterosexuality is not a biological reality but a way of thinking, an ideology, an expression of culture springing from and helping to reproduce a way of living that privileges some—those who are cisgender, those who are heterosexual, and those who are men—over others."[1] Horsey love is counter to this mandatory heterosexual love; it is counternormative.

The horse-crazy girls I spoke with described experiencing themselves as "belonging" in their relationships with horses, often in contrast to other parts of their girl lives. As girls who had some access to actual horses, they found a place to fit, to grow and develop with less regard to cultural norms. This horsey relationship provides a freedom from the demands of heteronormative love. Girls offer care to their horses and gain courage from their horse relationships, and they experience intimacy, love, and freedom with horses. Horse-crazy girls, with both fantasy and real horses, challenge the ways they might not fit in other areas of their lives. To some extent, the girls refuse gender norms and become themselves in their horsey relationships. In the case of girls who are in some way more socially marginalized, like those with disability, horses offer a challenge to marginalization and a place where they have control and choice. They make decisions and not only for themselves; they choose together with their horses.

The Well of Loneliness

In 1928 Radclyffe Hall published her famous novel, *The Well of Loneliness*, about (among other things) a horse-crazy girl named Stephen Gordon. Like her character Stephen, and like a good number of the women I interviewed, Hall was queer—or, in the term of her time, an "invert." In a time of profound oppression of queer people, Hall courageously wrote her novel from, she told her publisher, "a deep sense of duty." She stated, "I am proud indeed to have taken up my pen in defence of those who are utterly defenceless, who being from birth set apart in accordance with some hidden scheme of Nature, need all the help that society can give them." Journalist and historian Neil Miller calls *The Well of Loneliness*, about horse-crazy and queer Stephen, "the most influential lesbian novel of the twentieth century."[2] In a world with very few options for queer women, Hall's character Stephen finds love and belonging with horses.

Stephen wants to be a boy, and she loves and desires girls. Her first crush—her first love really, aside from her deep love for her father—is on her wealthy family's housemaid, a young woman of twenty named Collins. Stephen is seven years old when one morning she suddenly noticed Collins. That day, Hall writes, "Collins looked up and suddenly smiled, then all in a moment Stephen knew that she loved her—a staggering revelation!"[3] Hall describes when, after a brief conversation, Collins gives the child a quick kiss. "Stephen stood speechless from a sheer sense of joy. . . . At that moment she knew nothing but beauty and Collins, and the two as one, and the one was Stephen—and yet not Stephen either, but something more vast, that the mind of seven years found no name for." Seven-year-old Stephen is in love. "From now on Stephen entered a completely new world, that turned on an axis of Collins" (12). Stephen's days revolve around thinking about Collins, dressing up for Collins, searching for Collins, "who might have to be stalked to the basement," and showing off for Collins (13).

Stephen's private and passionate love for Collins ends painfully when she finds Collins and the "tall and exceedingly handsome" new footman kissing in a shed in the garden. She responds by throwing a piece of a broken pot at the footman's face and then turning and running away, crying hysterically. Her father finds her, consoles her, and fires both the poor maid and the wounded footman (23–24).

When Stephen's father gives her a pony for Christmas that year, Stephen chooses to name the pony after Collins. Hall writes, "Collins was comfortably transmigrated. It was Stephen's last effort to remember" (38). Stephen being a queer girl in a world where she does not fit, her pony Collins and later her horse Raftery become her closest, at times her only, friends, her loves.

On Love

෴ As a girl, I knew love. I knew the soft, vibrating love of my Siamese cat, Thomasina Love Tittlemouse (yes, that was the middle name I gave her at age eight or so, adding to the other two names, which my mother chose based on a Beatrix Potter character), and the gentle nudging love of my beautiful chestnut red horse, Snipaway, whom my father bought for me when I outgrew my Shetland pony. I did not merely receive love, I gave it too. I loved these animals with all my heart. I devoted myself to them and, given the opportunity or the need, very likely would have died for them. I longed to see them when away from them. I thought and dreamed and wondered about them. If I had someone human to talk to, I talked about them. When with them, I talked to them, particularly Snipaway. As things happened to me, I remember thinking about telling, planning to tell, Snip about them. I remember discussing life with him as we rode. I remember watching his red ears turn back toward me listening, then flicking forward again. I groomed and cared for these two beings. I worried ceaselessly over them.

I can remember how in my childhood I turned my attention to the matter of love, this amorphous thing that I needed so desperately and knew to be in short supply. Once, riding my bicycle on the way to my horse, I remember panicking. Perhaps I was wrong about my love for Snipaway; perhaps I was wrong about his love for me. Maybe he did not love me; maybe I did not love him. The panic, so intense, threatened to explode me into tiny parts all over that small road. I did not know what love was, could not put my finger on it or find words to describe it. But I did know that without this love that I shared, this love between my red horse and me, I could not go on. Without it, I would cease to be.

Relationships with Horses: An Alternative to Binary Gender and Heteronormativity

In what follows, I first explore counternormativity through the work of social theorist Elspeth Probyn, who theorizes the relationship between girls and horses, including her own childhood horse love. I also invoke Donna Haraway's concept of companion species, which offers an example of counternormativity. Next, I discuss my conversations with former horse-crazy girls and other research that investigates counternormative lived experiences of girls. Finally, I look at groups of girls who are in some ways outsiders to heteronormative society, including queer girls, "misfits," and girls with disabilities, whose experiences with horses offer them a place to belong.

Even in their fantasy games, horsey girls are strong and graceful because in their imagining they are on horseback or are themselves horses.[4] We see this in Finland where the fantasy horseback rider has even become a legitimate athlete with hobby-horsing, "a sport with gymnastic elements that has spawned a social media subculture among Finnish teen girls." In hobby-horsing almost ten thousand people, "nearly all of them between the ages of ten and eighteen" and most of them girls, compete in otherwise "traditional equestrian events" such as dressage and show jumping. Yet instead of a live horse, the girls ride a hobby-horse. The sport is physically strenuous (as was playing horses outside with my friends as a child). And reinforcing my claim that girls gain some of the same benefits from imaginary horses that they do from real ones, some hobby-horsers argue it is similar to being with live horses. For example, in an article in the *Finnish American Reporter*, the secretary general of the Equestrian Federation of Finland, Fred Sundwall, says, "We think it's simply wonderful that hobby-horsing has become a phenomenon and so popular. . . . It gives a chance to those children and teens who don't own horses to interact with them also outside stables and riding schools."[5]

In the lived experiences of girls, I postulate that horse love allows them to refuse gender norms like the heteronormative social demand to prioritize relationships with and desire for boys above all else. In this heteronormative ideal, girls are understood to be emotional and gentle caregivers (of boys, children, and other animals), while boys are rational, strong, and competitive (they compete to provide for girls). Ultimately, in a heteronormative society, heterosexuality is assumed to be the standard, and we are pushed into heterosexual relationships.

Heteronormative demands are everywhere—from the Disney princesses to the characters in prepubescent novels that girls read. Our society tells girls that they must desire to be part of a heterosexual, binary boy-girl (mind-body) pair. Girls get the message that this heterosexual relationship should matter more for them, as girls, than anything—more than school, more than their relationships with girlfriends and mothers and teachers, and more than the work they might do. And yet this boy-girl relationship often does not fulfill many of the things girls have been socialized to desire, like one-on-one conversations and intimate exchanges of feelings. Nor is it often equally fulfilling, equally supportive to girls as it is to boys.[6] All too often the boy-girl relationship disempowers the girls and is emotionally, physically, or sexually violent.[7]

Life can be hard for girls in the contemporary United States. Many girls live in poverty, and many can look to a life of poverty as women. On average, in 2016 women earned seventy-nine cents for every dollar earned by men,[8] and women have historically been, and continue to be, significantly more likely than men to be poor.[9] As happened with my mother raising me and my siblings after she left my father, single women with children are even more likely to be impoverished than other women. U.S. girls live surrounded by, and white girls live in white communities that perpetuate, racism. Girls live with everyday forms of sexism, homophobia, and sexual bigotry. All U.S. girls live within a social order that prioritizes profit over (human and non-human) life.

Moreover, U.S. girls face a world where sexual and other forms of gendered violence present real and everyday threats to girls and women. As radical feminists in the 1970s eloquently argued, the all-too-normal experience of gendered violence is one way that girls and women become "normal" girls and women.[10] The #MeToo movement that has blossomed in the United States and many other places starting in 2017 makes clear the ongoing reality of, and presents a challenge to, the everyday harassment and violence that women and girls face.[11]

Because violence against girls and women is so prevalent in what scholars of violence have called our rape culture,[12] I briefly explore here this normative and gendering form of violence in the United States. One example, from a plethora of research on gendered violence, comes from the Rape, Abuse & Incest National Network (RAINN), an organization that works to stop sexual violence and support survivors of such violence. RAINN reports that "one out of every six American women has been the victim of an attempted or completed rape in her lifetime." In their book on rape in the United States, Emilie Buchwald, Pamela R. Fletcher, and Martha Roth cite a statistic from the time period during which I grew up, writing that even the relatively conservative FBI's Uniform Crime Report data reported "1.5 million female survivors of forcible rape or forcible rape attempts in this country" between 1972 and 1991. This, they clarify, was the most moderate number "available and should be considered the baseline or minimum rape figure." For generally the same time period, the National Crime Victimization Survey, the largest nationally representative crime survey in the United States, records the much higher number of "2.3 million rapes of females during the time period of 1973 to 1987."[13]

As reporting has changed, the numbers of such violent and gendered crime have risen over the most recent decades.[14] The Centers for Disease Control and Prevention's nationally representative survey of adults found that "1 in 5 (18.3%) women and 1 in 71 men (1.4%) reported experiencing rape at some time in their lives." Many of the rapes happened during girlhood, as

"42.2% of female rape victims were first raped before age 18."[15] Addressing other forms of gendered violence in 2017, the National Coalition Against Domestic Violence claims that one in three women "have been physically abused by an intimate partner." Many girls, as I did, face gendered violence in their homes, the places they live and grow and develop.

In my own childhood, perhaps an example from the edge of the continuum of human experiences involving everyday intimate violence, I lived in a state of normalized fear. Neither home nor school felt safe. At home, violence periodically burst through the day-to-day, taking me hostage, sweeping me away. I never knew when or where the violence might appear: in our garage where my drunken father killed my little sister's cat, in our bedroom at home where she and I were sexually assaulted, taken as a small child from my grandfather's home to his Ku Klux Klan meeting. The feeling of being afraid was for me the norm, the baseline from which all other feeling experiences developed.

My horse was my refuge. With him, I was safe, with him I could be. And so with him, I became something that refused the sharply gendered binary frame that was the rest of my life, a girl-life outside of my horse that was, at times, not a life worth living.

She Just Loved Horses

Reflecting this girl-horse love relationship in the pony book genre, Alison Haymonds writes, "Pony stories are, after all, love stories—girl meets pony, girl loses pony, girl gets pony."[16] Indeed, Michael Korda claims that parents actively use horses and ponies as a way to keep their daughters away from boys. Korda writes that "somewhere back in the minds of most parents even today" is the thought that "the longer you can keep a girl interested in horses, the longer you can put off the moment when she starts being interested in boys." Korda elaborates, "From that point of view, encouraging a girl's interest in riding early on can be seen as a prudent step, if it accomplishes nothing more than keeping her away from boys for a crucial year or two of her adolescence." Aside from the issue of gendered violence, here we see the double standard around sexuality. Boys are supposed to be sexual and desire sex. Girls are not. Nowhere does Korda mention that horses might keep boys away from the girls who desire boys sexually. Implicit in this (solidly heteronormative) thinking is the idea that boys' sexual desire is good for boys but dangerous to girls. We do not worry about girls' sexual desire for boys. We assume that girls want to caregive (horses in this case) but do not actively seek out opportunities to be sexual. We assume that boys want sex but do not want to caregive (horses or anyone). And of course in this heterosexist framework, no one worries about keeping girls (and their sexual desire for other girls) away from girls.[17]

Heteronormative parents and their worries aside, horse-crazy girls find other ways to become, and other ways to, as Probyn writes, "be-long." Probyn explains, "Within popular culture this generalized coupling of girls and horses ('pony mad') then operates in opposition to that of girls and boys ('boy crazy')."[18] Again and again, the women I spoke with told me that they "just loved horses." That explanation seemed enough to explain their ongoing and profound childhood passion. Reflecting this, the American Horse Publication Equine Industry Survey also revealed the profoundly intimate relationship that many humans have with their horses: "Respondents were most likely to view their horses as family members (67.4%), companion animals (62.7%), performance partners (57.6%) and/or best friends (55.9%)."[19]

Probyn describes an advertisement by Nike depicting the opposition between horse-crazy and boy-crazy girls. "The eight-page advertisement for athletic shoes tells the teleological narrative of women moving from girlish indecision to mature choice. . . . [T]he ad text goes from equine images ('you wanted to own a horse/you wanted to be a horse') to images of girl-girl friendship (finding a 'best friend'), and to the loss of the best friend when 'you' become a 'steady girlfriend.'"[20]

Instead of the focus of life being on becoming a girlfriend to a boy and living a heteronormative fairy tale, Probyn argues that horse-crazy girls find alternative ways to have identity, but more than identity, alternative ways to "become," alternative ways to be "caught up in the process of wanting to be." About this process, this way of being that she calls be-longing, Probyn clarifies,

> I want to briefly outline a model of thinking identity through singular images of desire. While identity can be seen to stand in for any number of terms—sexual identity, sexual preference, sexual orientation or choice—what I am primarily interested in are issues of "be-longing." In fact, I find the term "identity" rather staid; "be-longing" may be kitsch, but it captures for me some of the movement of

desire, longing, nostalgia, and sheer "being" caught up in the process of wanting to be. (23)

There is a lack of boys in horse worlds, a lack present in the actual stables and riding communities where girls go to find horses, and, to some extent, in the whole popular culture of horses. Probyn writes, "From the pony-club stories and experiences of my youth, I can only remember girls and girls together with horses and not a boy to be seen." Yet these friendships are more than mere freedom from boys, more than a movement away from heteronormativity. They are also relationships where girls experience, as Probyn writes (above), "the movement of desire" and "sheer 'being' caught up in the process of wanting to be."

Referring to the Nike advertisement, Probyn writes, "The line about owning/being a horse vividly recalls for me the image of how girls get together with girls around horses and of how my best friend and I seemingly consciously chose each other and our ponies over boys" (23). One lesbian woman and former horse-crazy girl whom I spoke with described her and her lesbian friends as disproportionately interested in horses. She believed more queer girls are horse crazy than heterosexual girls. When I asked Sonya, who participated in my study and is lesbian, what she thought about this, she said, "I think that there might be something to the notion of girls being interested in riding who are interested in being independent and having a sense of themselves and not adhering to gender roles."[21] Gwen, a lesbian woman in her seventies, agreed with this idea. She argued that "normative girls don't quite fit in a horsey world. A girl has to be a little different, a little tough or something" to be involved with horses.[22]

In this relationship, girls often lead as they become together with their horses. And their girl-horse relationships support their becoming.[23] Probyn asserts, "[I]mages of girls and girls and horses have no essence, no fixed reference. . . . [T]hey can, however, express longing; they do throw us forward into other relations of becoming. For example, in a poem by Ruthann Robson, an image of a 'stampede of wild horses' throws the narrator forward into a realization 'that what you want is to become.'"[24] As quoted in chapter 4, in her children's book, *The Magic Pony*, Patricia Leitch describes this "relation of becoming" and a girl's experience of oneness with her pony, Shantih. Leitch describes Jinny riding Shantih across the moors in the United Kingdom, leaping ancient dry stone walls as they ran. Jinny experiences profound joy "in this flying freedom," joy that "sang through Jinny's whole being." On her Arab mare, Leitch writes, Jinny rode "entranced" as her pony Shantih became "part of her."[25]

Like the relationships described by the women I interviewed, the bond between Jinny and Shantih, and between the ponies and girls described by Probyn, resonates with Haraway's concept of "companion species." Haraway explores relationships between humans and dogs that are in some ways similar to that between horses and girls. She writes, "Living with animals, inhabiting their/our stories, trying to tell the truth about relationship, co-habiting an active history: that is the work of companion species, for whom 'the relation' is the smallest possible unit of analysis."[26] In other words, the smallest unit of analysis in that relationship is neither the human nor the dog but the human-and-dog. Following Haraway, we can see how girl and horse, as companion species, together become a single unit of analysis, co-becoming in culture and history. Love is at the heart of the story.

Haraway does not romanticize the love between humans and nonhuman animals. Nonhuman animals like dogs do not, she clarifies, love "unconditionally." Nor are nonhuman animals the "children" of humans. Haraway writes, "[B]oth of these beliefs are not only based on mistakes, if not lies, but always they are in themselves abusive—to dogs and to humans" (33). These mistaken ways of understanding human and dog love, and human and horse love, are profoundly binary. Just as humans and animals are not on opposite sides of a binary split, their loves are not all or nothing; they are neither simple nor perfectly clear. Like all loves, they are untidy, even chaotic; they are bound up in the gritty nature of day-to-day life.[27] "Receiving unconditional love from another," Haraway argues, "is a rarely excusable neurotic fantasy; striving to fulfill the messy conditions of being in love is quite another matter." Haraway writes, "The permanent search for knowledge of the intimate other, and the inevitable comic and tragic mistakes in that quest, commands my respect, whether the other is animal or human."[28] Echoing Haraway is one former horse-crazy girl I interviewed named Ruth, a woman in her late seventies who still rides. She explained that being with horses has pushed her to work toward understanding "reality from somebody else's point of view," that is to say the point of view of the horse.[29]

Yet, Haraway argues, love is not all there is to the story. Both horses and girls pull history and culture into their relationships; they alter history, and they shape culture. In particular, the relationship of girls to horses simultaneously informs, reinforces, and subverts gender norms. Several women used a term from gender-normalizing culture, "I was a tomboy," as they explained their childhood love of horses. Horses were a place where their challenge to girly culture could be expressed.

As discussed in chapter 5, horse love can also be normalized as an aspect of the "natural," as when girls and women describe themselves, and popular literature describes them, as having a "natural female instinct" that makes females better able to interact with, train, and connect with horses that, in this binary schema, are also "natural" and of the body. (In this binary split, males are associated with science and the rational mind.) Yet in the lived reality of girls, horse love allows them to refuse gender norms, like the heteronormative social demands that they prioritize relationship with and desire for boys above all else. Horsey girls prioritize horses. About this, Haraway employs a term ordinarily used to describe romantic human relationships, "significant others." And indeed, horses and girls are just that, they are significant others.

Many of the women I spoke with described their strong commitments to and with their horse partners. One woman described her (also horse-crazy) daughter, Lauren, a very talented and highly competitive rider, who had the potential to compete and win with many horses. Yet when Lauren's own horse was injured, she chose to stop competing rather than compete without him. She waited for him to recover before going back to showing. As significant others, their showing together was a partnership. Lauren's waiting for her horse to heal enacted Haraway's concept. Lauren's mother and her grandmother were also horse-crazy girls. Lauren's mother, Penelope, described summertimes when her parents leased a horse for her for the summer. At the end of the summer, Penelope had to return the horse to its owner, and albeit having lasted only a couple of months, Penelope spoke poignantly of the pain and upset she would feel saying goodbye.[30]

Girl-Horse Oneness

Like relationships with romantic significant others, girl-horse relationships are in large part lived through bodies, and body-on-body connections that are grounded in physiology. Korda discusses oneness as a goal that good horseback riders have for their riding. He writes, "The aim of riders everywhere is to maintain control of the horse with the bare minimum of effort and force, and to do so gracefully, harmoniously, and within the limits of the possible, with the horse's full cooperation."[31] Korda describes his spouse Margaret on her horse Nebraska:

> Nebraska would make any rider look good, but with Margaret aboard she seemed to skim over the ground effortlessly, so responsive that it was as if she were reading Margaret's thoughts rather than responding to a signal.
>
> And perhaps she was, at that. I'm not a skeptic when it comes to that kind of communication between animal and person, and in fact there is a level of riding that's only possible if horse and rider are communicating mentally. (285)

One way this merging of horse and girl—which I experienced, and have heard other women describe—might happen is in the mutual release of a hormone called oxytocin, a biological response to touch in mammals.[32] About her experience of horseback riding, Ruth explained to me, "It is a physicality. But the feeling also opened up other things, the impact of a motion. You know, the oxytocin. You know, the movement, which opens up the oxytocin, the touching, which has an impact. So all those things, you know, which were not part of my life were suddenly opened up. [My] body began to feel."[33]

Oxytocin plays a critical role for humans and other mammals in giving birth, lactation, and orgasm. In *Boundaries of Touch,* I discuss the role of oxytocin in breastfeeding. When breastfeeding mothers see their hungry infants or hear them cry, they will experience a rush of oxytocin in their systems that signals to their bodies to let down the milk in their breasts so that the infant can nurse. Oxytocin makes breastfeeding humans feel calmer and happier. Both sex and giving birth also involve oxytocin, and so does mere gentle physical contact between humans. In other words, physical contact, touch, is powerful; it can elicit oxytocin. And studies increasingly show that we need it, touch, to grow and develop as children and to survive and thrive as adults. About the hormonal response that touch can evoke, Meg Daley Olmert writes, "Oxytocin lowers heart rate and stress hormones." She claims, "It makes people more trusting and trustworthy. It can even relieve some of the antisocial tendencies of autistics."[34]

Touch is powerful between humans, and it is powerful between different (and among other) species. There is a growing literature on the biomedical impact of human contact with nonhuman animals and the role of oxytocin. We do not have to touch or be touched by other *humans* to experience benefits of oxytocin. As Ruth indicates above, physical contact with nonhuman animals can also elicit oxytocin in both of those involved, human and nonhuman. Indeed, not only touch but other kinds of friendly, loving exchanges between (human and other) animals can prompt a flood of oxytocin in the animals involved.[35]

Our contact with other animals, human and nonhuman, physical and visual, impacts on us. And for humans, studies show that our contact with nonhuman animals can be as powerful if not more powerful than our contact with other humans. In one late 1970s study, done at the University of Maryland on "the survival effects of human social support on heart patients," the researchers found that above and beyond human support, "pet ownership made the biggest difference in who survived and who didn't." Erica Friedmann had been part of the research team as a postgraduate student. Friedmann decided to repeat the study in 1995 with 369 patients.

> This time she found that dog ownership was the big survival factor in the first year following a heart attack. Of the eighty-seven subjects who owned dogs, only one died; nineteen of the non-dog-owning patients did. When weighed against the other top survival factors (strength of heart, absence of diabetes, and regularity of heartbeat), owning a dog gave a heart attack victim a significantly greater chance of being alive one year later.[36]

Horses offer humans some of the same benefits that dogs do. And in part, this is why horses and horseback riding are used as therapy for a wide range of conditions, including developmental, physical, and psychiatric disabilities like mine. Research indicates that contact with horses helps calm anxious humans, focuses and connects humans limited in their abilities to engage socially, and develops the physical capacities of humans with physical limitations. Some argue that the primary benefit for humans in being with horses (and other animals) is the increase in our level of oxytocin. Indeed, both the humans *and* the horses seem to experience this increase of oxytocin in their systems from humans merely being in the presence of horses, but more particularly through the physical contact of stroking, grooming, and riding horses.

Jean, the hero in Christine Pullein-Thompson's *Phantom Horse* series, who had been worried and upset about her family's pending move, describes the peace and joy that came to her while grooming her horse. "I groomed Phantom that evening until his tail was like cream silk and his coat gleamed like gold. I oiled his elegant two-coloured hoofs and imagined myself riding him down the lane to Sparrow Cottage, and suddenly I felt happier than I had ever felt before."[37] Ultimately, the becoming of girls-with-horses happens in bodies, bodies in contact with bodies.[38]

Before she started riding, Ruth, mentioned above, said, "I was not very aware of my body." Riding opened "another side" of her.[39] In my interviews, to some extent this body connection between girls and horses came out in an *absence* of words, or a limit to the words women offered. Often the words did not adequately cover the emotion in the voice of the woman who was speaking. At times, the woman cried and the words did not fully explain why. Nor did the words fully justify the extensive time the women had given and many were still giving to horses. Many of the women themselves said that they could not explain the love. They did not have words for it. When I asked one woman why she loved her horse, she said, "If you need to ask, you don't understand."

I myself had trouble explaining why I loved my horse, why I spent hours with him in freezing cold Montana weather, grooming and riding him; why I rode my bicycle twelve miles round trip in the summer sun to be with him every day of summer vacation; why I spent my weekend nights bussing tables at a local restaurant so that I could afford to keep him. I too had trouble finding the words to explain and describe and write about this love.

I argue that this struggle itself, this struggle to find words, offers insight. If my relationship with my horse was not mutual in spoken language, it was in physicality. I did spend hours talking, talking, talking to him. Yet our mutual conversations, and of course his responses to me, had little to do with the English language.

⮑ We spoke back and forth to each other through a leg squeeze, a turn of chestnut red ear going back and then forward, a nicker and nuzzle, a humph sound. I clicked to my horse and he trotted forward. I laid my head backward on his rump and watched the sky; he slowed down, grabbed a quick bite of grass. The tension I lived with, gripping the muscles of my body, most days, most of the time, relaxed a little. I breathed deeply and, even for moments, shut my eyes. My relationship with him was corporal. And it went beyond my body simply being next to or on top of his body. In some strange way, our bodies merged, and in my experience, his became an extension of mine, and I an extension of him.

In *The Well of Loneliness*, Hall describes a similar love between her queer character, Stephen Gordon, and Stephen's beloved horse, Raftery. When Stephen Gordon's father, Sir Philip, gives Stephen her horse, Raftery, "a real thoroughbred hunter," it was "love at first sight." Hall explained,

> [T]hey talked to each other for hours in his loose box—not in Irish or English, but in a quiet language having very few words but many small sounds and many small movements, which to both of them meant more than words. And Raftery said: "I will carry you bravely, I will serve you all the days of my life." And she answered: "I will care for you night and day, Raftery—all the days of your life." Thus Stephen and Raftery pledged their devotion, alone in his fragrant, hay-scented stable. And Raftery was five and Stephen was twelve when they solemnly pledged their devotion.[40]

Healing and Horses

Horse relationships can bring a sense of peace. When I was a teenager, my mother once commented about how calm I always was when I came back from riding my horse. She noted that even if I was extremely upset when I left to go riding, I always came back tranquil and centered. We knew nothing about oxytocin, but in retrospect my mother's reflection probably speaks in some way to the power of this hormone and its role in horse-girl love. In a *New York Times* article, Alia Volz describes her ongoing experience of peace while riding horses. Her mother, a single parent like mine, managed to buy her daughter and help her keep a horse, "a scrappy pinto named Tango." Volz writes, "Maintaining a horse habit was no easy feat for a single parent with an iffy income. We were always broke. 'Well,' my mom would say, 'it's cheaper than a lifetime of therapy.'" Finding a way to ride as an adult by volunteering, Volz writes,

> They say that if you do what you love, you'll never work a day in your life. During the two decades I didn't ride, every day felt like work. But when I began donating

Thursday afternoons to the Mounted Patrol, it felt like coming home to myself. . . . All these years later, Mom is still right: My weekly sessions with the Mounted Patrol horses do more for my peace of mind than any shrink could.[41]

These strong horsey relationships are counternormative, a challenge and an alternative to the type of relationships girls are supposed to have. Grounded in bodies, relationships with horses offer girls a different and more empowering way to be embodied than heteronormative culture—with its all-too-common obsession with thinness and normalized experience of sexual violence. Jenny, a participant in my study discussed in earlier chapters, said that even as little girls, she and her sister "had a sense of the lurking violence of masculinity."[42] This girl had spent eight years, from around the ages of six to fourteen, obsessed with horses. She did not own a horse and only rarely had the opportunity to ride, but she filled up her childhood with fantasy games involving horses and reading books about horses. Jenny talked about her own and other girls' passion for horses and the many fantasy games they played, games in which the girls played heroic, powerful, and central roles. Those games, she claimed, helped girls to manage, to handle, the "lurking violence of masculinity." The girls borrowed from the power of the imaginary horses, gaining strength and speed and grace. About her, her sister, and her girlfriends' fantasy horse play, she mused, "Maybe that's one way of dealing with it. I mean . . . that whole imagination. Because I think of it now in very concrete terms, I mean masculinity is, there is something really wrong with it."

In horse worlds, along with freedom from the male gaze, girls also gain some freedom from actual boys and men. Horse worlds are places socially marked as female and often dominated by girls. Boys and men are rare. As in an all-girls school, girls in horse worlds gain liberty from the normative pressure to compete for the attention of boys. Girls can focus on being seen as actors and good with horses instead of objects, thin, beautiful, sexy, and attractive to boys. About this, psychologist Delphi M. Toth writes:

The adolescent girl brings more emotional needs to her relationship with a horse. She is feeling normal age-related insecurities, emotional turmoil, self-doubt, and intense self-consciousness. Her relationship with her horse is a contrast to the hypercritical world of adolescence and high school. She and her horse form a tiny clique characterized by unconditional and noncritical acceptance. The girl who feels unattractive, awkward, and unsure of herself becomes empowered and protected when with her beautiful, graceful, and sure-footed equine friend.[43]

Horses heal girls. In contrast to the wild beast, the male, tamed by a (beautiful) female in George Gilder's cautionary Beauty and the Beast tale (discussed in chapter 5), horses as beasts also tame, or rather "heal," girls in the stories and in the self-understanding of the former horse-crazy girls with whom I spoke. In the fictional books and in my interviews, women insist, as though they expect opposition, that their girlhood relationships with horses are powerful, profound, and mutual, such as one might expect with a very close friend. And they assert that the horses in their lives helped them to learn, challenged their shut-downness, pushed them to face their feelings, made them more self- and other-aware, and made them better riders and better human beings.

One woman with a disability posted the following question on Facebook. She included a close-up photograph of a horse's face: "Has a horse helped you heal? Please add his/her name to our Healers Honor Roll." In words printed over the photograph, she claimed that horses sense our emotions, even those we work to hide, and "do not judge" us; "they accept us as we are and help us to heal."[44] Another woman, Joanne Tortorici Luna, expresses this in the title of her article about her experience of becoming horse crazy, "The Horse, My Healer and Guide."[45] Luna writes about the time she spends with horses, "Lucky me, I get to spend time with my equine buddies who every day teach me what it means to be more authentic, more focused, stronger, more playful, more supportive, and congruent. Becoming more like a horse, I have become a better human" (22). Indeed, Luna writes about horses' "seemingly uncanny capacity to perceive and reflect a person's internal state, kind of like living biofeedback." Sounding very similar to the descriptions many girls and women might offer about a good friend, Luna says, "A horse will tell you if you are being patronizing, pushy, wimpy, or mean. If you are smiling on the outside and crying on the inside, you can count on the horse to let you know about it" (20).

Relationships with horses are primary or "significant other" relationships in many horse-crazy girls' lives. Christine Pullein-Thompson depicts this repeatedly through her character Jean, mentioned above, in her series about Phantom, Jean's formerly wild horse. For example, in one of the novels, *Phantom Horse in Danger* (1980), Jean is trying to save her horse from being sold to a slaughterhouse by a rich white criminal man, Geoff Craig, who made his wealth selling stolen and other horses for meat. Jean thinks, "This time tomorrow it will all be over.... Either we will have saved our horses or they will be dead." And she says, "I imagined life without Phantom and it felt as empty as a deserted building and just as pointless."[46]

In our heteronormative society, boys and girls are socialized to be in relationships in very different ways, and yet they are required to be romantic partners together. Boys are socialized to interact through group activities like sports and to avoid conversations about personal and intimate experiences. In contrast, girls are socialized to interact in pairs and to discuss their emotions and how they feel.[47] Given this very different socialization despite the demand for heteronormative relationships, some of the women I spoke with found the kind of connections they have been socialized to desire with animals, and in particular with horses.

When I asked the women I interviewed if their childhood horse was their friend,[48] all responded yes, and often with emphasis, like the participant who said: "I have ridden many different horses in my life, from a Welsh pony named Kelly, to a standardbred named Donna, a quarter horse named Lucky and even a Percheron named Sam. I considered all those horses my best friends. Particularly Donna the standardbred. She was my 'heart horse.'"[49]

One woman shared a childhood poem, entitled "Red and I," that she had written at age eleven about her beloved horse, Red.

> You and I are best friends
> Our love will never end
> Our hearts are mended in soft thread
> We share days and nights together
> All in different types of weather
> Our love will never end
> 'Cause we both live in thought
> A year ago today we met
> When I saw you I didn't fret
> You're the best gift I can ever have
> We will live together all our lives
> One day we'll be united in Heaven
> Our hearts will be woven together.[50]

(White) Girls on the Margins

Horse-crazy girls find meaning in their relationships with horses. Many of the women with whom I spoke described difficulties making human friends as girls. Only one of them was part of the "popular crowd" growing up. As one former horse-crazy girl put it, they were "misfits." Many were shy. As an only child growing up in a small town, Korda explains about his wife, Margaret, that her pony was "not only a friend, but a *best* friend."[51] Christine Pullein-Thompson's Jean character has trouble making friends because her family moved so frequently that her "local friends had disappeared, or made other friends." At one of the (many) times her horse Phantom was in danger, Jean "tried to imagine the future without Phantom. What would I do? How would I spend my weekends? I had no close friends. . . . But it had not mattered because I had had Phantom."[52]

Several women described themselves as introverted. Some felt they were outcasts and struggled with connecting to other humans. Some were lesbian and unable or unwilling to become "boy crazy," as our heteronormative culture demands of girls. Some called themselves "tomboys." Bella simply wanted to be a boy. She wanted the power and freedom and adventure that being a boy made possible. Six women had disability and in this found themselves limited by or marginalized from some aspects of normative culture. Four of the women with disability rode horses for horse therapy.

Through horses, these horse-crazy girls gained love, connection, and power. Those who used wheelchairs gained mobility and height. On a horse, they looked down, instead of up, at everyone else. Ultimately, in horses, girls gained a friend, a trustworthy and constant friend. These relationships, like those with good human friends, in large part lacked instrumentality. The relationships mattered for their own sake, and not merely for some end the girls attained through the relationships, such as winning competitions or strengthening their bodies.

In my study, the older generation of horse-crazy girls, in particular, was more likely to broadly challenge gender norms and heteronormativity. Six of these eight older women were among those who described themselves as "tomboys." Four of the women in the older generation identified as lesbian; one more had been in a long-term lesbian relationship. For all these women as girls, horses offered connection and intimacy, a place where they fit in and a sense of identity.

An older lesbian with no children and currently single, Gwen, eloquently described the connection she felt with horses. In our brief, forty-minute conversation, Gwen started to cry three times as she explained what horses mean to her. She claimed that horses see her for who she is, they understand her. Gwen told me that she rarely experienced this kind of connection with other humans, particularly when she was a child. About horses, she said, "They get me and I get them." In this deep intimacy, she claimed, "They can see inside me and I can see inside them."[53]

Gwen said that she was very shy and isolated as a child, and she had a very troubled family life. She had few connections outside of her relationships with horses. As in my own experience, Gwen told me that she might not have made it through her childhood if not for her intimacy with horses. These relationships went beyond understanding for Gwen. With horses she experienced a profound and mutual sense of trust, something that she did not really have with other humans. Again and again, women like Gwen told me of the powerful and "healing" connections they had, and in many cases continue to have, with horses. This language cut across generations.

I understand this insistence on both the depth of connection and on the language of healing, as a claim to an alternative normalcy, to a world that is both real and distinct from the normative world where girls also have to function. In a larger culture where girls do have less power as girls—less power than women, less power than boys, and of course less power than men—the world of horses is a place where they gain both belonging and power. With horses and other horsey girls, they fit, and even more, they lead. They lead their horse partners, and they work *with* them. In horseback riding, girls make decisions: to ride or not to ride, where to ride and how fast or how slow, which way and when they turn, how much time they spend grooming, and so on. With horses, girls gain a kind of power that they have limited opportunity to achieve anywhere else.

Almost all the horse-crazy girls that I spoke with described themselves as animal lovers. Many currently had what they described as intimate relationships with nonhorse animals past and present. Gwen told me about two beloved dogs, one deceased, the other with her as we spoke. During our interview, Donna had a cat resting on her lap and had many close relationships with other/nonhuman animals. Several women were involved in animal rescue work, including horse rescue and, in the case of Kathleen, fostering homeless dogs and cats. These women described intense and embodied relationships with animals, mutual relationships that they called friendships and described as familial, in language reminiscent of that used by queer "chosen families." Gwen described the closeness she has felt with individual horses over the years. She volunteered for a time at a riding stable in Manhattan that closed down in the early twenty-first century. She cried when she remembered saying goodbye to one particular horse at the stable, an elderly gelding. She thought it likely that he would be sent to a slaughterhouse. Gwen describes standing with the horse in his stall on the last day before the stable closed. She stood with him in the dark as the stable's lights were turned off for the last time, and he rested his muzzle against her in the silence. Gwen loved, and felt deeply loved by, this old and dignified horse.

Many women spoke about the love they felt from their animals and, in particular, from their horses. To help me understand how this love happens, they offered me examples of the animals' behavior. Donna, in her twenties, described her horse's response whenever she had to go to the hospital for brain surgery. (Due to her hydrocephalus, she has endured multiple brain surgeries.) Donna's horse would become so distraught he would stop eating. Her most recent hospitalization lasted ten days. Her horse's caregiver had to hold a telephone to the horse's ear, with Donna speaking to him from her hospital bed, so that he would hear Donna's voice and calm down.

It is hard to know what love is. When we recognize love, see it or feel it, what do we recognize? It is hard to know love between animals, between nonhuman animals and human animals, and also between human animals and other humans. In my study of ways of thinking about touching children, scientists like John B. Watson and Harry Harlow again and again equated love with touch, physical contact, because they had no way to know if *love* was what they saw happening between infants and parents. It is hard to know love. Yet many of us feel sure of our own experience of love for another. And many argue that they feel sure of the love of other beings, be they adult human or dog, infant human or horse.[54]

Horses are herd animals and usually do not like to be without other horses. Like humans, they also develop particular and close relationships, and they worry and fuss when separated from one another. Is this love? Chuck Culpepper, in a recent *Washington Post* article, wrote of what humans understood to be the love shared between two racehorses, Simonsig, "a very, very shy horse," and Triolo D'Alene, "a genuinely nice person as a horse," both male, both geldings. Shortly after encountering each other, the two became "inseparable." Culpepper wrote, about the humans caring for this pair, that they had never before "seen quite this level of inseparable." A human caregiver, Tracy Vigors, said that the horses were "very much bestie-mates. . . . They would stand together, eat together, walk together, trough together, eat out of the same manger." These two would "rest heads across each other, scratch each other's backs, share the food pot." Eventually their human caregivers even allowed the pair to share a stall, a rare treat for finan-cially valuable animals, whose humans do not want them hurt. In the case of Simonsig and Triolo D'Alene, "you knew they weren't going to kick each other," trainer Nicky Henderson said. If humans took one of the two horses away, "the other fretted unmistakably." Henderson noted, "So what you'd call Triolo and Simonsig, I don't know, but it was two boys that fell in love with each other."[55]

(Dis)ability and Horses

People with disability are marginalized on multiple fronts in our culture. Every human being lives on a continuum of ability. Yet binary mainstream culture frames us as either "normal" and able-bodied or "abnormal" and with disability. Disability studies doctoral student Danielle Lucchese explains that because she was born with hydrocephalus and has visual impairment and "balance issues," she is understood to be disabled and not "normal." Lucchese claims, "One's body either conforms to society's perception of normal and able, or it does not." People with disability challenge, and often experience marginalization in, (hetero)normative culture not only in terms of the able-bodiedness but also in terms of their sexuality.[56] As both Lucchese and cultural theorist Robert McRuer argue, having disability is often understood to mean *not* having sexuality. McRuer writes that disabled people are "com-monly positioned as asexual—incapable of or uninterested in sex."[57] Activist Anne Finger wrote about this marginalization of those with disability, "Sexuality is often the source of our deepest oppression; it is also often the source of our deepest pain. It's easier to talk about and formulate strategies for changing discrimination in employment, education, and housing than it is to talk about our exclusion from sexuality and reproduction."[58]

For girls with disability, like me with my trauma history, and like other girls who experience marginalization in our heteronormative society, horses offer a relationship within which one belongs. Indeed, because of the profound connectedness that some people experience with horses, as discussed above, in the United States horses are increasingly used in various kinds of therapy for a wide range of disabilities.[59] Four of the former horse-crazy girls that I interviewed rode horses as girls, in part, as therapy. A fifth former horse-crazy girl, Rosemary, in her seventies, took part as an adult in horse therapy, hippotherapy, for her physical disability. I also spoke with a mother of a girl who has disability and is horse crazy, who took part in both hippotherapy and equine-facilitated psychotherapy (EFP) at a summer camp each summer. Finally, to further explore horse therapy, I visited a southwestern horse therapy organization, Challenge New Mexico, just outside of Santa Fe.[60]

Formal horse therapy usually takes one of two forms, hippotherapy and equine-facilitated psychotherapy. Medical anthropologists Dona Lee Davis and colleagues define hippotherapy as "therapeutic horse-riding for people with physical or emotional disabilities."[61] Formal hippotherapy is often "conducted under the supervision of an occupational, physical, or speech therapist who is specifically trained to use the movement of the horse to facilitate improvements such as balance, coordination, and fine motor skills in the patient/client." Davis and colleagues write that equine-facilitated psychotherapy often involves "a legally credentialed mental health practitioner or therapist and is used for patients/clients who have issues associated with anger control, self-esteem, trust, empathy, and communication" (302).

I support Davis and colleagues in their argument for a more inclusive way of understanding horse therapy as something that can happen for humans without the formal assistance of (human) professional healers. They make a case for understandings of horse therapy that include broader forms and methods of healing, and against "rigid distinctions between popular/recreational and professional/therapeutic riding." In one study, they interview fifty-two women equestrians, all amateur or recreational, many of whom, like Volz above, repeatedly refer to their own recreational horseback riding, and time with horses, as therapeutic. These informants often refer to their horse as their therapist and recreational horseback riding as a therapeutic alternative to the biomedical model of psychotherapy. In other words, in contrast to traditional psychotherapy with a human psychotherapist, these women ride and spend time with horses. For example, one of their informants, Krusty, said in an interview, "Riding is something I love. It keeps me sane" (303). Another, Agnes, said about riding, "It's therapeutic." A third, JZ, explained, "Riding is my life, long and short of it. It is joy. It is therapy" (301).

The women, the former horse-crazy girls, whom I spoke with, perhaps because they were speaking about themselves as children, were less likely to use terms like "therapy." Yet many of them talked about horses and horseback riding as having gotten them through their childhoods, particularly those like me who had very difficult childhoods. Even when they did not make overt references to therapy, the women that Davis and colleagues interviewed related "horse-human relationships to the maintenance of well-being and everyday coping" (301).

The Professional Association of Therapeutic Horsemanship (PATH), founded in 1969, claims on its website that it "changes and enriches lives by promoting excellence in equine-assisted activities and therapies." Using many numbers to emphasize their claims, the PATH website asserts, "With nearly 4,500 certified instructors and equine specialists and 850 member centers around the globe, more than 7,500 PATH Intl. members help more than 54,000 children and adults with physical, mental and emotional challenges find strength and independence through the power of the horse each year." The website, like the committed and kind Challenge New Mexico staff, is a little vague as to how exactly it changes and enriches lives, and even more vague about exactly whom they help. The website states, "[M]embers, instructors and centers serve participants of all ages and with a range of physical, emotional, behavioral and cognitive challenges. Not all PATH Intl. instructors or programs serve every population, but the following is a very short list of conditions and challenges helped every day through PATH Intl. and EAAT [Equine-Assisted Activities and Therapies]." The "very short" list of twenty-four conditions ranges broadly and includes hyperactivity disorder, paralysis, substance abuse, visual and auditory impairment, and weight control disorders.

I wonder if the details—as to whom, with what disability, and how exactly horseback riding helps—matter. I loved that during my time visiting Challenge New Mexico, I was not sure who had and who did not have a disability. No one was reduced to her, his, or their disability, everyone was included, and each person seemed to take ownership of the place and its work.

When I arrived at Challenge New Mexico, someone introduced me to everyone there, literally everyone standing around or working or talking. Each one mattered, each merited introduction. And I as a visitor mattered too. Almost immediately following the introductions, someone else pointed me to the tack shed and instructed me to pick up a brush. And I, again like everyone else—volunteers, clients, and the director—took an active part in grooming, tacking up, and caring for the horses. Almost everyone (including all three volunteers) had a chance to ride.

Along with the physical contact and through increased levels of oxytocin, perhaps the program of getting people (clients with disability and volunteers who may or may not have disability) outdoors and exercising, around gentle animals, and in contact with other humans who like animals might simply be a good thing for most humans, those of us with and those of us with no known disability. Perhaps these are the central healing forces of horse therapy.

Ultimately, people with disability are more likely to live in poverty, and poverty tends to limit access to horses. Therefore, at the very least, programs like Challenge New Mexico make horses and horsey community more available to people who could not otherwise afford them. Maybe the full social situation—touching, smelling, seeing, and hearing horses; humans and horses being outdoors all together—offers healing. At the very least, horsey relationships bring love, connection, and greater power to the human girls and women in these relationships.

Additional benefits of horse therapy include developing one's abilities, physical exercise, oxytocin, and emotional regulation. In person, as on the website, the people at Challenge New Mexico claim that horses help people with physical, psychiatric, and developmental disabilities to grow and to gain greater ability. For example, they claim that horses help people like me suffering from post-traumatic stress disorder to recover and gain greater freedom from their symptoms. The four women with physical disabilities that I interviewed claimed horse therapy offered them the opportunity to be, as Donna said, "the same as everyone else."[62] Off horseback, Donna's hydrocephalus caused her to have trouble balancing, standing, and walking. On horseback, not only could she balance and easily move about, she became an internationally competitive horseback rider. Everything everyone else can do on horseback, she can do too. Indeed, compared to most of us, she can do it better. This leveling or equalizing of ability happens for women in general on horseback. As discussed in chapter 5, horseback riding is unique as a sport in which women can compete equally with men. As Josephine Pullein-Thompson said in an interview, "I think the reason horses appeal so much to girls is that when they are on horseback girls are absolutely equal, in fact in a lot of ways they are better."[63]

Corroborating my findings, two of the competitive riders with disability whom Katherine Dashper interviewed told her that when they ride, they are "not really different" from those without disability. Dashper writes about these two women, "Natalie relates with pride the fact that most people watching her ride 'just don't notice the disability' and that she attended a horse show for two years and the judge never noticed her impairment in all that time. Both of these young disabled women express pride in their ability to conceal their impairments, particularly when they are competing in an able-bodied environment."[64]

There are of course limits to the sameness a person with disability experiences on horseback. Shannon, whom I interviewed, herself a former horse-crazy girl and the mother of an eleven-year-old girl named Rose who has hydrocephalus, explained that Rose "was born horse crazy." When she was a newborn infant in the hospital, because of her condition, "they were not sure if she was going to be able to come home." Shannon said that Rose's father whispered in Rose's ear, "If you come home, I'll buy you a pony." Shannon laughed and said that her daughter's "love of horses was in her blood." To fulfill the promise, when the baby came home from the hospital, her parents gave her a toy pony, the only kind they could afford.[65]

Like most of the women I spoke with, eleven-year-old Rose is an animal lover. Horses, however, are "her first love," emphasized her mother. Rose has never been afraid of horses, even as a tiny infant. Rose started riding for horse therapy at the age of six and has been riding ever since. Because the family cannot afford a horse for Rose, she rides in the summer at a horse camp each year. Rose's parents had trouble finding a stable that would work with a child with hydrocephalus and shunts (to drain fluid from her brain). The place they found is an eight-hour-per-day camp forty-five minutes' drive from their home. Each day, Shannon drives a total of three hours going back and forth to the camp. She has three other children, so she drops Rose off, drives home, and then returns to the camp at the end of the day. To my comment about her driving, "Wow, that's a lot for you!" Shannon responded, "Yes, but it's worth it, for all that she gets out of it." Shannon told me about Rose's riding, "It makes her so much more independent when she's up there. She feels sort of in charge and is able to be, you know, just a regular kid. She feels empowered." Shannon continued, "With horseback riding, you know with certain activities, she feels more normal. You know, she feels that she can do what other kids can do."

In many areas of her young life, Rose's experiences are not like those of other children. Due to her hydrocephalus and the necessary surgeries and treatment, Rose "misses a lot of school." Shannon described Rose's educational experience: "We have to get a tutor for her to get caught back up. She has trouble with math and remembering things. She has real trouble in school. It's like having a concussion every time she has surgery. You have to wonder what she's forgotten, what has to be relearned, where the gaps will show up."

About sports at school, Shannon said, "She has sports she wants to do, and it's not a good idea.... We have to cut back on sports where she can get hit in the head." Shannon added that about seven months ago, Rose did not have a headache for a period of time. During this respite, said Shannon, "she was able to run around on the playground when they had recess. And she could hang upside down on the monkey bars." Now the headaches have returned, and "she really can't do that" anymore.

Nonetheless, Shannon explained, even on horseback, Rose still does not have all the same abilities as everyone else. Due to her hydrocephalus, Rose regularly gets headaches. Wearing a helmet and riding in the summer heat also offer challenges for Rose and tend to exacerbate her headaches. Indeed, Shannon said, "It is probably not a good idea" to put Rose in a helmet, but they do. Rose "loves the horse camp so much that she would ignore her headache. And you know it's therapy," Shannon said, "it's doing something that you love." Because of how much she loves it, Rose "wouldn't notice the headache until she is done" with the ride. When Rose's head hurts before she leaves to ride, Shannon makes her stay home. When this happens, "She cries. She's miserable. She so wanted to do it."

At the age of eleven, Rose has already had "about fourteen surgeries." Shannon explained, "The last year and a half have been more difficult because she really hit a rough patch where she had four surgeries." She missed her horse camp the previous year "because she was in the hospital for most of the summer. So this summer she can't wait to get back."[66]

Horse crazy from about five years of age, Fiona, a woman who has spina bifida, is paraplegic, and uses a wheelchair, started horseback riding because of her disability. She described riding as "definitely therapeutic." She said, "You get to sit on a giant beautiful animal, feel its every breath and movement underneath you, and you can just ride off anywhere you want . . . and go into your own little world."[67] More specific than others, Fiona also explained that horseback riding helped her "maintain the strength in my body and get some physical exercise that I would not have otherwise been able to easily achieve."

In chapter 6, I note that for girls with disability like me as well as for girls marginalized in other ways, horses offer a place of belonging and connection. Many girls with disability gain strength and even relief from their symptoms in horseback riding. From a position of marginalization, girls with disability can become "the same as everyone else." Indeed, as Josephine Pullein-Thompson said above about all girls, on horses, "girls are absolutely equal, in fact in a lot of ways they are better."

This equality, this challenge to normative culture, happens in the context of relationship. My connection with my beloved childhood horse, Snipaway, started when my father bought him for me. I was thirteen, and Snip, a yearling, lived for twenty-five years. When Snip died, I stopped riding, completely, for eight years. I did not even sit on a horse from 2004 to 2012. Aside from my profound grief, it was hard for me to imagine riding outside of my relationship with my one, particular, and unique horse. About life without her horse Phantom, Christine Pullein-Thompson's character Jean thinks, "I shall never have another horse; I won't want one either, not after Phantom."[68]

Both in fictional accounts and in my interviews, girls experience a connection with horses like no other connection in their lives. They claim that horses understand them. And they understand horses. In many stories, the central girl character tames a once-untamable horse. For her, and often for her alone, this wild animal becomes docile. Although my sweet horse was very gentle and well mannered, I never let anyone else ride him until I shared him with Dave (discussed in chapter 4) out of necessity. I knew he would allow other riders to ride him, so I stipulated that I just did not want anyone to be rough on, or damage, his mouth. Looking back, I think I wanted our relationship to be unique, as special to him as it was to me.

About our relationships, our entanglements with each other, Michel Foucault argues that we are never done thinking. We are never free from ambiguity about normative culture, gender, girls, or horses. There is no Truth for us to rest on in these matters. As I discuss in chapter 5, girls ride (on real and on imagined horses) dangerously close to normative ideologies about "natural" girlness, about girlish instincts and innate connections to horses and other animals. Although horsey girls may come uncomfortably close to these normative ways of performing gender, I argue like Probyn that they also, and principally, create a space in girlhood that resists gender norms and challenges binary culture. I invoke Haraway in describing horses and girls as companion species. This space of girl-horse relationships entails independence *and* caring, leading *and* working with, all at once. And in horsey worlds, girls matter for what they *do*, not how they appear. Of course Foucault will not let us off the hook, so to speak, here. Everything is dangerous, he argues. Nonetheless, it seems to me that the challenge horsey girls offer to the grip of normative gender shakes it, a bit, loose and brings us a little closer to a kind of liberty. In their challenge, in Foucault's words, horsey girls offer "new impetus . . . to the undefined work of freedom."[69]

Horses

Life, Death, and Rescue

In *Horse Crazy*, I have been exploring horse history, the pony book genre, mainstream ways of thinking about girls, and why so many girls, like me, love horses. Throughout this book, I investigate the ways social power shapes human and nonhuman animal lives. I have shown how social power helps define human meanings and experiences of life in terms of phenomena like gender. In other words, gender is a social form that life takes, and a form that is *socially* made, in part, by power. Power works both to create meanings of life and death, and to shape and control life and death. In this argument, as discussed in chapter 1, I rely on Michel Foucault's concepts of normalization and biopower and Nicole Shukin's animal capital. Most importantly, in *Horse Crazy*, I examine the ways that life—girl life and other life—pushes back on the normative demands about how to live.

In chapter 2, I explored horse history in the United States. In this concluding chapter, I turn to the contemporary realities of horse lives. What do horse lives mean?[1] How do horses live and die? How and why and when do horse lives matter? It is perhaps banal to say that, of course, humans manipulate the lives of domestic and other animals. Humans form the meanings of animal lives. We bring some animals, and some horses, to life. We send some to death, or we simply leave them to die. We understand some animals as beings to love, others as food to eat, and still others as pests to be controlled and exterminated. Humans relate to nonhuman animals in ways that are sometimes instrumental and sometimes not. These ways of relating are almost startling in their seeming randomness. For example, I receive petitions attempting to challenge horse-eating (and dog-eating) practices in communities outside of the United States, but none attempting to challenge the eating of pigs here. Why do many people in the mainstream United States find it abhorrent to eat a horse (or a dog) but not a pig, even though many know that pigs are very social animals and significantly more intelligent than almost all breeds of horses and dogs?

In human and nonhuman animal life alike, power pushes for giving life to some and death to others. Among humans, the lives of some people are supported and fostered through, for example, public health campaigns about healthy eating, while the lives of others, such as people living on the streets of New York City, are neglected. In the case of horses, organizations develop around breeds of horses—those who fit a breed, are pure-blooded, and have the characteristics required (like spots on the rump, the very spots that were absent on the rump of my horse, Snipaway). These animals might be highly valued and extremely well cared for with special foods, insulated stalls, and elaborate medical care. Other horses, perhaps even horses with a pedigree who qualify as a special breed, become old, can no longer be bred or ridden or used in any way, and are sold to slaughter.

The arbitrariness and inconsistency surrounding animal lives, around the meanings we humans make of them, are endless: one three-year-old thoroughbred horse, who produces significant material capital through his racing, sells for $600,000. The three-year-old's full sibling (one year older, from the same mare, and by the same sire) is badly injured and no longer able to race. This four-year-old thoroughbred horse sells for a few hundred dollars and is shipped for thirty hours in an overcrowded truck, without water or care, to its death at a slaughterhouse in Canada. At the slaughterhouse, the four-year-old is transformed into meat for dogs and cats in the United States and humans in Europe to eat. At the same auction where the four-year-old is sold for meat, another thoroughbred, a mare, also with a racing history but one in which the mare consistently lost races, is likewise destined for the slaughterhouse. Yet this mare has no injury and is bought by a thirteen-year-old girl's parents for her to ride and show. The mare lives for many years as a pampered pet until the girl goes to college, when the mare is sent back to the auction.

A family's beloved poodle-mix dog lives fifteen years and is buried in a graveyard filled with hundreds of beloved dogs, the former pets of hundreds of humans. Another dog, also a poodle mix, is euthanized at six years of age because the shelter cannot find an owner for it. Its body is transformed into food for other animals, perhaps even for the beloved dog-family members of humans. We humans construct the value of horses (and dogs) in this somewhat arbitrary way, and in that we construct what a horse or a dog is.

With human-horse relationships, as with most stories of cross-species relating, there are a multitude of ambiguities. We eat the meat of and yet also love edible nonhuman animals. We shake our heads at the crazy cat lady down the street with her eight cats and donate thirty dollars a month to programs like Meals on Wheels that bring food to elderly people like her who live in poverty; and yet we spend thousands of dollars on surgery for our own sick cat. We are vegetarian, yet we buy the meat of animals killed brutally at a slaughterhouse to feed our family dog.

In this book, I have examined how human beings, particularly girls, involve themselves with horses in noninstrumental ways, involvements that are in the moment and for their own sake. And yet I am also interested in what happens next. Girls grow up. And horses grow old, endure injury, or simply become less useful. And then, some horses' value and meaning for humans shift from the noninstrumental to the instrumental. In a global capitalist society, I claim, most lives that matter—be they girl or horse—are lives that produce something for power.

In this chapter, I briefly investigate horse lives, reproduction, and care to illustrate the biopolitical definition and manipulation of life. I also use the example of a famous horse who lived a century ago in Europe, Clever Hans, to consider what horses know and to wonder about how our human knowing of what horses know shapes the meanings we make of horse life. Next I explore horse death and the possibility of death at slaughterhouses. Finally, I briefly look at the horse rescue movement, where I believe horse-crazy women continue the challenge to a society and economy that values almost everything in terms of the instrumental, in terms of profit. These women labor to care for horses that have little instrumental value. They do so because they believe these horse beings matter too. Those rescuing the horses establish their meaning; they make the horses matter through care, through relationship. And through love.

Horse Lives

Animals, humans and horses alike, are a mass of living, breathing cells, cells that take shape at conception, cells that are born and develop and change, cells that grow old if given that opportunity. At some point, always, cells die and return to the earth in one way or another. And then those former cells become again, and become something else.

Controlling Horse Reproduction

As animal capital, horse bodies offer diverse possibilities for profit. Humans manage horse and other animal lives from reproduction to death to transformation into other materials. In the United States, wild animals like mustangs reproduce efficiently in the wild. Humans past and present cut down mustang populations by capturing them, by killing and processing them in slaughterhouses, and by taming them for human use. Humans have handled the reproduction of other (domestic) horses, and other animals, in various ways. For example, today in the United States most humans want their small animal pets, those like my chihuahua, to be spayed or neutered.

Historian Katherine C. Grier explains that this preference in "people's attitudes toward and methods of coping with sexual maturity and fertility" signals a fundamental difference between past and modern humans. "Although unwanted cats and dogs remain a significant problem in many communities, a recent survey suggested that most modern pet-lovers do not want to own sexually intact cats or dogs."[2] Before the twentieth century, humans had little choice when it came to their pet animals' reproductive capacity. When some pet animals reproduced, such as rabbits, the young could be eaten, although Grier writes, "by the 1870s this was becoming an uncomfortable proposition for many children" (101). People also drowned the newborn offspring of their pets, "sparing one infant for the mother to nurse" (104).

Livestock like horses and cattle were not pets, and males were regularly castrated. While pet owners could have followed the example of livestock castration, Grier claims that the owners were wary about having their small animals castrated because the few veterinarians who did it could be "cavalier about sanitary precautions." As to anesthesia, Grier explains, it "was considered optional, although the text warned that without it, care had to be taken not to suffocate the animal when subduing it. One textbook illustrated a tomcat restrained by being pushed headfirst into a rubber boot" (101).

In the 1910s and 1920s, it was the disappearance of horses in cities that led many large animal veterinarians to "convert their practice to pet clinics" and begin to spay and neuter pets more regularly. "One influential small-animal veterinarian even traveled the country during the 1920s demonstrating his 'easy spaying and castration techniques'" (102).

Humans have normally not spayed large animals like horses for safety reasons and because of the cost. As mentioned above, to control the reproduction of horses and the wild behavior of some male horses—stallions—in the United States (and many other cultures), human owners geld the male animals. Gelding horses means a more or less safe and pain-free removal of the horse's testes.

The British veterinarian widely read by animal-loving and horse-crazy girls in the late twentieth century is known by his pen name, James Herriot. He practiced veterinary medicine and, in his book *All Creatures Great and Small* (1972), wrote about his practice in a rural area of England. He described castrating horses as it had been done in pre-1940s England "for generations." He explained, "[T]he operation had been done by casting the colt and tying him up very like a trussed chicken. It was a bit laborious but the animal was under complete restraint and it was possible to concentrate entirely on the job."[3] In the 1940s, around the time that Herriot finished school and started work as a rural veterinarian, he writes that things began to change, and "standing castration" came to be the common practice. For this reason, Herriot dreaded what he called "the time of the horse," May and June, when one-year-old colts were castrated.

Standing castration "consisted simply of applying a twitch to the colt's upper lip, injecting a shot of local anesthetic into each testicle," and, as Herriot puts it, "going straight ahead." The twitch is a stick that has a loop of rope at the end. The loop is put on the horse's lip or ear and twisted to keep the horse subdued. About standing castrations in comparison to the "trussed chicken" technique, Herriot wrote, "There was no doubt it was a lot quicker." Yet, he explained, "The obvious disadvantage was that the danger of injury to the operator and his helpers was increased tenfold, but for all that the method rapidly became more popular." Herriot described a demonstration of this new technique at a local farm owned by Kenny Bright, "who considered himself an advanced thinker." Bright held the twitch on his colt. As soon as the horse specialist, the person gelding Bright's colt, "touched the scrotum with his antiseptic the colt reared and brought a forefoot down on Kenny's head." Herriot wrote, "He was carried away on a gate with his skull fractured and spent a long time in hospital." Perhaps knowledge about the danger of head injuries was limited in this 1940s rural British community. "The other farmers didn't stop laughing for weeks but the example failed to deter them. Standing castration was in" (149).

Herriot wrote over twenty books, the most famous published in the 1970s. Adults and children read his stories, and some of Herriot's books became international best sellers; there were also a television series and two films made from them. Unlike most twentieth-century children's literature, his books did not shy away from blood, pain, or sexual reproduction. One did not normally find discussions of gelding horses in the pony book genre. Children's book author Mary O'Hara offered an exception in her novel published in 1940, *My Friend Flicka*. There is no gentleness and no anesthetic in her description of gelding colts on a fictional rural Wyoming ranch.

The gelding process starts with the novel's male head of the family, Captain Rob McLaughlin; his veterinarian, Doc Hicks; Doc's assistant, Bill; and McLaughlin's hired help, Gus and Tim. The men work to get the first yearling colt from the McLaughlin herd running. "McLaughlin and Tim made their short ropes sing, whirling them, and they all yelled and shouted. The colt looked terrified, and began to gallop around the corral." Perhaps by way of explanation, Doc said, "The faster he goes the harder he falls." In the strange terms of the story and its all-too-familiar representation of western masculinity, one assumes that when he falls hard, the colt is stunned, which makes it easier to geld him. The colt is roped.

> Bill's eyes were as keen and steady as a marksman taking aim, as he stood in the middle, whirling the loop of his lariat. Suddenly it snaked out along the ground; both forefeet of the colt fell in it. He went down with a crash, and Tim was kneeling on his head before he could move. McLaughlin and Gus tied his feet. Doc went in with his knife, and the colt screamed and tried to struggle. It was over in a minute.[4]

After they let the colt go, he moves away, "head hanging down, blood streaming." About this brutal practice, O'Hara writes, "It wasn't only the blood and the cutting, it was the way the colts stood when it was over. They crowded into a bunch in the corner of the big corral and stood motionless and shocked, one or two off alone by themselves" (85). McLaughlin's son Ken, who is in the fifth grade, watches the process until he is so upset by it, he breaks down sobbing and runs away (87).

The procedure is less brutal in most places today. Often horses are gelded when they are yearling colts, but not always, as horses can be gelded at any age. The gelding frequently happens with minimal pain under either general or local anesthesia. The standing castration described by Herriot remains a practice. Like Herriot did, veterinarians use local anesthesia and a twitch. Yet today veterinarians are much more cautious about the possibility of getting hurt. A veterinarian writing for *The Horse* magazine, Christina S. Cable, explains, "The requirement for a standing castration is that the horse must be big enough for your veterinarian to lean under the belly to remove the testicles—no miniature horses! The horse must be trained well enough to be restrained properly—that means no standing castrations in foals." Cable herself rarely does standing castrations because of the danger. She notes, "I perform 99% of castrations with horses anesthetized." This is safer for the veterinarian as the horse is completely sedated and lying down on the ground for the operation.

Horse Care

Common thinking about proper horse care, like common thinking about the care of human infants, has varied over time. Foucault shows that social power shapes these changing ways of thinking. For both horses and human infants, there is a lot of self-help material available—for a price—to tell you how to do things correctly. As the culture changes, the advice does too. One final comparison: in the cases of both horses and infants, there have been important social movements arguing that the care (of both) should be done "naturally." For human infants, this movement is currently called attachment parenting and, for horses, natural horsemanship (briefly discussed in chapter 2). In an interview with sports and gender studies scholar Lynda Birke, and using circular reasoning, a woman named Cassie explains about natural horsemanship (although she could be describing attachment parenting too): "The method itself is superb because it is natural. Nature itself is a perfect system. However, you have to learn to become natural in what you do. . . . [Horses] are cared for naturally by the human, and this is always beneficial because horses evolved to live naturally."[5]

Two natural horsemanship–based changes in thinking about horse care, in my own life experience, concern "turning out" horses and leaving them "barefoot." The idea behind natural horsemanship, and both "turning out" horses and horses going barefoot, is that it is better for domestic horses to live as they would in the wild. About the practitioners of natural horsemanship, Lynda Birke writes, "For many, being natural meant abandoning metal shoes, having horses unrugged in winter, living in herds, [and] having a natural diet" (227). Because horses on this continent come from domestic horses brought over originally from Spain, for examples of wild horses we have to look at the wild descendants of domestic horses, mustangs. Mustangs, of course, are perpetually "turned out," that is, living outside, barefoot, and with at least a little room to roam and graze.

In contrast to the natural horsemanship people, many in the United States over the past century have believed that, ideally, horses should be kept inside. As a child and young adult, I could not afford to pay for space in a stable, so my horse, Snipaway, lived his whole life outside, turned out in a pasture. I used to worry about my horse being always out in the cold Montana winters. I worried that living outside would hurt his health and shorten his lifespan. Yet today, many people argue that horses stay healthier living outside and, at a minimum, should be turned out to pasture for as much time as is possible each day. Journalist Christine Barakat writes in *Equus* magazine, "The simple act of turning your horse out for as long as possible every day can improve his health in many ways." Barakat quotes veterinarian Robert Magnus of the Wisconsin Equine Clinic and Hospital: "'Being outside twenty-four hours a day is a wonderfully healthy way for a horse of any age to live,' says Magnus. 'Just because a horse is older doesn't mean he needs to be kept indoors. In fact, turnout can help prevent many of the problems we typically see in older horses.'"[6]

As with being turned out, largely for financial reasons, Snipaway normally went barefoot. Because of this I was careful to avoid riding him on hard cement and rocky roads. And like my concerns about having him live outside, I worried about damage to his hooves because of keeping him barefoot. Today the natural horsemanship people indicate I worried needlessly. For example, film producer and director Joe Camp, who created the Benji movie series (and made millions and millions of dollars from them to spend lavishly on horses), has become a horse person and supports natural horsemanship. He argues in his very popular book series on natural horsemanship that horses should not wear shoes. Camp explains that horse hooves should flex in each step taken and that "[the] simple act of flexing is just about the most important thing a horse can do for good health and long life." Camp writes that metal horseshoes (most horseshoes are made of a band of U-shaped metal) stop the hoof from flexing.[7]

In support of barefoot horses and horses living outside uncovered by a blanket, "unrugged," a woman named Karen whom Birke interviewed "spoke about how she preferred her own horse to be unshod and unrugged, even in winter." Karen said, "I love the fact that I'm not nailing shoes onto her beautiful hooves. . . . I feel she can regulate her temperature herself if I don't disturb her in any way. As far as I'm concerned, the more natural the better!"[8]

Camp describes the many horse people who now, with great success, keep their horses barefoot like Snipaway: "Eddie Drabeck, a specialist in Houston also using the wild horse model, helped take the entire Houston Mounted Patrol barefoot, and they are all doing terrifically, with lower vet bills than ever before, even though they work every day on concrete and asphalt."[9] If the natural horsemanship people are right, I was lucky. My financial limitations ended up shaping the care I gave my beloved horse, to be superior (perhaps) to the care those with money gave their horses. Or at least that is what the natural horsemanship people indicate.

For Foucault, natural horsemanship is no more a truth about horses than other ways of thinking about horse care. In some ways, natural horsemanship might be better horse care than other forms and, in some ways, worse. Yet following Foucault, I am interested in what is understood as better and worse, as these are created categories. Good and bad horse care categories shift and change over time and do not necessarily bring us closer to a Truth about what is best for horses (or babies). Deemed poor horse care at the time, according to natural horsemanship, I actually cared correctly for Snip. Yet other contemporary ways of thinking about horse care still understand Snip's care to have been poor.

Either way, horse lives in the United States defy human categories of naturalness. We have no natural wild horses in the United States, so we have to make do with "wild" horses that come from domestic ones. Natural horsemanship shapes horse lives and normalizes horse people. If you do not care for your horse naturally, we are told, then you are a bad horse person.

What Is a Horse (or a Person)?
And Does What We Know Shape Who We Are?

Our knowledge about horse (and infant) care changes. And as Foucault makes clear, this shifting knowledge does not develop in a progressive, linear way that brings us ever closer to a solid Truth. Human knowledge changes, and it is in myriad ways bound up with power. As material animal capital, U.S. horses went from productive animals in agrarian human societies in the nineteenth century, often living outside with land to move about and graze, to expensive pleasure animals largely living individually cloistered in stalls, to animals increasingly turned out as natural horsemanship requires.

Our approach to nonhuman animals, that is, how such animals are shaped through human activity, is based partly on how we define the status of the animal. Some animals hold the status of family members and others the status of food, in spite of the fact that many in both categories can be eaten and have sentience. In other words, lots of animals including horses are edible, but many of those animals we do not eat in the mainstream United States today. In spite of the counterexample of highly intelligent and commonly eaten animals like pigs, the status of animals depends in part on our assessment of their intelligence. (Vegetarians like me try to convince people to stop eating pigs by pointing out their high intelligence.)

How intelligent are horses? What do they think? What exactly does a horse know when she knows something? What, *who*, do we humans know when we know a horse? Wilhelm von Osten owned Hans, an Orlov Trotter stallion who knew things. I pause uncomfortably as I write the words "von Osten *owned* Hans." Can one *own* another being, a being that comprehends, a being fully entangled in a world of knowing? Hans knew how to do a number of relatively sophisticated tasks, tasks that my daughter, Lena, took the first nine years of her life to learn.

The tasks Hans knew included adding, subtracting, multiplying, dividing, working with fractions, telling time, and differentiating musical tones. For Lena, knowing these things matters. For example, to be understood as normal, to be understood as developing appropriately, Lena needs to know how to perform an array of tasks deemed by the current U.S. public school system as normal and appropriate. Knowing that other beings know matters. If a horse can know these things that Lena knows and that we thought horses could *not* know, then what is a horse?

Do we all know the same thing when we each know a particular thing? Did Hans know what my daughter knows about fractions and time?

Journalist Edward T. Heyn enthusiastically explained, in the *New York Times* on September 4, 1905, that nine-year-old Hans had "never been used for riding or driving" and that von Osten gave "the animal systemic instruction such as he would give a child," a child such as my daughter would receive at nine years of age. Heyn wrote that von Osten and his horse "astonished" the neighborhood as they "beheld him and Hans at a certain hour of the day standing in the court before a blackboard and counting machine."

> Herr von Osten, undismayed by ridicule . . . instructed the stallion by showing him the balls on the machine, and influencing him to indicate a number by stamping down his right hoof. At the same time, while the horse was doing this his instructor spoke the name of the number. Then every time Hans put down his foot correctly he would be rewarded by a carrot or a piece of sugar. All other things the intelligent animal learned by seeing certain objects and at the same time hearing their names. In this way words to him became signs for visible objects, and he used footsteps as signs for his perceptions according to the same psychic laws as we use a language to make others understand.[10]

Hans had numerous skills valued highly by humans. He seemed to know all kinds of things, things like mathematics, that many humans do not know. Yet one wonders, what exactly did Hans know? And *how* did Hans know what he knew?

As a teacher, I recognize there are multiple paths to knowing. My students' knowing, my own knowing, my daughter's knowing deepens across time and experience. For example, I myself have read a book I teach, Emile Durkheim's *Suicide* (1951), many times. We readers all know that the first time we read a text, we know it differently than the second or the fifth or the twenty-fifth time. The first time I read *Suicide*, I vaguely understood that Durkheim used this startling and individual human behavior to show, to prove, that the social exists. Society, the social, influenced the phenomenon of suicide. By the second reading, Durkheim convinced me that one cannot understand suicide without recognizing the role played by society, by the social, in human suicides. If one mapped out all the causes of suicide including the psychological and biological, to be complete in understanding suicide, one must recognize the role of society. Reading Durkheim, the third and fourth time, my own periodic desire for the relief of death became something inextricably webbed in the moment and culture in which I live. Suicide became for me something more, more than an individual decision. It became a choice made in a social context. In the fifteenth reading, Durkheim's argument moved me by its detail and structure. I see and understand tiny bits of the frame he slowly built, leading me to a particular recognition.

In part, in my knowing, I probably memorized pieces of Durkheim's text. Like a photocopy machine, I reproduced the information in Durkheim's study in my memory. Yet the knowing happened in other ways too: as I came to understand Durkheim's argument, it changed me, it changed my relationships with the world, with the phenomenon of suicide, with my own periodic desire for relief from life, with the social world around me. I understood that in our contemporary, modern society, suicide is common, and the desire for, the thinking of suicide extremely common. I believed Durkheim's claim that alienation and anomie, disconnection and change, influenced humans in my culture to consider suicide. In a visceral way, I felt my experience, my suffering, bleed into the world around me. I became, and I became someone else, someone whose suffering lived as a part of the world, lonely but not alone, singular but still the same as so many other beings all around me.

Was Hans "merely" memorizing? This is something my colleagues and I worry over regarding our students. Rather than memorizing in the liberal arts, we want our students to, as we say, "think critically." We want our students to engage with the material in such a way that the engagement makes them different, the world different, and their own knowing different. Did Hans "think critically"?

Surely Hans memorized, and just as surely that is a form of knowing. Yet his skills seemingly exceeded memorization; he knew how to *do* things with his knowledge. Hans knew how to divide numbers and spell names. Hans reacted. Or so humans thought.

And, as we humans came to believe, Hans seemed to know how to trick the humans. Equally interesting in regard to Hans's intelligence was that his intelligence was eventually debunked. In 1907, after careful (scientific) study, psychologist Oskar Pfungst established the "Clever Hans effect." This term refers to "the experimenter effect by which researchers inadvertently give their subjects the answers to their questions."[11] Pfungst determined that Hans was not able to actually spell words or divide numbers; instead, Hans found his answers in the involuntary movements of the humans around him. In particular, Hans knew his owner, von Osten, well. Hans watched—Hans's other senses were probably involved too—he waited, for von Osten to give him the answers to the questions offered him. Von Osten did not *know* that he was giving the answers to Hans, but he did give them, argued Pfungst.

Pfungst believed that Hans learned the answers to the questions by being attentive to the ways the humans told him the answers, albeit unintentionally. To support his hypothesis, Pfungst devised a "blind test" in which one person, Schillings, would ask Hans a question and leave, when another person, von Osten, who did not know the question (and thus did not know the answer), would come to receive the answer from Hans. With this blind test, Hans made more mistakes. Animal studies scholar Vinciane Despret writes, "Hans's silence or stray responses to the blind questions marked him as guilty of having tricked the humans" (78). Pfungst believed that Hans's errors showed that Hans was a "dumb beast" merely reacting to signs, unwittingly given him by the humans asking the question, as he answered each question.

Pfungst's work with Hans happened in the midst of a "critical moment of the bifurcation of psychology: the transformations of Hans herald the transformation of subjects. One can read, engraved in this history, the first signs of the advent of behaviourism." In this moment in Europe and the United States, many humans were beginning to understand human behavior differently. Human knowledge, what humans knew about other humans in this place and time, changed. Despret clarifies,

> Pfungst reduces the conduct of the horse to simple mechanisms, he makes Hans pass from the animal who responds into the "animal that reacts." Reaction is at the heart of the whole affair, it is the real transformation that announces that living beings, as the objects of these sciences that make psychologists dream, will finally submit to the laws that govern the universe. Only the conversion of response into reaction can enable this passage. (80)

Hans Knew Things Humans Cannot Know

Despret challenges Pfungst's findings and locates his arguments in their historical moment. She claims Hans was not merely reacting, not merely offering a learned response to a stimulus. "Pfungst's solution," Despret writes, "despite its coherence and all the accumulated experimental evidence, leaves here and there unexplained residues, peculiarities, details that do not settle well with the whole and which suggest that there might be another explanation." As her translator Matthew Chrulew asks, "Must the spectre of Hans's cleverness remain an ironic epithet—an accusation of falsity and bête stupidity—or can we recast it as an alternative intelligence, a remarkably attentive capacity to be affected?" (77–78).

Like all horses, Hans had a finely tuned ability to take in sensory information. Hans's ability might have been sharper and more variant than that of other horses. Yet horses in general read others, humans and nonhuman animals alike, very closely and with seemingly little to no information. Horseback riders sometimes find their horses doing what they had only begun to think about but had not yet signaled to the horse. Despret elaborates, "The horse normally uses several sensorial channels, each of its senses is involved in what it perceives—it is, in the words of ethologists, a polysensorial being." Horses use various senses to interpret what to humans are normally invisible, if not nonexistent, elements of reality. Despret explains,

> Certainly, the horse uses his vision, but, in the lovely expression of Jean-Claude Barrey, "he will never believe his eyes," he always has to confirm it with his nose. At the same time, muscular sensations are not perceived by the body alone; at the slightest movement of the rider, the ears of the horse lie down: he listens to the effect of his sensation-movements in his body, he uses his ears "as the eyes of the body." Merely to say in the same breath that muscular sensations are heard by the "eyes" or that scent confirms vision gives us an idea of the difficulty of determining both how the horse perceives and what can produce the neutralization of just one of his senses.

Despret notes that Hans did answer questions correctly at times when his human questioner was incorrect. Pfungst recorded seven such cases. Despret describes two such instances in the early period of Pfungst's study. She writes, "A few days before the meeting started, some members of the commission had begun the work with him, in order to do some tests and to establish a good connection with the horse."

> From this preparatory work, the Count zu Castell has returned quite surprised: on the 8th of September he had asked Hans the date. Hans had responded with eight taps of his hoof. Yet zu Castell was convinced that it was the 7th. He was about to correct Hans when somebody pointed out to him that the date was indeed the 8th, and not the 7th. On another visit, still in the course of this week, zu Castell presented to Hans a slate bearing the numbers 8, 5 and 3, and asked him to add them. In his excitement, zu Castell thought that the total was 10. Hans went up to 16. (79)

Despret explores Pfungst's work on these seven "occurrences" of Hans being correct seemingly on his own, seemingly *without* a knowing human. Using the theory of Hans merely reacting, it is hard to explain these seven cases. Perhaps the human knew the correct answer on some deeper level of consciousness, and Hans reacted to that deeper consciousness. Or perhaps Hans made a mistake (and another mistake and another), and it just happened to be correct, seven different times.

Despret offers "another more radical interpretation." She writes that perhaps "the Hans before Pfungst's experiment and the Hans after it were not the same." She argues, "The horse would have been transformed by the way Pfungst worked with him, by the suspicion, by the manner of addressing him" (79). Perhaps early in his education, Hans learned to know in one way, perhaps the very way that Pfungst suggested, through sensing the answers that the knowing humans inadvertently indicated. And perhaps after dealing with Pfungst, Hans came to find another way of knowing, a way that did not work as well—a way without humans indicating—but another way? And albeit with more error, Hans still knew, he knew enough to know the answer seven times when the humans present inadvertently told him the incorrect one?

Over one hundred years later, with Hans and von Osten and zu Castell and Pfungst all dead, it is still hard to know what—or how—Hans knew what he knew. Did Hans change as Despret suggests? Does what we know shape who we are? In some small part, are we beings in the world made through our knowing?

Horse Death

Raftery's Death

What do we love when we love a horse? And what do we kill when we kill a horse? What dies when a being dies?

In *The Well of Loneliness*, Stephen Gordon's mother, Lady Anna, wishes her daughter dead. Lady Anna finds out about Stephen's relationship with another woman, a married neighbor named Angela Crosby, and tells Stephen,

> I would rather see you dead at my feet than standing before me with this thing upon you—this unspeakable outrage that you call love in that letter which you don't deny having written. In that letter you say things that may only be said between man and woman, and coming from you they are vile and filthy words of corruption—against nature, against God who created nature. My gorge rises; you have made me feel physically sick.[12]

Although Stephen deeply loves her Morton home, she leaves because her mother claims, "[W]e two cannot live together at Morton—not now, because I might grow to hate you." Through this ordeal, Stephen's horse Raftery remains one of her few and closest friends.

Stephen moves from Morton to London, with her childhood teacher and her horse. In London, Stephen becomes a successful writer. Yet even as all else goes by the wayside except her writing, Stephen remains committed to her beloved horse. "Only one duty apart from her work had Stephen never for a moment neglected, and that was the care and welfare of Raftery" (239).

Stephen loves her horse intensely. So when, in London at age eighteen, Raftery goes "very lame," everything else in Stephen's life "was forgotten." Being wealthy, Stephen brings in a series of experts to assess the situation. "Every good vet in London was consulted." They each give the same grim diagnosis, "No cure, no cure, it was always the same, and at times, they told Stephen, the old horse suffered." But this Stephen "knew well—she had seen the sweat break out darkly on Raftery's shoulders" (248–249). So Stephen prepares to take Raftery by train back from London where they are living, to Morton where she grew up, and from which she was banished by her mother because of her love affair with Angela.

Stephen sends her groom, Jim, away to ride in the third-class compartment of the train, and she rides with Raftery "on the seat reserved for a groom." Stephen opens the window by her seat, whereupon Raftery's muzzle came up and his face looked out of the window. She fondled the soft, grey plush of his muzzle. Presently she took a carrot from her pocket, but the carrot was rather hard now for his teeth, so she bit off small pieces and these she gave to him in the palm of her hand; then she watched him eat them uncomfortably, slowly, because he was old, and this seemed so strange, for old age and Raftery went very ill together. (250)

Raftery spends one last night in his old "spacious loosebox." "But," Hall wrote, "when the sun came up over Bredon, flooding the breadth of the Severn Valley, touching the slopes of the Malvery Hills that stand opposite Bredon across the valley, gilding the old red bricks of Morton and the weather-vane on its quiet stables, Stephen went into her father's study and she loaded his heavy revolver" (251–252).

Stephen takes her beloved horse out to one of the family's fields. With Jim holding Raftery's bridle, Stephen says to Raftery,

"I'm going to send you away, a long way away, and I've never left you except for a little while since you came when I was a child and you were quite young—but I'm going to send you a long way away because of your pain. Raftery, this is death; and beyond, they say, there's no more suffering." She paused, then spoke in a voice so low that the groom could not hear her: "Forgive me, Raftery."

Stephen puts her gun "high up against Raftery's smooth, grey forehead" and fires. Raftery "dropped to the ground like a stone, lying perfectly still." And Stephen instructs Jim to bury Raftery there near a "mighty hedge" over which Stephen used to jump him and that had "set the seal on his youthful valour" (252). Hall described Stephen's profound grief: "She could not work, for a great desolation too deep for tears lay over her spirit—the great desolation of things that pass, of things that pass away in our lifetime. And then of what good, after all, are our tears, since they cannot hold back this passing away" (255).

Even Horses Pass Away

One woman I interviewed, Sonya, kept thinking, "I really do need to give up the horse. And so every once in a while I'll advertise her." Once a woman even came to look at Sage. So Sonya and her spouse, Maya, "went out and looked at her farm." Sonya explained, "And you know we just got a bad feeling. We said, you know, 'This is not to be a companion horse. It's going to be a glue factory horse.' And so we were not going to do that."[13]

Horses are expensive and require a lot of care. In old age, illness, and death, horses and ponies present the obvious problem of size. Whereas their humans might love them as much as humans love dogs and cats, caring for an old horse, a horse too old or frail to ride, and burying an old horse takes space—land—and money. Slaughterhouses offer a ready solution; they put the horse down and dispose of the body all while the owner makes, rather than spends, money. Animal rights activist and journalist Gail A. Eisnitz writes, "There are a lot of unwanted horses in this country. In fact, according to the USDA," Eisnitz explains, "between one and three hundred thousand pleasure and race horses find themselves at the business end of the captive bolt gun."[14] Yet while owners might think they are simply putting their horse down, euthanizing the animal, and making a bit of money simultaneously, the American Society for the Prevention of Cruelty to Animals (ASPCA) states otherwise: "The term 'horse slaughter' refers exclusively to the killing and processing of horses for human consumption. Horse slaughter is *not* humane euthanasia. While 'euthanasia' is defined as a gentle, painless death provided in order to prevent suffering, slaughter is a brutal and terrifying end for horses."[15]

For one year, Eisnitz documented "the conditions of slaughter-bound horses at auction houses." Horses experience not only the slaughter itself, but many also experience neglect and abuse before being shipped to slaughter. "With photos showing the animals' conditions—broken bones, burns, infections, starvation so severe they could barely stand up," Eisnitz worked to convince "a prosecutor to raid a horse auction and prosecute the abusers." It is extremely important work, but as Eisnitz herself argues, in the case of the raid, it only addresses one auction, one time, and not the broader problem.[16]

Horses killed in U.S. slaughterhouses have been processed as pet food as well as sent to Europe for humans to eat there.[17] Because humans in the twentieth-century United States have increasingly understood horses (and our relationships with them) as similar to or even the same as cats, dogs, and other pets, a social movement developed protesting the killing of horses in slaughterhouses. In the United States, people have expressed and continue to express horror at the slaughter of horses for meat and at the eating of dogs in China. This points to the somewhat socially arbitrary nature of pet status. As noted above, pigs are more intelligent than dogs, clean, and potentially very loving and loyal to humans. Yet we ruthlessly breed millions of pigs, breeding hogs, who "spend their entire lives inside crates so small they can never turn around." We raise and slaughter pigs in factory farms with little expression of social concern.[18] These conditions are considered "normal agricultural practices" and thus are exempt from anticruelty laws.[19] Pigs aside, the concern over slaughterhouse killing of horses has led to various laws passed by Congress attempting to curtail the process for horses.

Signed into law in 2005, the Agriculture, Rural Development, Food and Drug Administration, and Related Agencies Appropriations Act, 2005–2006, "led to the closure of horse slaughterhouses in the United States."[20] The ASPCA explains, "The last three U.S. slaughterhouses—two in Texas and one in Illinois, all foreign-owned—were shuttered in 2007. In 2006, these facilities killed and processed more than 104,000 horses for human consumption, shipping the meat overseas."[21] Surprisingly, this law closing in-country horse slaughterhouses in some ways *worsened* the life and death conditions of U.S. horses. Humans abandon more horses now, leaving them to die of starvation and illness. Journalist A. G. Sulzberger writes that more horses "are being neglected and abandoned, and roughly the same number—nearly 140,000 a year—are being killed after a sometimes grueling journey across the border."[22]

Now, instead of selling horses to slaughterhouses in the United States, owners sell their horses to be slaughtered where it is still legal, in Mexico and Canada. Horses being shipped to slaughter do not need to arrive at the slaughterhouse in good condition. They are valuable to the slaughterhouse as long as they are alive and able to walk (more or less) to their deaths. Thus one does not need to spend time or other resources protecting the horses on their sometimes long journeys driving to slaughter. Horses can be shipped in carriers not made for animals their size, crowded together, uncomfortable at best. Such shipping can cause grave injury to the horses. Those shipping the horses do not need to water or feed the animals unless the shipping takes so long that the animals would otherwise die without water. On their website, the ASPCA writes,

> Horses bound for slaughter (who may include pregnant mares, foals and horses who are injured or blind) are commonly shipped for more than twenty-four hours at a time in crowded trucks without food, water or rest. The methods used to kill horses rarely result in quick, painless deaths for these animals and sometimes they even remain conscious during dismemberment.[23]

The information we have about death in a slaughterhouse is quite limited. Yet what we do know indicates that, as animal rights organizations claim, slaughterhouses in Mexico and Canada have most of the same issues that they have in the United States.[24] For obvious reasons, slaughterhouses work to avoid any such news reaching the public. For example, today the limits on slaughterhouse information in the United States are so extreme, it is illegal to even photograph the outside of slaughterhouses. "Ag Gag" laws, as they are known, "protect the industry by making whistleblowers into outlaws."[25] Journalist Leighton Akio Woodhouse explains, "Ag Gag laws take aim at camera-wielding undercover whistleblowers, whose videos have provided some of the few unvarnished glimpses the public has seen of where their food comes from—and it's not a pretty sight." What we do know about slaughterhouses is that they can be brutal places for animals to die, unsafe for workers, bad for the environment, and toxic for the food produced there. "In processing plants, ever-increasing disassembly line speeds have increased the risks of injury to knife-wielding slaughterhouse workers, who tend to be poor, often undocumented migrants from Mexico and Central America, while compounding the risk of some animals being skinned and dismembered while still alive."[26] Given our probusiness and antianimal legal systems, those who work to expose brutality on factory farms and in slaughterhouses often do so illegally.

This is not to say that there are no laws protecting farm animals, or the workers who raise and slaughter them, or the food that comes from the meat industry. There are some legal protections, but they are very limited. And where such protections do exist, oversight to be sure the laws are followed is also very limited.

When, at the turn of the twentieth century, Upton Sinclair published his famous novel *The Jungle* about slaughterhouses in the United States, the public outcry about the state of our meat, a situation brought to light in the book, was extensive. Indeed, meat sales fell 50 percent after *The Jungle* (1906), came out, and immediate action was taken to protect the public from bad meat. President Theodore Roosevelt himself campaigned for the Federal Meat Inspection Act of 1906. Along with subsequent legislation, the new law established slaughterhouse sanitation standards and federal inspection of meat shipped between states and out of the country.[27]

Personally less concerned about the food issues, Sinclair really wanted to make the public aware of the horrible working conditions and treatment of workers in the slaughterhouses. While the Federal Meat Inspection Act and the Federal Food and Drug Act passed remarkably fast, within the year *The Jungle* came out, "no legal or other formal changes were made on behalf of meat industry workers or of the animals-to-be-meat."[28] A disappointed Sinclair noted, "I aimed at the public's heart, and by accident I hit it in the stomach."[29]

Death by Slaughterhouse

The animals-to-be-meat went largely unnoticed during Sinclair's time, and they continue to garner little attention today. In Mexico, where we send thousands of horses to be slaughtered each year, as of this writing, it is legal to slaughter and process a conscious animal, one that is not properly stunned. The United States is only slightly better.

Today in the United States there is one, and only one, very limited law called the Humane Slaughter Act protecting animals slaughtered in meat industry slaughterhouses. This law came out first in 1958. The federal government updated it in 1978 and added an amendment in 2002. The Humane Slaughter Act dictates that animals be rendered unconscious quickly, in one blow or stun, before being butchered. Once unconscious, they can be shackled, pulled up by the shackled limb to a hanging position, bled out, and processed into meat. Using a cow as an example, Eisnitz describes the slaughter process once the animal is stunned and shackled. She explains that a worker called a "sticker" takes the next step.

> The sticker makes a vertical, not horizontal, incision in the animal's throat, near where the major vessels issue from the heart, to cut off the flow of blood to the animal's brain.
>
> Next the cow travels along the "bleed rail" and is given several minutes to bleed out. The carcass then proceeds to the head-skinners, the leggers, and on down the line where it is completely skinned, eviscerated, and split in half.[30]

The Humane Slaughter law represents the U.S. federal government's attempt to obtain a relatively pain-free death for farm animals. The heart of the matter is that the animal must not be able to feel pain, it must be unconscious, before the butchering begins.

There are a number of problems with the law. First and foremost, the law is not adequately regulated. In effect, the U.S. government leaves the meat industry to regulate itself. On the rare occasion that a slaughterhouse is charged with a violation of this law, they receive only a symbolic penalty. Because the meat industry is interested in and concerned about profit above and beyond all else, the industry has a great incentive to ignore the Humane Slaughter Act if it is profitable to do so. And it is, indeed, profitable to do so.

The issue with slaughterhouse animal abuse, in the United States, Canada, and Mexico, is time. As Benjamin Franklin himself noted, in a capitalist economy, time is money.[31] The more animals slaughtered each day in a given slaughterhouse with a given number of workers, where labor and equipment costs remain the same, the more money is gained. In the United States, where at least this law protecting animals does exist, it takes extra time to slaughter an animal following the conditions of the Humane Slaughter Act. Wanting to maximize profit, slaughterhouses strive to limit the time it takes to slaughter more and more animals.[32] It takes time to stun an animal properly. If a slaughterhouse rushes the animals through processing, some are likely to be conscious after being stunned or, rather, after not being properly stunned. As undercover animal rights activists have also discovered, again and again slaughterhouse workers told Eisnitz in interviews that, on a regular basis, animals were butchered while still conscious. For example, United States Department of Agriculture worker Timothy Walker described shackled animals "kicking and thrashing as they hung upside down." He said, "A lot of times the skinner finds out an animal is still conscious when he slices the side of its head and it starts kicking wildly." Workers would sometimes try to cut the spinal cord of the conscious animal. "This practice paralyzes the cow from the neck down but doesn't deaden the pain of head skinning or render the animal unconscious."[33]

The rushing of animals through processing also leads to accidents for the human workers laboring to stun, bleed, skin, and eviscerate the animals. Slaughterhouse workers have little to no training. In the United States, these vulnerable workers are poorly paid, without unions, often immigrant, and often undocumented. Add to this situation humans working packed together with sharp knives, and, periodically, large animals being processed while still conscious and fighting, and it takes little imagination to understand many of the risks. Yet there are less obvious risks too. For example, because of the intense pressure to work fast in a cold slaughterhouse environment (cold to preserve the meat), workers suffer many musculoskeletal disorders. Journalist Peggy Lowe writes about the United States, "The workers, most often immigrants and resettled refugees, slaughter and process hundreds of animals an hour, [and are] forced to work at high speeds in cold conditions, doing thousands of the same repetitions over and over, with few breaks."[34]

On top of the danger presented to the animals and the workers, factory farms and industrial food slaughterhouses are also bad for the environment, and the meat they produce is arguably bad for humans.

Horses are rarely if ever *raised* for meat in the United States. Yet they are sold for meat when their usefulness for other purposes, such as riding, racing, jumping, or showing, comes to an end. And then, as with other animals (those like cattle and pigs, actually raised for death in slaughterhouses), the risk of a terrible death is real. The ASPCA writes, "Looking at data from 2012 to 2016, an average of 137,000 American horses are trucked over our borders each year to slaughter facilities in Mexico and Canada. Reopening slaughterhouses in America is not the answer to ending this form of cruelty." The ASPCA explains that we need to ban the slaughter of horses for meat in the United States as well as ban their "export abroad for that purpose."[35]

How should horses die? As sentient beings that engage in profound and close relationships with one another and with humans and other animals, I argue for a noninstrumental death, a death that happens more naturally out to pasture with other horses. If the horse's humans do not have the money or space to retire their horse in a pasture, a more humane alternative to a slaughterhouse death is to hire a veterinarian to gently euthanize the animal. One organization, the Homes for Horses Coalition, which works "to end horse slaughter and other forms of horse cruelty," claims the "average cost of having a horse humanely euthanized by a veterinarian and its body disposed of is approximately $250." On their website, they argue that this is a "virtual drop in the bucket when it comes to the overall expense of keeping a horse. This cost is simply a part of responsible horse ownership."[36]

And Rescue

In a capitalist economy such as ours, power pushes to transform everything, every cell, every life, every death into profit. Horses are large and expensive animals. Once no longer useful to their humans, or once the humans caring for them no longer can afford to do so, the horses often have to move on, in one way or another. Those whose humans cannot, or will not, give them a comfortable horse retirement at pasture might be sold to another human to be used for another end. They might be left to die like the three malnourished horses "dumped on the highway" that state livestock inspectors found near Edgewood, New Mexico.[37] They might be killed at a slaughterhouse and turned into some other profit-making material, as Sonya worried one potential buyer would do with her horse, Sage. Alternatively, they can be "rescued." Why are some animals deemed worthy of being rescued whereas others are euthanized or slaughtered? The answer is determined in the activity. The meaning of animals to humans is determined in the various choices humans make.

We live in a moment in the United States where the animal rescue movement has salience and shapes the lives of many domestic animals. Animals in one part of the country can be at the brink of death in an animal shelter with a kill policy. (Some shelters have no-kill policies, usually meaning they will keep the animals in their care until the shelter finds a more permanent home for the animal.) At kill shelters, for example, animals who are deemed adoptable are normally put up for adoption, given a set amount of time to wait, and, if not adopted during that time frame, ultimately killed.

From the perspective of profit, either route—adoption or euthanasia— works well. Adoption means the animal is likely to live in a home with enough financial salience to pour thousands of dollars into the pet food and supplies industry over the animal's remaining years. Euthanasia at a kill shelter means that the animal will likely be rendered, itself, into something else, perhaps pet food for other animals to eat.

My Tiny, Terrible Rescue

Coming from the rural western United States where small dogs are not considered real dogs and no one has them, I knew nothing about chihuahuas. And so I made the mistake of adopting, indeed "rescuing," one. While my chihuahua is passionate in his love and adoration for me, he seems to hate everyone else, vehemently. He bites the elderly and small children alike. When he is not viciously attacking someone, he is likely to be yapping and yapping and yapping (and yapping). I saddled myself, and my family, with this animal by going online and searching for opportunities to "rescue" a small dog. Many dogs are gathered in the southern United States by rescue organizations. The explanation for the plethora of dogs coming from the South is that spaying and neutering animals has not become the norm there, as it is in the Northeast and other areas of the country. Because of this, more animals are (re)produced than the available number of human homes for them, and large numbers end up in kill shelters. The rescue organizations go to kill shelters and take animals whom they believe they might be able to find homes for and begin to work on finding them homes. It is common to post the dogs' photographs and descriptions online where people like me, in New York City, search through them, pick one, and arrange to adopt—to rescue— the animal. When I adopted him, my nine pounds of chihuahua became a reliable, daily dog food consumer for seventeen years. Had he not been rescued, his nine pounds would have been transformed into other material, possibly even dog food, to sell.[38] Nine pounds one way or nine pounds the other, there are profits to be made.

Like the Girls in the Pony Books, Women Rescuing Horses

As I finish this book, thirteen years after the death of my horse Snipaway, I have started riding again. I cannot afford a horse, or rather I cannot afford to board and care for a horse where I live in the urban Northeast, so here, the primary way to gain access to horseback riding is to pay for lessons. In the summer of 2018 my daughter and I started taking lessons together. I like the stable we chose, Getner Barn, both because they work to make horses accessible to low-income children through their nonprofit program, "Wishes for Horses," and because they rescue horses. Indeed, they rescued the sweet gentleman, a paint gelding named Liberty, that I rode for my lessons.

What does it mean to rescue horses? Not so different from rescuing chihuahuas or other domestic animals, the idea is to save the horses from being killed in a slaughterhouse by buying them at auctions—or, when possible, from being neglected or abused by their current owners by purchasing them. One program, Front Range Equine Rescue, describes its origins:

> Little Red was a three-year-old paint gelding found emaciated and crippled at a local auction back in August 1997. Front Range purchased Little Red to end his history of suffering. An equine veterinarian examined Little Red and confirmed our initial diagnosis. . . . Little Red had been neglected and abused for too long and could not be rehabilitated successfully. Humane euthanasia was the kindest option. Since Little Red, Front Range Equine Rescue has expanded its programs to a national level. Now, Front Range's rescue horses are kept in Colorado, Virginia and Florida.

Horse rescue often means buying injured or old horses that can no longer be ridden. The rescuers then keep and care for and in some cases never ride or otherwise use the horses until their death. The practice of rescuing horses offers a powerful example of engaging with horse lives in a noninstrumental way. Ten of the twenty-five former horse-crazy girls whom I interviewed, including Kathleen (discussed in chapter 5), were currently or had been involved in horse rescue, either by volunteering at a horse rescue organization or by rescuing horses themselves. Against her veterinarian's advice and at great expense, Kathleen bought a lame gelding, who cannot be ridden, to ensure that the horse would not be sold into an abusive situation or to a slaughterhouse. Women involved in horse rescue told me that the majority of the horse rescue workers are women and that the majority of workers are also unpaid volunteers.

Concluding Thoughts

In a world where value almost always means instrumental gain or profit, horse-crazy girls offer an alternative way of being. They love horses for the sake of the love. Horses matter for no reason outside of the reality of their existence.

These animals whom U.S. girls love first came into being here in North America and then disappeared from this continent thousands of years ago. They returned in the service of human colonization, but horses, like all existence, had and have life outside of human intention. As the objects of U.S. girls' passion, horses bring girls possibilities for being, being girls in the world, that shake power loose, that challenge normative culture and its at times deadly demands on girls. The pony book genre, primarily published in the United Kingdom from the 1930s to the 1970s and read passionately by horse-crazy girls, then and now, exhibits the ambiguities of horsey-girl lives. The books normalize whiteness and capitalist class structures yet simultaneously challenge oppressive aspects of mainstream girlhood such as the conservative demand that girls focus on caregiving beyond all else.

Still today in the United States, girls face this caregiving imperative. Simultaneously, mainstream liberal feminists require that girls focus on successful careers in the working world. In their self-assertion with and loving care of their horses, what I call their vital care, horse-crazy girls challenge both of these models for life.

Social power grips us tightly, but life pushes for itself. Horse-crazy girls foster horse lives. These girls foster the mattering of horses' lives and for reasons beyond, between, and around those of capital. Horsey girls offer us an example of alternative meanings and noninstrumental ways of being, of vitalism. Many grown-up former-horse-crazy girls and many current horse-crazy women continue the challenge made in girlhood that I discuss in chapters 5 and 6; that is, they as adults continue to love and care for horses and even for rescued horses that are at times, in an instrumental sense, useless.

There are pressures on all of us to live in normalized ways. Normalized life can be deadening, but, to a degree, horse-crazy girls find their ways around normalized models for being girls and live a more vital life. Together with their horses, horse-crazy girls find a kind of freedom. They gain strength and share love in their horsey relationships. And together they offer the rest of us a model, an alternative way of being in the world, with life itself as its own telos, a way where each one matters for her own sake, and each moment is alive unto itself.

Epilogue

The Boys Who Love Ponies

At the age of eight I had a little pony, my Shetland, Dolly. Growing up in Manhattan, my daughter, Lena, cannot have a pony like Dolly. When she was eight, *her* little pony was pink and mass produced. Lena had the exact same little pony thousands of girls—and some boys—had, My Little Pony.

Like horse-crazy girls and women, some boys and men, too, engage in a vital, counternormative experiment in living. Some are known as bronies, human males who are enthusiastic about My Little Pony. In their creation of a community through the vital activities of writing, sharing, and enacting, bronies resist the normative constraints of traditional masculinity.[1]

To the extent that girls are pushed toward one side of a gender binary in mainstream debates, boys are pushed to the other side. For conservatives, white girls play the role of Beauty in the old story, and white boys play the Beast. The white-boy-as-Beast is a powerful being with deeply competitive, violent, and sexual drives. "Boys will be boys" is the underbelly of this story. The white-girl-as-Beauty is a gentle lady, the Madonna, who can tame him such that he becomes her provider and focuses his sexual attention on her alone. For conservative (and homophobic) writer George Gilder, gay men are just men being men, having as much sex as possible with others, who, also men, also want as much sex as possible. Being gay is just one of the ways the Beauty and the Beast story can run off its tracks. Raping and pillaging is another way. In both cases, normative understandings hold, as was echoed in the local response to the seven teenage boys who raped an intellectually disabled girl in Glen Ridge, New Jersey: boys will be boys.[2]

My Little Pony (also called MLP and discussed briefly in chapter 1) offers young girls a chance to be horse crazy and girly all at once. The ponies do normative girl things like dressing up and combing each other's hair as well as having girl-oriented adventures about developing friendships with other ponies and learning life lessons, with no battles and with minimal athletics. My Little Pony first came out in 1982. Little girls loved and continue to love each generation, but it is in the fourth generation that the ponies' repertoire of nongirly activities began to expand. Fourth-generation My Little Ponies also do nonnormative things like committing to friendships with other girl ponies beyond any other relationships, and exhibiting bravery and courage. Perhaps not coincidentally, it was also the fourth generation that caught the attention of the boys. This generation of My Little Pony began in 2010 with the television show *My Little Pony: Friendship Is Magic*, developed by animator Lauren Faust.[3] Writing for the conservative magazine the *Weekly Standard* about the brony phenomenon, Matt Labash describes the Hub, the channel that airs the show, "a cable network co-owned by toymaker Hasbro, who thought it a keen idea to program a slate of low-quality cartoons (like *Pound Puppies* and *Transformers: Prime*) to help hawk toy lines to susceptible children." Labash says, "The new MLP wouldn't have seemed like anyone's idea of revolutionary animation, nor was the intent to appeal to adult men." The dialogue was "a bit snappier" than earlier My Little Pony generations, "but it was still little-girl fare, with ponies such as Twilight Sparkle and Rainbow Dash cantering around the mythical land of Equestria with their 'cutie marks' (like brands, only cuter), bantering about the magic of friendship."[4]

   In the interest of understanding, in early 2013 I myself carefully watched the full run of *My Little Pony: Friendship Is Magic* with my then six-year-old daughter, Lena. As a child, in sharp contrast to my daughter, I was neither a television watcher nor a girly girl. Given this, I had my doubts about how engaged the forty-five-year-old me would be in girly early-childhood television. Yet, snuggled up with my daughter in front of my computer, watching the episodes recorded by a friend who was the father of a seven-year-old girlfriend of Lena's, I became, for the first time in my life, wrapped up in children's television. That winter my daughter and I visited London, and what I remember most about the trip was watching *My Little Pony* in the odd hours of the night with Lena in a friend's freezing-cold London home.

In his article, Labash mocks bronies: "Like so many American men, they wish to be forever suspended in childhood. Except this time, they want to be six-year-old girls." I wonder what exactly is wrong with playing at being a six-year-old girl. Being six was not a great time in *my* life, but my daughter seemed to really enjoy that year.

To find out more about the brony phenomenon, I interviewed three white men who identified as bronies. About its origins, one brony, Jack, explained to me, "The movement started—could only have started—with an online community. Men saw this show, with younger siblings or even daughters, and actually enjoyed themselves. People who love any one piece of culture tend to swarm to the internet to form community based around it." About the brony movement, Jack explained, "It gained notoriety for its perceived 'weirdness' based in its challenge to gender norms." He added, "I guess what they say is true; there isn't such a thing as bad press."[5]

Labash might not like it, but the brony movement has spread. He writes, "One terrifying 'State of the Herd' survey estimates that there are as many as 12.4 million, which if true would mean that if Bronies had their own state, it would be the seventh most populous in the nation."

While the brony movement does not seem to focus or center on sexuality, homophobic stereotypes about the bronies abound. Labash perpetuates some of this bigotry in his statement that "despite their fascination with pastel talking ponies, there's no evidence that Bronies are mostly gay or pedophiles." Labash seems to believe pastel colors, pedophilia, and gayness all go together. Of course, in mainstream thinking like Labash's, gender and sexuality *do* go together; that is, if a man loves girly things, then he is both *not masculine* and *gay*. And, in this ugly thinking, if he is gay, he is also likely to be a pedophile.

As Jack indicated, in their love for My Little Pony, the bronies challenge normative gender. The challenge is not explicitly stated or direct. Bronies explain their passion with reference to the innocence of the show, the fun celebrated in the series, the tolerance exhibited, and the community of bronies enjoying the show together.[6] One brony, an Army drill sergeant at Fort Benning, explained to Labash, "A good part of the appeal is that wholesomeness and innocence." Some argue that *My Little Pony: Friendship Is*

Magic is just "good television." A brony named Santi described the appeal of the show to me:

> Some bronies are in it because they like to see a show so idealistic and cartoony while most things on the media, nowadays, are so dark and gritty. Some bronies really like the songs. Others like the storytelling. Others, the characters.... and so on. My opinion is that it's a little bit of everything, it's the combination of all those factors that make *My Little Pony: Friendship Is Magic* such an interesting show.

Santi clarified, "It has great writing, good characters, excellent voice-acting.... Of course, you're hearing all of this from a brony. So, don't quote me on this." He paused before adding, "Or do."[7]

Good television aside, community, openness, and having fun together seemed central to the movement's appeal. Liam, another brony I spoke with, said, "The brony community is a really solid space for a couple of reasons. First, it's a fun community full of primarily nonjudgmental people who just like to have a good time. Secondly, it produces a lot of enjoyable fan material including music, fan fictions and numerous videos."[8] On the theme of community, Liam explained, "The simple presence of the community makes the show more enjoyable. Half the fun is seeing how certain people reacted to an episode, watching fan spoofs, and seeing if *Friendship Is Witchcraft* [a spoof series produced by fans] has released another goofy fan episode."[9] Santi summed up the appeal of the brony community and of the *My Little Pony* show; friendship is very important in both. "The bronies themselves are a wonderful community. They are as welcoming as can be ('Love and Tolerate' is our motto), they don't take themselves too seriously." And, he added, bronies "are fun as heck. They even have charity initiatives all around the world."

Jack compared *My Little Pony* to other children's shows that young-adult males enjoy.

> These shows tend to have a typical thematic structure of a young hero who represents a pure good against some enemy who represents a pure evil. There is little ambiguity and the powers of love, friendship, et cetera tend to play an important role. I think humans desperately seek for such a simple world, as a reprieve from the utterly complex grey morality of the real world. The difference here is that this particular trend challenges gender norms.[10]

Central to the theme of Michel Foucault's work is how the individual is "constructed" from the diverse powers that proliferate in modern life. This

construction produces thought that both constrains but also resists constraints. Horse-crazy girls and bronies resist and live more vitally in the
shared world they create. Jack describes the vital meanings in his community. He saw tolerance as central to both the community and the show. About
"what makes the show good," he said, "I think it has a lot to do with the great
animation and nostalgic effect it has on its viewer with regard to its general
themes of friendship and empathy." According to Jack, those themes resonate throughout the community. He explained that "an oft-quoted brony
meme" is "I'm gonna love and tolerate the shit out of you."[11]

Notes

Chapter 1. Horse Crazy

1. Schowalter, "Some Meanings of Being," 501.

2. I signal the personal-narrative writing as distinct by changing not only the writing style or voice but also the margin (one is indented more than the other) and alignment (one is justified, one is ragged right), and by adding an icon. These are common ways to note a shift in register among scholars who incorporate personal narrative, memoir, and experimental writing into their scholarly work. For another example, see Grace M. Cho's beautiful and award-winning book, *Haunting the Korean Diaspora*.

3. Interview by author on April 6, 2013. I have changed the names of this person and almost all those who participated in my study to protect their privacy.

4. Birke and Brandt, "Mutual Corporeality," 196.

5. I am especially grateful to Francesca Degiuli for this idea about the uniqueness of horseback riding as a form of empowerment for girls.

6. Interview by author on April 6, 2013.

7. Haraway, *When Species Meet*.

8. In her fascinating study of gender integration in equestrian sport in the United Kingdom, discussed briefly in chapter 5, Katherine L. Dashper also offers a strong challenge to binary culture in "Beyond the Binary."

9. Haraway, *Companion Species Manifesto*, 6.

10. Along with Haraway and other animal studies scholars, I draw from texts such as Margo DeMello's *Animals in Society* and Kay Peggs's *Animals and Sociology*. DeMello's book, the first textbook offering an overview of human-animal studies, makes a wonderful backdrop to my study and justifies the need for it. Peggs

challenges sociology to rethink its disciplinary boundaries. She argues for stretching the traditional understanding of sociology as a discipline focused only on humans. Like DeMello's, Peggs's text offers a frame for and validates my exploration of the special relationship between girls and horses.

11. Probyn, "Girls and Girls."

12. Interview by author on May 10, 2014.

13. Halley, *Boundaries of Touch*.

14. Dashper, "It's a Form of Freedom."

15. Interviews by author on September 10, 2013; February 12, 2014; and April 21, 2014.

16. Olmert, *Made for Each Other*.

17. Foucault, *Discipline and Punish*.

18. Jacob Segal in personal correspondence with the author, February 24, 2018.

19. Foucault, *Discipline and Punish*, 223.

20. Halley, *Parallel Lives*, 16–17.

21. The obsession with thinness is a useful example for a book about U.S. girls because of its prevalence—it is something experienced by many girls. To some degree, horse-crazy girls are finding alternatives to such heteronormative obsessions.

22. Foucault, *History of Sexuality*, 144. Page numbers to works cited in the previous note are given parenthetically in the text to avoid the use of *ibid.* as possible.

23. Halley, *Parallel Lives*, 13.

24. Foucault, *Society Must Be Defended*, 252–253.

25. Foucault, *History of Sexuality*, 144.

26. Shukin, *Animal Capital*, 12.

27. I am grateful to Melissa Hope Ditmore for alerting me to this website, Lore Sjoberg, "Porn Star or My Little Pony?" Quizzes, *The Brunching Shuttlecocks*, http://archive.is/Wy2mC (accessed September 23, 2018).

28. The enormously popular *My Little Pony* movie, released June 6, 1986, grossed $5,958,456 domestically.

29. Sanchez, "Every Time They Ride," 259.

30. Dashper, "Strong, Active Women," 358.

31. Grier, *Pets in America*.

32. Haederle, "Economic Crisis."

33. Kilby, "Demographics," 200.

34. Oakeshott, "Voice of Poetry," 537.

35. Rose, *Powers of Freedom*, 282.

36. Foucault, "What Is Enlightenment?" 315. For more on this essay by Foucault, see Segal, "Michel Foucault and Michael Oakeshott."

37. I used similar methodologies in two of my previous books, *Boundaries of Touch* and *The Parallel Lives of Women and Cows*. In this I follow Robert R. Alford, *The Craft of Inquiry*, and others who encourage triangulation of methodologies.

38. My adviser, media studies scholar and historian Stuart Ewen, worked closely with me in writing my dissertation that became my first book, *Boundaries of Touch*, on ways of thinking about touching children in the mainstream United States. Following Ewen, in *Horse Crazy*, I use a theoretical framework grounded in cultural studies, media studies, and the work of Foucault. In *Boundaries of Touch*, I explore thinking about touching children via analyzing self-help books on child-rearing and other popular cultural material in terms of what I call ideologies of touch. I examine the meanings of these ways of thinking in terms of social power and the impact the ideologies had on women, men, and others who parent. Using Foucault, I argue, "Ideologies of adult-child touch are part of larger patterns of social 'power' that reveal and reproduce mainstream conceptions of gender, sexuality, race and class. In other words, these ways of thinking are normative; they expose social power 'in action.' And social power *happens* through them" (2). Child-rearing advice is a bit like popular cultural material for horsey girls. It both challenges sexist restrictions on mothers (and horsey girls) and reproduces such restrictions. Popular truths about parenting, much like popular truths about being a girl who loves horses, are born from a cultural context and are, to some extent, expressions of power in that cultural context.

39. Personal-narrative writing is sometimes also called memoir, autoethnographic, or experimental writing.

40. See Patricia Ticineto Clough's *End(s) of Ethnography*, and the volume Clough and I edited, *The Affective Turn*, for more on this methodology.

41. Alford, *The Craft of Inquiry*.

42. Numerous sociologists have published their experimental writing. These include books by Grace M. Cho, Patricia Ticineto Clough, Norman K. Denzin, Carolyn Ellis, Laurel Richardson, and Allen Shelton. Indeed, Cho's beautiful book about trauma and the Korean War, *Haunting the Korean Diaspora*, won a major American Sociological Association award. There is also a burgeoning of social thought about personal-narrative writing dating back two decades.

About experimental writing, Clough notes that some sociologists critique feminist, queer, and other modes of critical sociological inquiry, including experimental writing or autoethnography, because they see it as operating against rational modes of doing sociology (2007). In response to this critique, like Clough, I argue that there is an unconscious (unrecognized) element to rational sociological discourse. Critical sociological inquiry such as that in the form of experimental writing works as a critique of the belief that our social-scientific work is fully conscious, fully rational.

Because knowledge and production are now indissoluble, earlier assumptions about the separation between knowledge and power no longer work as social models (Aronowitz and DiFazio, *The Jobless Future*). Experimental writing is one methodology that helps us think through this contemporary knowledge/power tangle. About this, in *The Order of Things*, Michel Foucault claims that he meant "to reveal the positive unconscious" of the social sciences (xi). Foucault argues that this unconscious was "a level that eludes the consciousness of the scientist and yet is part of scientific discourse."

43. I changed the names and other identifying characteristics of all those I interviewed, except for one woman, an important animal studies and feminist scholar who gave me permission to use her real name, Carol J. Adams.

44. I write at length about this personal history in my book *The Parallel Lives of Women and Cows*.

45. For example, see "The Legacy of the Black West" at the New York City Federation of Black Cowboys, http://nycfederationofblackcowboys.com/legacy_of_the_black_west.html (accessed August 3, 2017).

46. Halley, Eshleman, and Vijaya, *Seeing White*.

47. Interview by author on February 3, 2013.

48. GaWaNi Pony Boy, *Of Women and Horses: Essays*.

49. In particular, I wonder about the experiences of Native American girls. There is a popular idea, perhaps based in part on white fantasy and the racist association of Native Americans with nature and all things animal, that Native Americans in general are horse people. A newspaper article by Leslie Linthicum, "Delicate Balance in Horse Nation," notes the importance of horses and describes a debate, in local indigenous communities, about whether to send wild horses to slaughter. The author quotes a member of the Sioux community, Sandy Schaefer, who believes that "[t]o slaughter a horse is greedy, disrespectful, and contrary to the Native Americans' relationship with its brother nation, the horse nation."

Perhaps some indigenous groups, including some living in the southwestern United States, do ride and use horses more than the population at large. Do Native American girls experience horse craziness? If so, what role do horses play in the lives of Native American girls? And for those who do not have actual horses, are some girls still horse crazy? What is the meaning of horses to indigenous girls?

50. Halley, Eshleman, and Vijaya, *Seeing White*.

51. For more on social class and equestrian culture in Ontario, Canada, see Kendra Coulter's intriguing article, "Herds and Hierarchies," and her book chapter, "Horse Power."

52. Korda, *Horse People*, 234.

53. Pierson, *Dark Horses and Black Beauties*, back cover.

54. Forrest, *If Wishes Were Horses*.

55. Haraway, *When Species Meet*, 3.

56. Haraway, *When Species Meet*, 301.

57. Adelman and Knijnik, *Gender and Equestrian Sport*. The recent anthology *Equestrian Cultures in Global and Local Context*, edited by Miriam Adelman and Kirrilly Thompson, also addresses equestrianism globally but without the focus on gender.

58. Davis and Maurstad, *Meaning of Horses*.

59. Birke and Brandt, "Mutual Corporeality." Katherine Dashper is a prolific and important scholar of animal, gender, and sports studies. For example, see Dashper's "Tools of the Trade?" and her "Listening to Horses."

60. Interview by author on February 3, 2013.

61. Korda, *Horse People*, 83.

62. Adrian Franklin, *Animals and Modern Cultures*, 1.

63. For more on this, see Katherine Dashper, "Strong, Active Women"; Dorré, *Victorian Fiction*; Plymoth, "Gender in Equestrian Sports"; and Thorell and Hedenborg, "Riding Instructors, Gender, Militarism."

64. Cunningham, "Seizing the Reins," 65.

65. Dashper, "Strong, Active Women," 351.

66. Gilder, *Men and Marriage*. Regarding recent evidence of the influence of Gilder's work, Rich Lowry, editor of the conservative *National Review*, refers to Gilder's "classic book" *Men and Marriage* to support his argument in "The Wages of Polygamy." And in "Four Legacies of Feminism," popular conservative writer Dennis Prager notes that Gilder's "classic book on single men" supports Prager's argument about feminism.

For more on liberal feminist and other debates around gender and care-work, see my first book, *Boundaries of Touch*, in which I explore these debates and the various positions taken by U.S. feminists on care-work.

Chapter 2. U.S. Horse History from Colonization to Recreation

1. Foucault, *Society Must Be Defended*, 252–253.

2. Foucault, *History of Sexuality*, 138.

3. Shukin, *Animal Capital*, 11.

4. Foucault, *History of Sexuality*, 143.

5. Shukin, *Animal Capital*.

6. Dashper, "Strong, Active Women," 351.

7. As noted in chapter 1, for more on this, see Dashper, "Strong, Active Women"; Dorré, *Victorian Fiction*; Plymoth, "Gender in Equestrian Sports"; and Thorell and Hedenborg, "Riding Instructors, Gender, Militarism."

8. Franklin, *Animals and Modern Cultures.*

9. Williams, *Horse*, 95.

10. Stillman, *Mustang*, 37.

11. Williams, *Horse*, 93 (Kindle edition 94).

12. Stillman, *Mustang*, 38.

13. Wilson and Reeder, "Equus Caballus."

14. Stillman, *Mustang*, 40.

15. University of California Museum of Paleontology, "The Pleistocene Epoch."

16. Hoig, *Came Men on Horses*, 3.

17. Viola, "Introduction," 7.

18. Hoig, *Came Men on Horses*, 3.

19. Viola, "Introduction," 7.

20. Kilby, "Demographics," 179, 186–189.

21. Viola, "Introduction," 10.

22. James, *Home Ranch*, x.

23. James, *Home Ranch*, 55–56.

24. Zeigler, "Cowboy Strike of 1883."

25. McMurtry, *Lonesome Dove*, 136.

26. Halley, *Parallel Lives*, 23.

27. Stillman, *Mustang*, 132–133.

28. Ibid., 140–141.

29. Ibid., 143–144.

30. Shukin, *Animal Capital*, 20.

31. Stillman, *Mustang*, 196.

32. Ibid., 196–197.

33. Library of Congress, "Thomas Edison Patented the Kinetoscope."

34. Stillman, *Mustang*, 199.

35. National Mustang Association, "What Is a Mustang?"

36. Stillman, *Mustang*, 237.

37. Stillman, "Wild Horses Aren't Free."

38. Stillman, *Mustang*, xii.

39. Ibid., 262–263.

40. Ibid., 244.

41. Ibid., 236–237.

42. Ibid., 239.

43. Ibid., 249.

44. Ibid., 241.

45. Ibid., 248.

46. Ibid., 247.

47. Henry, *Mustang*, 83.

48. Ibid., 84–85.

49. Stillman, *Mustang*, 250.

50. Henry, *Mustang*, 86–87.

51. Stillman, *Mustang*, 252.

52. Ibid., 253.

53. Stillman, "Wild Horses Aren't Free."

54. Oklahoma State University Department of Animal Sciences, "Breeds of Livestock: Mustang (Horse)."

55. Stillman, *Mustang*, 265.

56. Interview by author on March 26, 2013.

57. Interview by author on April 6, 2013.

58. See my earlier book *Boundaries of Touch*, particularly 28–38, for more information about these sociohistorical shifts.

59. Cunningham, "Seizing the Reins," 65.

60. Limerick, *Legacy of Conquest*.

61. Hall, *Well of Loneliness*, 228.

62. Maines, *Technology of Orgasm*, 89.

63. Interview by author on August 26, 2013.

64. Tucker, *Child and the Book*, 163.

65. Korda, *Horse People*, 102.

66. Ibid., 103.

67. Roberts, *Man Who Listens to Horses*, 21.

68. Birke, "Learning to Speak Horse," 237.

69. Writer Nicholas Evans used Buck Brannaman as the model for his character Tom Booker in the novel *The Horse Whisperer* (1995). This book was turned into a 1998 film with the same title, and Robert Redford produced, directed, and acted in the film as Tom Booker. Brannaman assisted in making the film and acted as Redford's double.

70. Birke, "Learning to Speak Horse," 224.

71. Olmert, *Made for Each Other*, 85.

72. Roberts, *Man Who Listens to Horses*, 4.

Chapter 3. Dreaming of Horses

1. Interview by author on May 22, 2013.

2. Interview by author on October 16, 2013.

3. Interview by author on April 6, 2013.

4. Interview by author on March 27, 2013.

5. Korda, *Horse People*, 78.

6. Here and throughout the book, I use "pony" and "horse" interchangeably. Both are equines; ponies are just smaller equines as they are under 14.2 hands. (Hands are the units commonly used to measure horses and ponies. Each hand is four inches.) In contrast to ponies, horses are at least 14.2 hands.

7. Badger, *Heroines on Horseback*, 96; and Kendrick, "Riders, Readers, Romance," 184.

8. Korda, *Horse People*, 105.

9. Pullein-Thompson, *Phantom Horse Disappears*, 25.

10. The scholarly literature about pony and horse stories for children is extremely limited. I found fewer than ten scholarly articles. In an early example of this literature, Bernard Poll ignores gender yet still makes an argument that to some extent supports mine, that is, that the horse in horse stories "attracts children because of the role it plays in fulfilling [children's] needs" for "uncompromising, unqualified" love (473).

11. Haymonds, "Rides of Passage," 51.

12. Haymonds, "Pony Books."

13. Haymonds, "Rides of Passage," 53.

14. McCabe et al., "Gender in Twentieth-century Children's Books."

15. Badger, *Heroines on Horseback*, 87.

16. In online Google searches, and along with *Black Beauty*, these three books— *My Friend Flicka* (1940), *The Black Stallion* (1941), and *Misty of Chincoteague* (1947)—come up on list after list of the top, the best, the most-read horse books. For example, see Goodreads, www.goodreads.com/list/show/245.Best_Horse _Books (accessed June 20, 2017). They are even listed as the best horse books on lists for adult readers such as this one at *Horse Illustrated* ("30 Best Horse Books," December 15, 2006), www.horsechannel.com/horse-fun/30-best-horse-books.aspx (accessed June 20, 2017).

17. Haymonds, "Rides of Passage," 57.

18. Pullein-Thompson, *Fair Girls and Grey Horses*, 130.

19. "Obituary of Josephine Pullein-Thompson," *The Guardian*, June 22, 2014, www.theguardian.com/books/2014/jun/22/josephine-pullein-thompson (accessed July 26, 2016).

20. Tucker, *The Child and the Book*, 162.

21. Badger, *Heroines on Horseback*, 96.

22. Thiel, "Dark Horse," 112–122.

23. Haymonds, "Rides of Passage," 52.

24. Badger, *Heroines on Horseback*, 89.

25. Haymonds, "Rides of Passage," 51.

26. For example, see Haymonds, "Rides of Passage"; and Kendrick, "Riders, Readers, Romance," 184.

27. On their website, Barnes & Noble claims that since the novel came out in 1877, over fifty million copies of *Black Beauty* have been sold. It is one of the best-selling books of all time and has, the website states, been "translated into 50 languages," www.barnesandnoble.com/w/all-time-bestseller-anna-sewell/1105013694?type= eBook# (accessed September 16, 2018). And in 2017 Google listed *Black Beauty* seventh in a list of books "popular on the web" (accessed June 20, 2017).

28. Pullein-Thompson, *Fair Girls and Grey Horses*, 129.

29. Badger, *Heroines on Horseback*, 10–11.

30. Dorré, *Victorian Fiction*, 109.

31. Dorré, *Victorian Fiction*, 112.

32. Of books from the twentieth-century United Kingdom and United States, I have yet to find a pony book, or a reference to a pony book, that has children of color as primary characters.

33. Sewell, *Black Beauty*, 1.

34. Dorré, *Victorian Fiction*, 109.

35. Badger, *Heroines on Horseback*, 10.

36. Haymonds, "Rides of Passage," 53.

37. Badger, *Heroines on Horseback*, 10.

38. Kilby, "Demographics," 176, 177.

39. Korda, *Horse People*, 90.

40. Badger, *Heroines on Horseback*, 10.

41. Haymonds, "Rides of Passage," 66–67.

42. Golden Gorse quoted in Badger, *Heroines on Horseback*, 13.

43. Stacey Gregg quoted in Badger, *Heroines on Horseback*, 83.

44. Badger, *Heroines on Horseback*, 20.

45. Pullein-Thompson, *Phantom Horse Disappears*, 12.

46. Haymonds, "Rides of Passage," 67.

47. Badger, *Heroines on Horseback*, 100.

48. Ibid., 45.

49. Diana Pullein-Thompson quoted in Badger, *Heroines on Horseback*, 45.

50. Badger, *Heroines on Horseback*, 46.

51. "Obituary of Christine Pullein-Thompson," *The Telegraph*, December 6, 2005, www.telegraph.co.uk/news/obituaries/1504796/Christine-Pullein-Thompson.html (accessed July 24, 2016).

52. Badger, *Heroines on Horseback*, 39.

53. Ibid., 32.

54. Ibid., 20.

55. Enid Bagnold quoted in Badger, *Heroines on Horseback*, 21.

56. Bagnold, *National Velvet*, 67.

57. Tucker, *Child and the Book*, 163.

58. Farley, *Black Stallion Returns*, 231.

59. Farley, *Island Stallion*, 2200–2207.

60. Farley, *Black Stallion's Courage*, 339–346.

61. Badger, *Heroines on Horseback*, 58.

62. Ibid.

63. Ibid., 96.

64. Pullein-Thompson, *Phantom Horse: 1*, 5–6.

65. Pullein-Thompson, *Phantom Horse Comes Home: 2*, 164.

66. Haymonds, "Rides of Passage," 51.

67. Ibid., 57.

68. Turner, *Frontier in American History*, 2–3.

69. Halley, *Parallel Lives*, 26.

70. Turner, *Frontier in American History*, 3.

71. Halley, *Parallel Lives*, 27.

72. O'Hara, *My Friend Flicka*, 12.

73. See Walter Farley's Black Stallion series, published between 1941 and 1989.

74. Farley, *Black Stallion*, 103.

75. Interview by author on May 22, 2013.

76. Badger, *Heroines on Horseback*, 146.

77. Interview by author on April 6, 2013.

78. Chincoteague Chamber of Commerce, "Pony Penning History."

79. Henry, *Misty of Chincoteague*, 32.

80. Henry, *Misty of Chincoteague*, 70–71.

81. Interview by author on May 22, 2013.

Chapter 4. The Past That Is Still Present

1. Rose, *Powers of Freedom*, 282.

2. Halley, *Parallel Lives*, 12.

3. Korda, *Horse People*, 83.

4. "An Introduction to the Wind River Indian Reservation of Wyoming," Jackson Hole Historical Society & Museum.

5. "Crow Nation," Montana.gov.

6. My friend Rakesh Rajani wondered about the real origins of the name Buck.

7. Patricia Leitch quoted in Badger, *Heroines on Horseback*, 140.

8. Raban, "Unlamented West," 63.

9. See my book *The Parallel Lives of Women and Cows*, in particular 74–75, for a brief history of fences in the western United States.

10. In *The Legacy of Conquest*, Patricia Nelson Limerick explores the history of this all-too-common thinking of many white westerners about property ownership and their own right to the land. I do not know if the old woman was white or of color, but she seemed to share this thinking with many white people living in the West.

Chapter 5. Ways of Thinking about Normal in the United States

1. Halley, *Boundaries of Touch*, 2.

2. Foucault, *Discipline and Punish*.

3. Rose, *Powers of Freedom*.

4. As discussed in chapter 3, pony books, like other elements of horse-crazy girl culture, *do* normalize along with their challenge to normalization. The books, for example, exclude girls of color along with other marginalized groups. And they support contemporary capitalist ideology by proposing that if one tries hard enough, there are no limits to what one can achieve.

5. For example, see the opening story in George Gilder's *Men and Marriage*, 12. As I argue in chapter 1, note 66, Gilder's work continues to be very relevant and influential.

6. Korda, *Horse People*, 76.

7. Plymoth, "Gender in Equestrian Sports," 337.

8. See chapter 6 for more information on horse therapy, including the two common forms, hippotherapy and equine-facilitated psychotherapy (EFP).

9. Folse, *Smart Woman's Guide*.

10. Interview by author on May 11, 2013.

11. Interview by author on March 26, 2013.

12. Interview by author on May 7, 2013.

13. As mentioned previously, I changed all my participants' names to protect their privacy except in the case of Carol J. Adams.

14. Dashper, "Strong, Active Women," 353.

15. Plymoth, "Gender in Equestrian Sports," 336. Also see Katherine Dashper's intriguing study "Together, Yet Still Not Equal?" Dashper makes clear that integration at the Olympic level does not automatically bring equality. "Although sex integration," she writes, "may be an important step towards breaking down gender hierarchies in sport, without accompanying wider changes in gender norms and expectations, sex integration alone will not be enough to achieve greater gender equality in equestrian sport" (1).

16. Interview by author on June 25, 2013.

17. Halley and Eshleman, *Seeing Straight*.

18. Hochschild with Machung, *Second Shift*.

19. Interview by author on February 12, 2014.

20. Ojanen, "You Became Someone."

21. Interview by author on May 7, 2013; one woman, Toni, who grew up working class (interview by author on June 25, 2013), told me about inheriting her love of horse racing from her father. She grew up in a large city in New Jersey where her father owned a tavern. She and her father along with much of his family followed racing closely. Toni described skipping school to go to the racetracks and, one day, bumping into her uncle there. As he was *also* supposed to be somewhere else, he suggested that neither one had seen the other, and they quickly parted ways.

22. Interview by author on March 15, 2013.

23. Anderson, "Marriage."

24. Barnes, "Right Finds a Fresh Voice."

25. Prager, "Four Legacies of Feminism."

26. Gilder, *Men and Marriage*, 12.

27. Prager, "Four Legacies of Feminism."

28. Gilder, *Men and Marriage*, 16.

29. Prager, "Four Legacies of Feminism."

30. Gilder, *Men and Marriage*, 19.

31. Pullein-Thompson, *Fair Girls and Grey Horses*, 339.

32. I discuss the mind-body split and the association of women with the body, men with the mind, at length in chapter 1 of *Boundaries of Touch*.

33. Halley, *Boundaries of Touch*.

34. Midkiff, "An Intuitive Edge," 82.

35. Badger, *Heroines on Horseback*, 89.

36. For example, see the Jean character in Christine Pullein-Thompson's Phantom Horse series of six books published between 1955 and 1985.

37. Plymoth, "Gender in Equestrian Sports," 345.

38. Dashper, "Beyond the Binary," 48.

39. Eisenstein, *Feminism Seduced*, 57–58.

40. Halley, *Boundaries of Touch*, 131–150.

41. bell hooks, *Feminist Theory*.

42. Hochschild with Machung, *Second Shift*, 2012.

43. Halley, *Boundaries of Touch*, 131–150.

44. Dashper, "Strong, Active Women," 351.

45. Sanchez, "Every Time They Ride," 259.

46. For a moving and powerful example of struggling with and recovering from a horseback-riding injury, see Katherine Dashper's "Getting Better."

47. Thorell and Hedenborg, "Riding Instructors, Gender, Militarism," 659.

48. For an important review of horse-related risks and safety practices, see Thompson, McGreevy, and McManus, "Critical Review of Horse-Related Risk."

49. In many places, including the mainstream United States, horses are normally trained to be saddled and mounted on the left side. As a child, I was told that this is because when horses were used in war, soldiers carried their swords on the left (so that they could grab their sword with their right hand). Other riders confirmed that this was the reason they learned too.

50. Interview by author on March 15, 2013.

51. Interview by author on May 22, 2013.

52. Interview by author on April 6, 2013.

53. Badger, *Heroines on Horseback*.

54. Haymonds, "Rides of Passage," 66.

55. Cunningham, "Seizing the Reins," 65.

56. Ojanen, "You Became Someone," 150.

57. Adams, *Sexual Politics of Meat*.

58. Interview by author on September 10, 2013.

59. Korda, *Horse People*, 81.

60. Toth, "Psychology of Women and Horses," 34.

61. Patricia Leitch quoted in Badger, *Heroines on Horseback*, 137.

62. Korda, *Horse People*, 181.

63. Interview by author on May 7, 2013.

64. Interview by author on March 15, 2013.

65. Normally, all female horses (called fillies when young and mares when adults), and some male horses (called colts when young and stallions when adults), remain intact and able to reproduce. In the United States today, most male horses, like my childhood horse Snipaway, are gelded or castrated and called geldings.

66. Interview by author on May 21, 2013.

67. Ojanen, "You Became Someone," 139.

68. Slaughter, "Why Women.".

69. Other feminist scholarship on care-work and domestic labor that I draw from for this project (and used in *Boundaries of Touch*) includes but is not limited to Linda M. Blum's *At the Breast*, Chris Bobel's *The Paradox of Natural Mothering*, Stephanie Coontz's *The Way We Never Were*, Ann Crittenden's *The Price of Motherhood*, Barbara Ehrenreich and Deirdre English's *For Her Own Good*, Anita Garey's *Weaving Work and Motherhood*, and Julia Grant's *Raising Baby by the Book*.

70. Slaughter, "Why Women," 86.

Chapter 6. Horsey Girls

1. Halley and Eshleman, *Seeing Straight*, 67.

2. Miller, *Out of the Past*, 166.

3. Hall, *Well of Loneliness*, 10.

4. Even when I had my own pony, I played innumerable fantasy games. For example, with a neighbor girl down the street, Cora, we were both horses, racing around my front lawn, wild and free. The Junie B. Jones series of books for elementary school-age children also offers one, among many, examples of girls playing at being horses. Junie B. herself is a horse named Brownie. For instance, see *Junie B. Jones Is Not a Crook!* by Barbara Park.

5. Tanner, "These Folks."

6. S. Thompson, *Going All the Way*.

7. See, for example, Feinberg, *Stone Butch Blues*; Scholinski with Adams, *Last Time I Wore a Dress*; and Tanenbaum, *Slut!*

8. Maloney and the Joint Economic Committee Democratic Staff, *Gender Pay Inequality*; see also DeNavas-Walt and Proctor, *Income and Poverty*.

9. DeNavas-Walt and Proctor, *Income and Poverty*.

10. Halley, *Boundaries of Touch*.

11. Johnson and Hawbaker, "#MeToo."

12. Buchwald, Fletcher, and Roth, *Transforming a Rape Culture*.

13. Buchwald, Fletcher, and Roth, *Transforming a Rape Culture*, 8–9.

14. Buchwald, Fletcher, and Roth, *Transforming a Rape Culture*, 8–9; Human Rights Watch, "U.S."

15. Center for Disease Control and Prevention, "Sexual Violence."

16. Haymonds, "Rides of Passage," 64.

17. Korda, *Horse People*, 78.

18. Probyn, "Girls and Girls."

19. Zoetis, "2015 AHP Equine Industry Survey."

20. Probyn, "Girls and Girls," 23.

21. Interview by author on March 15, 2013.

22. Interview by author on May 11, 2013.

23. Haraway, *When Species Meet.*

24. Probyn, "Girls and Girls," 27.

25. Patricia Leitch quoted in Badger, *Heroines on Horseback*, 140.

26. Haraway, *Companion Species Manifesto*, 20.

27. See Joseph Schneider's *Donna Haraway* for a beautiful overview of Haraway's work, including discussions of Haraway's challenges to binary thinking on, for example, pages 36–39 and 75–86.

28. Haraway, *Companion Species Manifesto*, 35–36.

29. Interview by author on April 21, 2014.

30. Interview by author on May 4, 2013.

31. Korda, *Horse People*, 291.

32. In my first book, *Boundaries of Touch*, I explore both the impact, and our thinking about the impact, of physical contact between human adults and children.

33. Interview by author on April 21, 2014.

34. Olmert, *Made for Each Other*, xv.

35. Ibid.

36. Ibid., 212.

37. Pullein-Thompson, *Phantom Horse Comes Home*, 22.

38. Olmert, *Made for Each Other.*

39. Interview by author on April 21, 2014.

40. Hall, *Well of Loneliness*, 60–61.

41. Volz, "Galloping Away to a Place."

42. Interview by author on May 22, 2013.

43. Toth, "Psychology of Women and Horses," 34.

44. Jean Halley, personal Facebook page, www.facebook.com/jean.halley/posts/10201966539223479 (accessed September 19, 2013).

45. Luna, "The Horse, My Healer and Guide,"

46. Pullein-Thompson, *Phantom Horse in Danger*, 121.

47. Thorne, *Gender Play.*

48. For a rich exploration of the issue of the relationship between humans and horses in competitive equestrian sports, see Dashper, "Tools of the Trade."

49. Interview by author on March 26, 2013.

50. Personal material shared by participant in interview by author on August 15, 2013.

51. Korda, *Horse People*, 81.

52. Pullein-Thompson, *Phantom Horse Disappears*, 100.

53. Interview by author on May 11, 2013.

54. Halley, *Boundaries of Touch.*

55. Culpepper, "Two Racehorses, Both Male,."

56. Halley and Eshleman, *Seeing Straight*, 87–88.

57. McRuer, "Disabling Sex."

58. Finger, "Forbidden Fruit"; quoted in McRuer, "Disabling Sex," 107.

59. For example, see All, Loving, and Crane, "Animals."

60. Visit by author on August 23, 2013.

61. Davis, Maurstad, and Dean, "My Horse Is My Therapist," 299.

62. Interview by author on April 6, 2013.

63. Haymonds, "Rides of Passage," 59.

64. Dashper, "It's a Form of Freedom."

65. Interview by author on April 6, 2013.

66. Interview by author on April 6, 2013.

67. Interview by author on March 26, 2013.

68. Pullein-Thompson, *Phantom Horse in Danger*, 116.

69. Foucault, "On the Genealogy of Ethics," 316; I discuss this in my earlier work, *Boundaries of Touch*, 163–165.

Chapter 7. Horses

1. For further exploration, see the engaging anthropological anthology *The Meaning of Horses: Biosocial Encounters*, edited by Dona Lee Davis and Anita Maurstad. These scholars grapple with the meanings of horse lives across historical and transnational lines.

2. Grier, *Pets in America*, 100.

3. Herriot, *All Creatures Great and Small*, 149.

4. O'Hara, *My Friend Flicka*, 84.

5. Birke, "Learning to Speak Horse," 227.

6. Barakat, "5 Ways."

7. Camp, *Soul of a Horse*, 81.

8. Birke, "Learning to Speak Horse," 227.

9. Camp, *Soul of a Horse*, 81.

10. Heyn, "Berlin's Wonderful Horse."

11. Despret, "Who Made Clever Hans Stupid?"

12. Hall, *Well of Loneliness*, 228.

13. Interview with author on March 15, 2013.

14. Eisnitz, *Slaughterhouse*, 109.

15. "Horse Slaughter."

16. Eisnitz, *Slaughterhouse*, 110.

17. About this, Justine S. Patrick writes, "The commercial pet food industry faces minimal substantive regulation, despite navigating several layers of regulation

from various groups including the FDA, the American Association of Feed Control Officials (AAFCO), and state regulators. The FDA entrusts AAFCO to issue regulations governing ingredients, feeding trials, labels and nutritional claims. But AAFCO's rules fall short of ensuring that America's pets receive adequate nutrition, or even foods that won't cause chronic digestive, skin, eye, and coat problems. The influence by the pet food industry over AAFCO manifests itself through AAFCO's irrational regulations, including ingredient definitions which effectively prohibit organic chickens and vegetables, while blindly permitting thousands of euthanized cats and dogs to make their way into pet foods through the unsupervised rendering industry."

18. Halley, *Parallel Lives.*

19. Eisnitz, *Slaughterhouse,* 110–111.

20. Potter, "Timeline of Horse Slaughter Legislation."

21. "Horse Slaughter."

22. Sulzberger, "Slaughter of Horses Goes On."

23. "Horse Slaughter."

24. For example, see the Canadian Horse Defence Coalition's blog, "Working to Ban Horse Slaughter in Canada"; Animal Equality, "Mexican Slaughterhouses."

25. Woodhouse, "Charged with the Crime."

26. Woodhouse, "Charged with the Crime."

27. Halley, *Parallel Lives,* 129.

28. Ibid., 130.

29. Spiegel, "Introduction," vi.

30. Eisnitz, *Slaughterhouse,* 20.

31. Benjamin Franklin quoted in E. P. Thompson, "Time, Work-Discipline, and Industrial Capitalism," 89.

32. Halley, *Parallel Lives,* 130.

33. Eisnitz, *Slaughterhouse,* 28–29.

34. Lowe, "Working 'The Chain.'"

35. "Horse Slaughter."

36. "Euthanasia," Homes for Horses Coalition.

37. Haederle, "Economic Crisis Weighs Heavily."

38. Simon, "Pet Food Report."

Epilogue. The Boys Who Love Ponies

1. Malaquais, *Bronies.*

2. Lefkowitz, *Our Guys.*

3. Labash, "Dread Pony."

4. Ibid.

5. Interview by author on May 6, 2013.

6. Zaslow, "Hybrid Masculinity."

7. Interview by author on March 14, 2013.

8. Interview by author on May 12, 2013.

9. Interview by author on May 12, 2013.

10. Interview by author on May 6, 2013.

11. Interview by author on May 6, 2013.

Bibliography

Adams, Carol J. *The Sexual Politics of Meat: A Feminist-Vegetarian Critical Theory.* 1990; rpt., New York: Bloomsbury Academic, 2015.

Adelman, Miriam, and Jorge Knijnik. *Gender and Equestrian Sport: Riding around the World.* New York: Springer Netherlands, 2013.

Adelman, Miriam, and Kirrilly Thompson. *Equestrian Cultures in Global and Local Context.* New York: Springer Netherlands, 2017.

Alford, Robert R. *The Craft of Inquiry: Theories, Methods, Evidence.* Oxford: Oxford University Press, 1998.

All, A. C., G. L. Loving, and L. L. Crane. "Animals, Horseback Riding, and Implications for Rehabilitation Therapy." *Journal of Rehabilitation* 65, no. 3 (July/ August 1999): 49–57.

Anderson, Ryan T. "Marriage: What It Is, Why It Matters, and the Consequences of Redefining It." *Backgrounder*, March 11, 2013.

Aronowitz, Stanley, and William DiFazio. *The Jobless Future: Sci-Tech and the Dogma of Work.* Minneapolis: University of Minnesota Press, 1994.

Badger, Jane. *Heroines on Horseback: The Pony Book in Children's Fiction.* Somerset, UK: Girls Gone By, 2013.

Bagnold, Enid. *National Velvet.* 1949; rpt., New York: Scholastic Book Services, 1965.

Barakat, Christine. "5 Ways to Help Your Horse Live Longer." *Equus Magazine*, May 22, 2007. https://equusmagazine.com/management/livelonger_052207-8303.

Barnes, Robert. "The Right Finds a Fresh Voice on Same-Sex Marriage." *Washington Post*, April 15, 2015. www.washingtonpost.com/politics/courts_law/a-fresh-face -emerges-as-a-leader-in-the-movement-against-same-sex-marriage/2015/04/15 /d78cf256-dece-11e4-be40-566e2653afe5_story.html.

Birke, Lynda. "'Learning to Speak Horse': The Culture of 'Natural Horsemanship.'" *Society & Animals* 15, no. 3 (2007): 217–239.

Birke, Lynda, and Keri Brandt. "Mutual Corporeality: Gender and Human/Horse Relationships." *Women's Studies International Forum* 32 (June 21, 2009).

Blum, Linda M. *At the Breast: Ideologies of Breastfeeding and Motherhood in the Contemporary United States*. Boston: Beacon Press, 1999.

Bobel, Chris. *The Paradox of Natural Mothering*. Philadelphia: Temple University Press, 2002.

"Breeds of Livestock: Mustang (Horse)." Oklahoma State University Department of Animal Sciences. May 7, 2002. www.ansi.okstate.edu/breeds/horses/mustang (accessed November 29, 2016).

Buchwald, Emilie, Pamela R. Fletcher, and Martha Roth, editors. *Transforming a Rape Culture*. Minneapolis: Milkweed Editions, 1993.

Cable, Christina S. "Castration in the Horse." *The Horse: Your Guide to Equine Health Care*. April 1, 2001. www.thehorse.com/articles/10024/castration -in-the-horse.

Camp, Joe. *The Soul of a Horse: Life Lessons from the Herd*. New York: Three Rivers Press, 2009, Kindle edition.

Cho, Grace M. *Haunting the Korean Diaspora: Shame, Secrecy, and the Forgotten War*. Minneapolis: University of Minnesota Press, 2008.

Clough, Patricia Ticineto. *End(s) of Ethnography: From Realism to Social Criticism*. New York: Peter Lang, 1992.

Clough, Patricia Ticineto, with Jean Halley, editors. *The Affective Turn: Theorizing the Social*. Durham, N.C.: Duke University Press, 2007.

Coontz, Stephanie. *The Way We Never Were: American Families and the Nostalgia Trap*. New York: BasicBooks, 1992.

Coulter, Kendra. "Herds and Hierarchies: Class, Nature, and the Social Construction of Horses in Equestrian Culture." *Society & Animals* 22, no. 2 (2014): 135–152.

———. "Horse Power: Gender, Work, and Wealth in Canadian Show Jumping." In *Gender and Equestrian Sport*, edited by Miriam Adelman and Jorge Knijnik, 165–182. New York: Springer Netherlands, 2013.

Crittenden, Ann. *The Price of Motherhood: Why the Most Important Job in the World Is Still the Least Valued*. New York: Henry Holt, 2001.

"Crow Nation." Montana.gov. https://tribalnations.mt.gov/crow (accessed December 4, 2016).

Culpepper, Chuck. "Two Racehorses, Both Male, 'Fell in Love' and Grew Inseparable." *Washington Post*, December 25, 2017. www.washingtonpost.com /sports/two-racehorses-both-male-fell-in-love-and-grew-inseparable-until -tragedy-did-it-for-them/2017/12/25/a771d3ca-e75e-11e7-833f-155031558ff4 _story.html.

Cunningham, Gail. "Seizing the Reins: Women, Girls and Horses." In *Image and Power: Women in Fiction in the Twentieth Century*, edited by Sarah Sceats and Gail Cunningham, 65–76. London: Longman, 1996.

Dashper, Katherine L. "Beyond the Binary: Gender Integration in British Equestrian Sport." In *Gender and Equestrian Sport: Riding Around the World*, edited by Miriam Adelman and Jorge Knijnik, 37–54. New York: Springer Netherlands, 2013.

——— . "Getting Better: An Autoethnographic Tale of Recovery from Sporting Injury." *Sociology of Sport Journal* 30, no. 3 (2013): 323–339.

——— . "'It's a Form of Freedom:' The Experiences of People with Disabilities within Equestrian Sport." *Annals of Leisure Research* 13, nos. 1–2 (2010): 86–101.

——— . "Listening to Horses." *Society & Animals* 25, no. 3 (2017): 207–224.

——— . "Strong, Active Women: (Re)doing Rural Femininity through Equestrian Sport and Leisure." *Ethnography* 17, no. 3 (2016): 350–368.

——— . "Together, Yet Still Not Equal? Sex Integration in Equestrian Sport." *Asia-Pacific Journal of Health, Sport and Physical Education* 3, no. 3 (2012): 213–225.

——— . "Tools of the Trade or Part of the Family? Horses in Competitive Equestrian Sport." *Society and Animals* 22, no. 4 (2014): 352–371.

Davis, Dona Lee, and Anita Maurstad, editors. *The Meaning of Horses: Biosocial Encounters*. London: Routledge, 2016.

Davis, Dona Lee, Anita Maurstad, and Sarah Dean. "My Horse Is My Therapist: The Medicalization of Pleasure among Women Equestrians." *Medical Anthropology Quarterly*, Volume 29, Issue 3, 2014: 299.

DeMello, Margo. *Animals in Society: An Introduction to Human-Animal Studies*. New York: Columbia University Press, 2012.

DeNavas-Walt, Carmen, and Bernadette D. Proctor. *Income and Poverty in the United States: 2013*. Washington, D.C.: U.S. Government Printing Office, 2014.

Despret, Vinciane. "Who Made Clever Hans Stupid?" Translated by Matthew Chrulew. *Angelaki: Journal of the Theoretical Humanities* 20, no. 2 (May 18, 2015): 77–85.

Dorré, Gina M. *Victorian Fiction and the Cult of the Horse*. London: Ashgate, 2006.

Durkheim, Emile. *Suicide: A Study in Sociology*. 1951; rpt., New York: The Free Press, 1966.

Ehrenreich, Barbara, and Deirdre English. *For Her Own Good: 150 Years of the Experts' Advice to Women*. Garden City, N.J.: Anchor Books, 1978.

Eisenstein, Hester. *Feminism Seduced: How Global Elites Use Women's Labor and Ideas to Exploit the World*. Boulder, Colo.: Paradigm, 2009.

Eisnitz, Gail A. *Slaughterhouse: The Shocking Story of Greed, Neglect, and Inhumane Treatment Inside the U.S. Meat Industry*. Amherst, N.Y.: Prometheus Books, 1997.

Evans, Nicholas. *The Horse Whisperer*. New York: Delacorte Press, 1995.

Farley, Walter. *The Black Stallion*. 1941; rpt., New York: Random House Children's Books, 2002.

———. *The Black Stallion Returns*. 1945; rpt., New York: Random House Children's Books, 2016.

———. *The Black Stallion's Courage*. New York: Random House Children's Books, 1956.

———. *The Island Stallion*. New York: Random House Children's Books, 1948.

Feinberg, Leslie. *Stone Butch Blues*. New York: Alyson Books, 1993.

Finger, Anne. "Forbidden Fruit." *New Internationalist* 233 (1992): 9.

Folse, Melinda. *The Smart Woman's Guide to Midlife Horses: Find Meaning, Magic and Mastery in the Second Half of Life*. Foreword by Koelle Simpson and introduction by Clinton Anderson. North Pomfret, Vt.: Trafalgar Square Books, 2011.

Forrest, Susanna. *If Wishes Were Horses: A Memoir of Equine Obsession*. London: Atlantic Books, 2012.

Foucault, Michel. *Discipline and Punish: The Birth of the Prison*. New York: Vintage Books, 1979.

———. *The History of Sexuality: An Introduction*. Translated by Robert Hurley. Vol. 1. New York: Vintage Books, 1980.

———. "On the Genealogy of Ethics." In *The Foucault Reader*, edited by Paul Rabinow, 229–252. London: Penguin Books, 1984.

———. *The Order of Things: An Archaeology of the Human Sciences*. New York: Pantheon, 1970.

———. *Society Must Be Defended: Lectures at the Collège de France, 1975–1976*. New York: Picador, 2003.

———. "What Is Enlightenment?" In *Ethics: Subjectivity and Truth*, edited by Paul Rabinow, 303–319. New York: Free Press, 1997.

Franklin, Adrian. *Animals and Modern Cultures: A Sociology of Human-Animal Relations in Modernity*. Thousand Oaks, Calif.: Sage, 1999.

Franklin, Benjamin. Quoted in E. P. Thompson. "Time, Work-Discipline, and Industrial Capitalism." *Past and Present* II (1967): 89.

Friedan, Betty. *The Feminine Mystique*. 1963; rpt., New York: Dell, 1974.

Front Range Equine Rescue. www.frontrangeequinerescue.org (accessed July 26, 2017).

Garey, Anita. *Weaving Work and Motherhood*. Philadelphia: Temple University Press, 1999.

Gilder, George. *Men and Marriage*. Gretna, La.: Pelican, 1986.

Grant, Julia. *Raising Baby by the Book: The Education of American Mothers*. New Haven, Conn.: Yale University Press, 1998.

Grier, Katherine C. *Pets in America*. Chapel Hill: University of North Carolina Press, 2006.

Haederle, Michael. "Economic Crisis Weighs Heavily on Horses." *Los Angeles Times*, July 17, 2012: A6.

Hall, Radclyffe. *The Well of Loneliness*. Garden City, N.Y.: Blue Ribbon Books, 1928.

Halley, Jean. *Boundaries of Touch: Parenting and Adult-Child Intimacy*. Urbana: University of Illinois Press, 2007.

——— . *The Parallel Lives of Women and Cows: Meat Markets*. New York: Palgrave Macmillan, 2012.

Halley, Jean, and Amy Eshleman. *Seeing Straight: An Introduction to Gender and Sexual Privilege*. Lanham, Mich.: Rowman and Littlefield, 2017.

Halley, Jean, Amy Eshleman, and Ramya Mahadevan Vijaya. *Seeing White: An Introduction to White Privilege and Race*. Lanham, Mich.: Rowman and Littlefield, 2011.

Haraway, Donna J. *The Companion Species Manifesto: Dogs, People, and Significant Otherness*. Chicago: Prickly Paradigm Press, 2003.

——— . *When Species Meet*. Minneapolis: University of Minnesota Press, 2008.

Haymonds, Alison. "Pony Books." In *International Companion Encyclopedia of Children's Literature*, edited by Peter Hunt, 481–489. 2nd ed. London: Routledge, 2004.

——— . "Rides of Passage: Female Heroes in Pony Stories." In *A Necessary Fantasy? The Heroic Figure in Children's Popular Culture*, edited by Dudley Jones and Tony Watkins, 51–72. New York: Garland, 2000.

Henry, Marguerite. *Misty of Chincoteague*. Skokie, Ill.: Rand McNally, 1947.

——— . *Mustang: Wild Spirit of the West*. Skokie, Ill.: Rand McNally, 1966.

Herriot, James. *All Creatures Great and Small*. MFJ Books, 1972.

Heyn, Edward T. "Berlin's Wonderful Horse: He Can Do Almost Everything But Talk—How He Was Taught." *New York Times*, September 4, 1904.

Hochschild, Arlie, with Anne Machung. *The Second Shift: Working Families and the Revolution at Home*. New York: Penguin Books, 2012.

Hoig, Stan. *Came Men on Horses: The Conquistador Expeditions of Francisco Vázquez de Coronado and Don Juan de Oñate*. Boulder: University Press of Colorado, 2013.

hooks, bell. *Feminist Theory: From Margin to Center*. Cambridge, Mass.: South End Press, 1984.

"Horse Slaughter." American Society for the Prevention of Cruelty to Animals. www.aspca.org/animal-cruelty/horse-slaughter (accessed July 26, 2017).

"An Introduction to the Wind River Indian Reservation of Wyoming." Jackson Hole Historical Society & Museum. http://jacksonholehistory.org/an-introduction-to-the-wind-river-indian-reservation-of-wyoming (accessed December 5, 2016).

James, Will. *Home Ranch*. Missoula, Mont.: Mountain Press, 1935.

Johnson, Christen A., and K. T. Hawbaker. "#MeToo: A Timeline of Events." *Chicago Tribune*, March 19, 2018.

Kendrick, Jenny. "Riders, Readers, Romance: A Short History of the Pony Story." *Jeunesse: Young People, Texts, Cultures* 1, no. 2 (2009): 183–202.

Kilby, Emily R. "The Demographics of the U.S. Equine Population." In *The State of the Animals IV*, edited by Deborah J. Salem and Andrew N. Rowan, 175–205. Washington, D.C.: Humane Society Press, 2007.

Korda, Michael. *Horse People: Scenes from the Riding Life*. New York: HarperCollins, 2003.

Labash, Matt. "The Dread Pony: Life as a Cartoon." *Weekly Standard*, August 26, 2013. www.weeklystandard.com/the-dread-pony/article/748495.

Lefkowitz, Bernard. *Our Guys: The Glen Ridge Rape and the Secret Life of the Perfect Suburb*. Berkeley: University of California Press, 1997.

Limerick, Patricia Nelson. *The Legacy of Conquest: The Unbroken Past of the American West*. New York: W.W. Norton, 1987.

Linthicum, Leslie. "Delicate Balance in Horse Nation." *Albuquerque Sunday Journal*, August 18, 2013.

Lowe, Peggy. "Working 'The Chain,' Slaughterhouse Workers Face Lifelong Injuries." National Public Radio, August 11, 2016. www.npr.org/sections/thesalt/2016/08/11/489468205/working-the-chain-slaughterhouse-workers-face-lifelong-injuries .

Lowry, Rich. "The Wages of Polygamy." *Townhall.com*, April 21, 2008. https://townhall.com/columnists/richlowry/2008/04/21/the-wages-of-polygamy-n824771 (accessed July 20, 2018).

Luna, Joanne Tortorici. "The Horse, My Healer and Guide." *Reflections: Narratives of Professional Helping* 15 (Winter 2009): 20–23.

Maines, Rachel P. *The Technology of Orgasm: "Hysteria," the Vibrator, and Women's Sexual Satisfaction*. Baltimore, Md.: Johns Hopkins University Press, 1999.

Malaquais, Laurent. *Bronies: The Extremely Unexpected Adult Fans of My Little Pony*. Pottstown, Penn.: MVD Visual, 2013.

Maloney, Carolyn B., and the Joint Economic Committee Democratic Staff. *Gender Pay Inequality: Consequences for Women, Families and the Economy.* Washington, D.C.: Joint Economic Committee United States Congress, 2016.

McCabe, Janice, Emily Fairchild, Liz Grauerholz, Bernice A. Pescosolido, and Daniel Tope. "Gender in Twentieth-century Children's Books: Patterns of Disparity in Titles and Central Characters." *Gender & Society* 25, no. 2 (April 2011): 197–226.

McMurtry, Larry. *Lonesome Dove.* New York: Simon & Schuster, 1985.

McRuer, Robert. "Disabling Sex: Notes for a Crip Theory of Sexuality." *GLQ: A Journal of Lesbian and Gay Studies* 17, no. 1 (2011): 107–117.

Midkiff, Mary. "An Intuitive Edge." In *Of Women and Horses,* edited by GaWaNi Pony Boy, 81–87. Irvine, Calif.: BowTie Press, 2000.

Miller, Neil. *Out of the Past: Gay and Lesbian History from 1869 to the Present.* New York: Alyson, 2006.

National Coalition Against Domestic Violence. https://ncadv.org/statistics (accessed June 12, 2017).

Oakeshott, Michael. "The Voice of Poetry in the Conversation of Mankind." In *Rationalism in Politics and Other Essays.* Indianapolis: Liberty Press, 1991. 488–541.

"Obituary of Christine Pullein-Thompson." *Telegraph,* December 6, 2005. www.telegraph.co.uk/news/obituaries/1504796/Christine-Pullein-Thompson .html.

"Obituary of Josephine Pullein-Thompson." *The Guardian.* June 22, 2014. www.theguardian.com/books/2014/jun/22/josephine-pullein-thompson.

O'Hara, Mary. *My Friend Flicka.* 1940; rpt., New York: Harper Trophy, 2008.

Ojanen, Karoliina. "'You Became Someone': Social Hierarchies in Girls' Communities at Riding Stables." *Young* 20 (2012): 137–156.

Olmert, Meg Daley. *Made for Each Other: The Biology of the Human-Animal Bond.* Cambridge, Mass.: Da Capo Press, 2009.

Park, Barbara. *Junie B. Jones Is Not a Crook!* New York: Random House, 1997.

Patrick, Justine S.. "Deconstructing the Regulatory Façade: Why Confused Consumers Feed Their Pets Ring Dings and Krispy Kremes." April 2006. https://dash.harvard.edu/bitstream/handle/1/10018997/Patrick06.html (accessed October 16, 2017).

Peggs, Kay. *Animals and Sociology.* New York: Palgrave Macmillan, 2012.

Pierson, Melissa Holbrook. *Dark Horses and Black Beauties: Animals, Women, a Passion.* New York: W.W. Norton, 2000.

"The Pleistocene Epoch." University of California Museum of Paleontology. www .ucmp.berkeley.edu/quaternary/pleistocene.php (accessed January 8, 2015).

Plymoth, Birgitta. "Gender in Equestrian Sports: An Issue of Difference and Equality." *Sport in Society* 15, no. 3 (February 23, 2012): 335–348.

Poll, Bernard. "Why Children Like Horse Stories." *Elementary English* 38, no. 7 (November 1961): 473–474.

Pony Boy, GaWaNi, ed. *Of Women and Horses: Essays by Various Horse Women.* Irvine, Calif.: BowTie Press, 2000.

———. *Of Women and Horses: More Expressions of the Magical Bond.* Irvine, Calif.: Bowtie Press, 2005.

"Pony Penning History." Chincoteague Chamber of Commerce. www .chincoteaguechamber.com/pony-swim/pony-penning-history (accessed December 31, 2016).

Potter, Leslie. "A Timeline of Horse Slaughter Legislation in the United States." *Horse Illustrated.* January 26, 2012. www.horseillustrated.com/horse-resources/ horse-slaughter-timeline (accessed July 26, 2017).

Prager, Dennis. "Four Legacies of Feminism: They Have Made Life—and Life for Women—Worse." *National Review Online,* November 1, 2011.

Probyn, Elspeth. "Girls and Girls and Girls and Horses: Queer Images of Singularity and Desire." *Tessera* 15 (Winter 1993): 22–29.

Professional Association of Therapeutic Horsemanship (PATH). www.pathintl.org/ about-path-intl/about-path-intl.

Pullein-Thompson, Christine. *Phantom Horse: 1.* 1955; rpt., Workshop, Nottinghamshire, UK: Award Publications, digital edition, 2012.

———. *Phantom Horse Comes Home: 2.* 1970; rpt., Workshop, Nottinghamshire, UK: Award Publications, digital edition, 2012.

———. *Phantom Horse Disappears: 3.* 1972; rpt., Workshop, Nottinghamshire, UK: Award Publications Limited, digital edition, 2012.

———. *Phantom Horse in Danger: 4.* 1980; rpt., Workshop, Nottinghamshire, UK: Award Publications Limited, digital edition, 2012.

Pullein-Thompson, Christine, Diana Pullein-Thompson, and Josephine Pullein-Thompson. *Fair Girls and Grey Horses: Memories of a Country Childhood.* 1996; rpt., London: Allison & Busby, 2014.

Raban, Jonathan. "The Unlamented West: Militias, Freemen and Mad Bombers— Why Do So Many Extreme and Dangerous Individualists Seem to Come from One Place?" *New Yorker,* May 20, 1996, 59–81.

Rape, Abuse & Incest National Network (RAINN). www.rainn.org/statistics/ victims-sexual-violence.

Roberts, Monty. *The Man Who Listens to Horses.* 1996; rpt., London: Hand Held, 2007.

Rose, Nikolas. *Powers of Freedom: Reframing Political Thought*. Cambridge, UK: Cambridge University Press, 1999.

Sanchez, Laura. "'Every Time They Ride, I Pray': Parents' Management of Daughters' Horseback Riding Risks. *Sociology of Sport Journal* 34, no. 3 (2017): 259–269.

Schneider, Joseph. *Donna Haraway: Live Theory*. New York: Continuum, 2005.

Scholinski, Daphne, with Jane Meredith Adams. *The Last Time I Wore a Dress*. New York: Riverhead, 1997.

Schowalter, John E. "Some Meanings of Being a Horsewoman." *Psychoanalytic Study of the Child* 38 (January 1983): 501–517.

Segal, Jacob. "Michel Foucault and Michael Oakeshott: The Virtuosity of Individuality." *Foucault Studies* 18 (October 2014): 154–172.

Sewell, Anna. *Black Beauty*. 1877, Kindle edition.

"Sexual Violence: Data Sources." Centers for Disease Control and Prevention. www.cdc.gov/violenceprevention/sexualviolence/datasources.html (accessed August 6, 2017).

Shukin, Nicole. *Animal Capital: Rendering Life in Biopolitical Times*. Minneapolis: University of Minnesota Press, 2009.

Simon, Stephanie. "Pet Food Report Leads to Pile-Up at Animal Shelters." *Washington Post*, January 27, 2002. www.washingtonpost.com/archive /politics/2002/01/27/pet-food-report-leads-to-pile-up-at-animal-shelters /51593661-2712-4bd1-974a-21dc2f28c880/?utm.

Slaughter, Anne-Marie. "Why Women Still Can't Have It All." *The Atlantic*, July 2012. www.theatlantic.com/magazine/archive/2012/07/why-women-still -cant-have-it-all/309020.

Spiegel, Maura. "Introduction." In *The Jungle*, by Upton Sinclair. 1906; rpt., New York: Barnes and Noble Classics, 2003.

Stillman, Deanne. *Mustang: The Saga of the Wild Horse in the American West*. New York: First Mariner Books, 2008.

——. "Wild Horses Aren't Free: Failure to Enforce a 1971 Law Endangers the Mustangs It Was Supposed to Protect." *Los Angeles Times*, June 2, 2008. http://articles.latimes.com/2008/jun/02/opinion/oe-stillman2.

Sulzberger, A. G. "Slaughter of Horses Goes On, Just Not in the U.S." *New York Times*, October 24, 2011, A1.

Tanenbaum, Leora. *Slut! Growing up Female with a Bad Reputation*. New York: Harper Perennial, 2000.

Tanner, Jari. "These Folks Aren't Just Horsing Around." *Finnish American Reporter* 31, no. 6 (June 2017): 13.

Thiel, Liz. "The Dark Horse: Ruby Ferguson and the Jill Pony Stories." *The Lion and the Unicorn* 26, no. 1 (January 2002): 112–122.

"Thomas Edison Patented the Kinetoscope August 31, 1897." Library of Congress. www.americaslibrary.gov/jb/gilded/jb_gilded_kinetscp_1.html (accessed January 20, 2016).

Thompson, Kirrilly, Paul McGreevy, and Phil McManus. "A Critical Review of Horse-Related Risk: A Research Agenda for Safer Mounts, Riders and Equestrian Cultures." *Animals* 5, no. 3 (2015): 561–575.

Thompson, Sharon. *Going All the Way: Teenage Girls' Tales of Sex, Romance and Pregnancy.* New York: Hill and Wang, 1996.

Thorell, Gabriella, and Susanna Hedenborg. "Riding Instructors, Gender, Militarism, and Stable Culture in Sweden: Continuity and Change in the Twentieth Century." *International Journal of the History of Sport* 32, no. 5 (2015): 650–666.

Thorne, Barrie. *Gender Play: Girls and Boys in School.* New Brunswick, N.J.: Rutgers University Press, 1993.

Toth, Delphi M. "The Psychology of Women and Horses." In *Of Women and Horses,* edited by GaWaNi Pony Boy, 31–42. Irvine, Calif.: BowTie Press, 2000.

Tucker, Nicholas. *The Child and the Book: A Psychological and Literary Exploration.* Cambridge, UK: Cambridge University Press, 1981.

Turner, Frederick Jackson. *The Frontier in American History.* 1920; rpt., Tucson: University of Arizona Press, 1994.

"U.S.: Soaring Rates of Rape and Violence against Women." Human Rights Watch. December 8, 2008. www.hrw.org/news/2008/12/18/us-soaring-rates-rape-and-violence-against-women.

Viola, Herman J. "Introduction." In *A Song for the Horse Nation: Horses in Native American Cultures,* edited by George P. Horse Capture and Emil Her Many Horses, 7–10. Golden, Colo.: Fulcrum, 2006.

Volz, Alia. "Galloping Away to a Place Beyond Words: A Spanish Interpreter Finds a Weekly Respite as a Mounted Volunteer Park Patroller." *New York Times,* August 30, 2015: 7.

"What Is a Mustang?" National Mustang Association. www.nmautah.org/wildhorse.htm (accessed January 20, 2016).

Williams, Wendy. *The Horse: The Epic History of Our Noble Companion.* New York: Farrar, Straus and Giroux, 2015.

Wilson, Don E., and DeeAnn M. Reeder, editors. "Equus Caballus." In *Mammal Species of the World: A Taxonomic and Geographic Reference.* 3rd ed. Baltimore, Md.: Johns Hopkins University Press, 2005.

Woodhouse, Leighton Akio. "Charged with the Crime of Filming a Slaughterhouse: So-called 'Ag-Gag' Laws Reveal the Lengths to Which the Agriculture Industry Will Go to Keep Their Business Practices Secret." *The Nation*, July 31, 2013. www.thenation.com/article/charged-crime-filming-slaughterhouse.

Zaslow, Shayne. "Hybrid Masculinity and Brony Fan Communities." Unpublished paper, 2018.

Zeigler, Robert E. "The Cowboy Strike of 1883: Its Causes and Meaning." *Texas Labor History*, edited by Bruce A. Glasrud and James C. Maroney, 65–78. College Station: Texas A&M University Press, 2013.

Zoetis. "2015 AHP Equine Industry Survey." American Horse Publications, July 31, 2015. www.americanhorsepubs.org/equine-survey/2015-equine-survey (accessed June 7, 2017).

Index

About the Author

Jean Halley is a professor of sociology at the College of Staten Island and the Graduate Center of the City University of New York (CUNY). She earned her doctorate in sociology at the Graduate Center of CUNY and her master's degree in theology at Harvard University. Her book about touching children, breastfeeding, children's sleep, gender, and heteronormativity, *Boundaries of Touch: Parenting and Adult-Child Intimacy,* was published in 2007. She also assisted Patricia Ticineto Clough in editing *The Affective Turn: Theorizing the Social* (2007) and co-authored, with Amy Eshleman and Ramya Vijaya, *Seeing White: An Introduction to White Privilege and Race* (2011). Her book *The Parallel Lives of Women and Cows: Meat Markets,* a combination of memoir and a social history of cattle ranching in the United States, came out in 2012. Most recently, she and Amy Eshleman published *Seeing Straight: An Introduction to Gender and Sexual Privilege* (2017) on gender and heteronormativity. Halley and her horse, Snipaway, grew up in the rural Rocky Mountains.